THE ART AND SCIENCE OF STANISLAW LEM

The Art and Science of Stanislaw Lem

Edited by
Peter Swirski

McGill-Queen's University Press
Montreal & Kingston · London · Ithaca

ISBN-13: 978-0-7735-3046-1 ISBN-10: 0-7735-3046-0

Legal deposit third quarter 2006
Bibliothèque nationale du Québec

Printed in Canada on acid-free paper

This book has been published in cooperation with the Wirth Institute for Austrian and Central European Studies, University of Alberta, Edmonton, Canada.

McGill-Queen's University Press acknowledges the support of the Canada Council for the Arts for our publishing program. We also acknowledge the financial support of the Government of Canada through the Book Publishing Industry Development Program (BPIDP) for our publishing activities.

"Solaris! Solaris. Solaris!" by Peter Swirski was originally published online in *Central Europe Review* (CER), 8 January 2003.
www.Culture.tol.cz/look/CER/article.tpl?IdLanguage=1&IdPublication=14&NRIssue=43&NrSection=3&NrArticle=8246
"(Un)masking the Agent: Stanislaw Lem's 'The Mask'"
by N. Katherine Hayles was originally published in *My Mother Was a Computer: Digital Subject and Literary Texts* (University of Chicago Press, 2005).

Library and Archives Canada Cataloguing in Publication

The art and science of Stanislaw Lem / edited by Peter Swirski.
Includes bibliographical references and index.

ISBN-13: 978-0-7735-3046-1 ISBN-10: 0-7735-3046-0

1. Lem, Stanislaw, 1921-2006 – Criticism and interpretation.
I. Swirski, Peter, 1963-

PG7158.L392A57 2006 891.8'537 C2006-901704-2

Typeset in New Baskerville 10.5/13
by Infoscan Collette, Quebec City

This book is dedicated to
Earle Waugh and Wacek Osadnik:
humanists and pedagogues.

Contents

THE ART AND SCIENCE OF STANISLAW LEM

INTRODUCTION

The Man behind the Giant

PETER SWIRSKI

Stanislaw Lem is no longer the obscure East European writer who invited prolonged discussions of context when his name began to infiltrate North American circles in the late 1960s. Today Lem is recognized as a literary grandmaster, a provocative and thought-provoking literary critic, and, not least, a sophisticated philosopher, diagnostician, and prognostician of science, tirelessly prospecting the outermost reaches of *technoscientia incognita*.[1] Over a career spanning more than half a century, he has accrued accolades as prestigious and eclectic as the books he has written, some of which are required reading in schools in his native Poland. Scholars declare him to be a literary movement in himself, contributing to bibliographies of Lem studies that run into hundreds of pages in all the major and many minor languages of the world in Europe, Asia, and both Americas.

A Renaissance polymath, Lem is also a social critic and philosopher of science *par excellence* and a much sought-after futurologist and policy advisor. Scientists from Carl Sagan to Douglas Hofstadter and philosophers from Daniel Dennett to Nicolas Rescher have professed respect for Lem's writings. His cyber-evolutionary hypotheses have been deliberated not only at top-level literary conferences but also at interdisciplinary symposia involving linguists, philosophers, sociologists, and cognitive scientists. Translated into more than forty languages, his books have sold by now almost thirty-five million copies worldwide, making him one of the most successful writers of the twentieth century. In the United States Lem has attracted praise from authors such as John Updike, Joyce Carol Oates, and Kurt Vonnegut, as well as from leading East Coast critics like Ted Solotaroff and Leslie Fiedler. Just about the only form of international acclaim that has eluded the leading European litterateur is the Nobel Prize, although for the past quarter-century he has been shortlisted several times for this honour.

Lem has published science fiction, contemporary novels, short stories, detective fiction, poetry, experimental writing, criticism, sociological and cultural analyses, philosophy, futurology, autobiography, television and radio plays, film scripts, and volumes of polemical writings. In between, he has co-founded the Polish Astronautical Society, taught literature and philosophy at the Jagiellonski University, been appointed a member of Commission POLAND 2000 (a think-tank division of the Polish Academy of Sciences), and hosted dozens of television series as the national spokesman on culture and science. He has received the highest cultural and state honours, numerous decorations, and a legion of others accolades, including awards from scores of magazines and radio and television cultural committees. By now there have been numerous international adaptations of his novels for cinema, including the Soderbergh/Clooney/Cameron version of Lem's best-known novel *Solaris,* itself a remake of the 1972 Cannes Festival-winning adaptation by Andrei Tarkovsky.

WHO IS THE MAN BEHIND THE GIANT?

Stanislaw Lem was born 12 September 1921, in Lvov, Poland (now in Ukraine).[2] His father was a laryngologist whose social status and prosperity assured that the boy's growing years were spent in comfortable affluence, with a French governess and a multitude of expensive toys. The mother, Sabine (née Wollner), of whom Lem speaks only with greatest reluctance, was a housewife who had scant influence on his life. In his later years the adult writer reconstructed his childhood as lonely and bookish, enlivened by his passion for literature and science but devoid of close and lasting friendships. The chubby, physically unexceptional boy found a close mentor and confidant in his father, of whom he said with fondness: "I always highly valued these small chunks of time which he tore for me out of his working day."[3]

Many of Lem's childhood recollections are faithfully reproduced in his 1966 autobiographical work, *Highcastle: A Remembrance.* Although many critics interpreted it as an unabashedly autobiographical fiction, Lem insists that *Highcastle* contains not a single fictive element. Among a mine of fascinating detail, the book describes one of the earliest manifestations of his extraordinary gift of imagination and inventiveness. Like every child, young Stanislaw delighted in the creation of imaginary worlds, fictional objects, and made-up stories, but he found a rather idiosyncratic point of entry into such worlds. Instead of fashioning them in his head, he would painstakingly design and manufacture wads of official-looking documents (diplomas, permits, passports, certificates, iron letters, etc.) that conferred on him various powers within his imaginary paper state. This secret realm was his refuge and his alternative universe, and no one – not his schoolmates, nor even his father – was allowed to learn of its existence.

The second lasting influence on Lem's development came from his endless fascination with books. As he recalls, his earliest target – locked up with a key that had to be pilfered on every occasion – was his father's medical library. Later, these encyclopedias – German and French books on anatomy, and other technical sources – gave way to literature at large: poems, novels, popular science books, biographies of famous people, etc. Lem's intellectual gifts were formidable even at that time; in the mid-1930s, IQ tests placed his scores at well above 180 (although he did not learn about this till much later). At that time he already spoke Polish, French, and Russian and, as the fate decreed, was soon to perfect his German during the devastating years of the Second World War occupation. Reflective, cerebral, irreverent, ironic, and boundlessly creative, he seems to have carried all these adolescent traits into his adult personality.

After high school Lem passed his entrance exams to a polytechnic university, but, owing to the political situation, his application was rejected. He ended up enrolling at the Lvov's Medical Institute, where (under the Russian occupation, which cemented the partition of Poland under the Molotov-Ribbentrob Pact) he studied until 1941, when the Wehrmacht troops marched into the city.

There is no doubt about the harrowing effect the war years had on the shaping of Lem's intellectual and emotional outlook on life. The mature writer's almost obsessive return to the subjects of chance, luck, survival, aggression, the military mindset, and the inhumanity latent in humanity is clearly rooted in the young man's experiences in the war zone. Similarly, Lem's relative indifference to the fates of individuals next to the magnitude and intransigence of problems facing the human race must have grown from the terrors perpetrated by the Nazi extermination machine, which did not distinguish between the death of an individual and the death of thousands.

Since he was in possession of the so-called green papers, i.e., a prewar driving licence, Lem survived the war years working in a German carshop as a mechanic and welder. With typical mordant wit the adult writer jested that his lack of mechanical or welding skills was so severe that he must have daily risked being accused of behind-the-lines sabotage! Yet the risks were real and constant, since the young mechanic used to smuggle inside his overalls combat supplies (ammunition, radios, bayonets) over to the Polish underground. Since Lem and his family lived with false papers under an assumed identity, each day brought with it the threat of exposure. The belief that one may be in full control one's life must have seemed like Faustian hubris to someone living in these conditions. The young Lem's profound conviction in the role of chance must have intensified after his near-brush with death during one of countless bombing raids. The memories of these dark years prompted him many years later to confess in *The New Yorker*: "it isn't mere chance that I attribute in my work such a prominent role to chance as the shaper of human destiny." In the same article he said of the dark and aberrant years of Nazi mass-murders and exterminations: "I have learned how human beings behave under extreme conditions – how their behavior when they are under enormous pressures is almost impossible to predict."

After the war, the family was repatriated from the Soviet-annexed Lvov to Cracow, where, except for several years during the politically turbulent 1980s, Lem has resided since. The young man resumed his medical studies but, even though he completed them in 1949, chose not to take his final exams since all those who did were drafted by the army not for the customary two years but for life. At about that time he met Barbara Leśniak, a medical student in radiology, whom he married in 1953 after a three-year courtship. At the beginning of the 1950s Lem's situation in the Stalinist Poland was not to be envied: without a medical degree or steady academic employment, temporarily expelled from the Literary Guild for not having a book to his credit, with a wife and no reliable source of income, in the eyes of the authorities he may have seemed a suspicious element. Fortunately, the publication in 1951 of his first science-fiction book, *The Astronauts*, marked the turning point in his life and the beginning of a full-time literary career.

Lem's first writing attempts date from the period shortly before the outbreak of the war. His first poems were juvenile lyrics that, during the occupation, affected a strong patriotic tone. These early efforts, lost in the turmoil of war, survived in his fascination with the poetry of Reiner Maria Rilke, whose two slim volumes, published in 1941, he read nonstop during those years (and has guarded until today). Not surprisingly, Rilke's style and phraseology permeate Lem's early novels, especially the long and intricate *The Magellan Nebula* (1955). Lem's entry into the writing world took place in 1946 when he started publishing poems and stories in the local weeklies. Today he laughs at this poetry (collected and published as *Youthful Poems*) and at the fact that, despite earnest advice from established poets, he could never be cured of fondness for a strict rhyme scheme and stanzaic versification. The subjects of his early stories varied, but among lyrical-romantic tales and stories about war and espionage, there was the first science-fiction piece as well as his first serialized novel, *Man from Mars* (1946).

Still, one may wonder why Lem should have ultimately been drawn to science fiction. For one, his first "serious" novel, *Hospital of the Transfiguration* (completed in 1948, but not published until 1955), follows the conventions of contemporary realism. Describing a mental asylum during the first days of the Second World War, it dissects the medical staff's moral dilemma between fleeing for safety or trying to save the helpless patients from Nazi extermination. Second, Polish literature, dominated by often romanticized nationalistic and sociopolitical concerns, has virtually no tradition in fantastic fiction. And yet, reflecting on his career in 1982, Lem expressed doubts whether he could have ever become a realistic writer. "Many artists are gifted with only a narrow path on which they can create something valuable," he observed, adding: "I think I was destined to end up working in the genre in which I write."

In some ways, however, Lem may have been writing science fiction for many years even before he published *The Astronauts*. His earliest book-length project, *Theory of Brain Functions*, written and rewritten during the mid to late 1940s, had originally been conceived as a serious academic study. Be that as it may, this ambitious, vast, and completely muddled piece of nonsense – as the mature author calmly summed it up – may have in fact been his first, painstakingly researched, work of science fiction. The long trial-and-error years when this scientific and philosophical study remained on the drawing table helped Lem refine his unique approach to writing. With hindsight, the scientific accuracy of his fictions – worlds apart from the *Star Trek* or *Star Wars* props of US space opera – may owe to the research habits formed at this stage of his life.

A turning point in Lem's intellectual development was a meeting with Dr Mieczysław Choynowski. After blasting the young man's *Theory of Brain Functions*, Choynowski took him under his tutelage as a research assistant for the science study group at the Jagiellonian University in Cracow. There, throughout the late 1940s, the young scholar pursued a back-breaking program of study and research, while at the same time teaching at the university, working as a full-time reviewer of current scientific publications for the journal *Życie Nauki* (*The Life of Science*), and laboriously learning English from Norbert Wiener's *Cybernetics* and other scientific sources. The love affair with cybernetics and its subsequent myriad subbranchings, such as robotics, artificial life, and artificial intelligence, has remained with Lem throughout his life. He is a long-standing member of the Polish Cybernetic Society and has played an active role in the rehabilitation of cybernetics in the Soviet Union after the subject had come under attack for political incorrectness.

Had the study group not been dissolved for political reasons in 1950, Polish science might have gained what world literature would have lost. But, on a visit to a mountain resort of Zakopane, another chance meeting changed the direction of Lem's life. During a casual talk with a corpulent gentleman (who turned out to be a director at a well-known publishing house), the young writer was offered a contract to write a science-fiction novel. The result was the immensely popular *The Astronauts*, and Lem never looked back, producing an almost unbelievably diverse body of writing. With almost fifty book titles to his credit, among them several multi-volume studies, he remains to this day an eagerly consulted literary and cultural critic, philosopher, futurologist, sociologist, essayist, and scientific commentator – and, of course, a bestselling writer.

Lem travelled extensively in his lifetime, albeit only within Europe; he steadfastly refused all invitations to North America, including the reception of an honorary doctorate from the University of Alberta, which he regretfully declined, citing health reasons and the rigours of transcontinental travel. The only time he spent several years abroad was when Poland was in the grip of martial law following the Solidarity upheavals in the early 1980s. Refusing to join the government-run Writer's Union, he left for Vienna, where he spent most of his time, although he also stayed for a year (1982–83) at the Institute for Advanced Study in West Berlin. It has been reported that he enjoyed the advantages of the West but was bothered by the commercialism; in many ways, his then-literary agent revealed, he found the intellectual life in Poland more interesting. After his return he continued to live in Poland, in his spacious and beautiful house in a picturesque suburb of Cracow. He continued to write at a furious pace, indicated by the frequent replacement rate of typewriter ribbons, but after his last novel, *Fiasco* (1986), he gave up fiction. Since he tended to shy away from computers, including his son's Apple, he typed on a manual Remington Underwood, which he received as a present from his father at the age of twelve.

Although more frail towards the end of his life than when I interviewed him in the early 1990s, Lem was a still stocky man whose passion for knowledge, conversation, and writing had not abated over the years (he had a domestic library of well over ten thousand titles).[4] During the last years of his career he contributed mostly social and cultural criticism, essays in various philosophical journals, and articles on artificial life and intelligence. Following his lifelong writing habit of getting up before five in the morning, he worked for hours on end, confessing: "When I was younger, I could write as long as my stamina held out; the power of my intellect gave way only after my physical prowess had been exhausted."

THE ART OF SCIENCE OF STANISLAW LEM

The Art and Science of Stanislaw Lem is a unique collection of essays on the writer hailed on more than one occasion as a literary Einstein.

Its uniqueness is assured by the diverse, though complementary, nature of articles from individuals who for many years have defined Lem scholarship. In a paradigmatic display of interdisciplinarity, literary and film scholars, translators and editors, a scientist, and a philosopher contribute articles with the view to evaluating Lem's influence on Western culture. Rather than study him as a science-fiction writer alone, each essayist commands a wider sphere of reference for the appreciation of Lem's artistic and scientific contributions. Each addresses a larger theme from the writer's multidimensional opus: agency and consciousness, social engineering and human violence, Freudianism and the creative process, evolution and the philosophy of the future, virtual reality and epistemological illusion, science fiction and sociocultural policy, all the way to the film legacy. Each addresses Lem's abiding concern for the social and cultural significance of the twin engines of our civilization's material progress: technology and science.

With the exception of the opening and concluding essays, the contributors to the book are culled from a select group of scholars invited to the first-ever North American conference devoted entirely to Lem's cultural and philosophical legacy. Organized under the aegis of the Wirth Institute for Austrian and Central European Studies and held in 2003 at the University of Alberta, Edmonton, "The World According to Lem: Science Fiction and Futurology" was a fitting tribute to the writer, whose fame continues to spread not only in his native Europe but worldwide. Nor surprisingly, therefore, following in Lem's footsteps, these essays investigate the creative partnering of art and science in his fiction and futurology. Faithful to his cognitive slant, they strive to come to grips with his intellectual legacy before looking at his work in more conventional literary terms. Each contributor has selected a different work and a different set of issues for analysis, in the process creating a polyphonic chorus of intellectual interplay that covers the entirety of Lem's career.

Stanislaw Lem himself contributes "Smart Robots," an essay tackling topics that range from intentionality and volition to the cognitive engineering of transcendence. It sets the stage for subsequent discussions, from the commentary on human and machine will through my own treatment of volition and conditions of its surrender, the twin pieces on evolution, the philosophical analysis of agency and illusion, down to the discussion of techno-imperialism.

N. Katherine Hayles's tour-de-force interpretation of a novella published in English in mid-1970s as part of *Mortal Engines*, "(Un)masking the Agent: Stanislaw Lem's 'The Mask,'" painstakingly sifts through the many layers of Lem's thinking about what constitutes agency and freedom to act, specifically in the context of being human or a gendered machine. "Betrization Is the Worst Solution … with the Exception of All Others" discusses the means of saving humankind from itself. Introducing the concept of betrization, loosely interpretable as salvation by cybernetics, it combines literary, philosophical, and empirical investigations of the concept as it applies to *Return from the Stars* and to the world outside our windows. Michael Kandel's "A Freudian Peek at Lem's *Fiasco*" continues in the tradition of literary interpretation, though this time enriched by Kandel's intimate knowledge of the work that he himself has translated. Illustrated with examples from the translator's draftboard, it attempts to interconnect a series of images and linguist constructs in Lem's farewell work of fiction.

With Peter Butko's "*Summa technologiae* – Looking Back and Ahead" the book shifts into another gear. From a working scientist's perspective, the essay compares the theses developed in Lem's futurological magnum opus to what we know of, or can predict from, the science of today. Close in its footsteps is "Models of Evolution in the Writings of Stanislaw Lem." Jerzy Jarzębski, Polish critic and author of multiple books on Lem, takes a synoptic view of the writer's penchant for evolutionary analyses of just about everything, from culture to society, science, literature, and art. Tackling the perennially fascinating topic of virtual reality and the illusions of reality it may or not foster, Paisley Livingston's "Skepticism, Realism, Fallibilism: On Lem's Epistemological Themes" revisits the Ijon Tichy stories and Descartes's *Meditations* in order to position Lem within the firmament of philosophic debates on the subject. From analytic philosophy we move on to technological empire and the set of historical correlations between the genre of science fiction and the empire-building ambitions of geopolitical powers; in "Lem, Central Europe, and the Genre of technological Empire" Istvan Csicsery-Ronay pursues these and cognate topics on the borderline between art and sociotechnological policy. In "Lem on Film," Polish scholar, Krzysztof Loska, surveys all adaptations of Lem's books and stories for television and cinema, from the lesser-known Polish, Czechoslovak, and German films, to the Russian and American versions of *Solaris.*

Finally, I wrap up our collective efforts with a closer look at the three "versions" of the best-known, and perhaps best, novel in the writer's corpus. The somewhat more colloquial "*Solaris*! *Solaris*. *Solaris*?" aims to provide a handy reference and a tripartite introduction to the novel as well as to the Cannes-winning (1972) and Hollywood blockbuster (2002) film adaptations.

NOTES

1 For standard critical introductions to Lem, see Swirski, "Stanislaw Lem: A Stranger in a Strange Land," in *A Stanislaw Lem Reader* (Northwestern University Press, 1997): 1–19; and "Stanislaw Lem," in *Science Fiction Writers; Revised Edition* (Charles Scribner's Sons, 1999): 453–66.

2 Parts of this research were originally developed for an article in *Beacham's Encyclopedia of Popular Fiction* (unpublished).

3 All translations from the Polish are my own; see Stanislaw Bereś, *Rozmowy ze Stanisławem Lemem* [*Conversations with Stanislaw Lem*], Kraków: Wydawnictwo Literackie, 1987.

4 The interviews are collected in *A Stanislaw Lem Reader* (1997).

1

Smart Robots

STANISLAW LEM
Translated by Peter Swirski

1 In recent times a great number of theoreticians and researchers of various disciplinary stripes have been drawn to that subfield of artificial intelligence which *sui generis* resembles the study of human consciousness, or, to generalize more carefully, of animal consciousness. What is the basis of such resemblance? The problem can be separated into two parts: *architectural* (e.g., what kind of neural nets or processors need to be constructed, if any) and *theoretical* – this one of a decidedly philosophical flavour. In what follows I will focus on the latter, since the question of a pseudomind's physical architecture is clearly subordinate to it. It seems analogous to the question of whether a particular terrain vehicle should run on treads or on a special type of wheels (like the ones finally adopted by both the Americans and the Soviets for their lunar rovers).

2 Condensed and reduced to its nucleus, the philosophical problem consists of the challenge of grafting onto a robot a *volitional* drive. Even the most accomplished chess program run on today's fastest computer does not have as much as a shred of volition. It exhibits as much drive towards an established goal as an iron ball wrecking a building, or a cannon projectile in mid-flight. In this sense the program is an extraneous substitute for the *desire* to reach a certain goal. The only difference between a cannonball in motion and a move in a game of chess is that, on its way to the target, the

projectile encounters no obstacles (i.e., it *should* encounter none considering the gunners' expertise, which *notabene* extends beyond the world of cannons and cannonballs). On the other hand, attaining the target (i.e., winning a game) is made more difficult for the program by the strategy of an opponent who calculates his moves precisely to render the program's checkmate impossible.

3 Of course it is possible to simulate acts of volition, i.e., of wanting something. This type of pure imitation has nothing to do, however, with an authentic act of will. Clearly, if a program were effectively to imitate volitional actions, the programmer would have to anticipate all possible obstacles on its path, as well as ways of overcoming them. The number of such obstacles could of course be vast, even astronomical.

It is a separate question whether it is necessary to write explicitly into a program – i.e., anticipate the entire closed set of – *all conceivable* obstacles. The answer is clearly no, this need not be the case. Natural evolution does not operate in a way that would allow "programs" run on living creatures to cope with *all conceivable* obstacles. We all know that common flies, "programmed" with an uncanny ability to slip out from under the swatter, are quite incapable of figuring out the secret of glass in the window pane.

Owing to their "lifestyle," the flies' capacity to *acquire knowledge* – i.e., the capacity of individual specimens to form conditioned reflexes – is relatively small in comparison to other insect species, like bees. Bees, for example, are known to have developed a signalling language in the course of their struggle for survival (of the fittest). This ability, which comes not from an outside programmer but is simply an outcome of a long phase of natural selection, is nowhere to be found in any robot constructed by humanity.

Surely enough, researchers continue to multiply imitations of an experiential "drive," compose learned treatises on the functioning of quasi-volition, and build increasingly intricate pseudoneural nets. Yet, for all this, they have no way of descending to the molecular level at which even viruses and bacteria skilfully "shuffle" their own genomes in such a way as to escape or repulse deleterious effects of drugs (e.g., antibiotics). Typically microorganisms do it by neutralizing the drug's negative (from their point of view) biochemical potential, or by altering their antigen structure so that the drug can no longer identify the malefactor. This metaphorical language is used here to avoid getting bogged down in lengthy and complicated expositions of physical, chemical, or biochemical data that naturally underlie these types of processes. All I am trying to convey at this point is that protean instances of "desire," these nuclei of volitional actions, can be found already in the most "primitive" living organisms.

4 We should remind ourselves that in this area of research nothing can be gained by burying the real issue under the ponderous weight of academic polemics, no matter how intricate or high-minded. Consider the following. The movement of clock hands can be secured with springs, electricity, or weights (in this last case the clock is directly dependent on Earth's gravity and thus unable to function in any other environment, e.g., in orbit). In each of these cases the movement of the hands is vector-oriented as if *from above* by the watchmaker/constructor. But we are after something else. We want a robot's "electronic brain" – its computer "mind" – on its own to anticipate, develop, and pursue on its own goals that it could eventually bring to completion. Naturally at this stage of the game there could no longer be any foreknowledge of the individual decisions adding up to produce an impression of a robot's "sensible" behaviour. The reason for this is the same as the reason for our inability to foresee the decisions made by human explorers in their drive to the pole, or to the top of Mount Everest. In other words, we are speaking here of an increasing, adaptively effective autonomization on the part of the robot that, in the last phase of its volitional evolution, may become equal to humanity.

5 Many experts still believe that human ingenuity can find a shortcut that will replace the need for the billions of years that led to the Cambrian explosion of species and thus to the polymorphous "survival of the fittest." If only we think really hard and absorb the needed theoretical sciences – or so it is held – soon we will find ourselves surrounded by robots replete with free will, which we can later "persuade" and teach to pursue goals dear to *us*.

Another alternative, which cannot be a priori ruled out, is that such robots may fail to reach prescribed goals not in the manner of an ill-aimed cannonball but more like a willful child or a hand-reared pet-turned-pest. Put simply, we cannot exclude the possibility that machines equipped with sovereign will may at some point begin to resist us. I am not thinking, of course, of a robot rebellion against humankind, so beloved by all primitive purveyors of cognitive magic. My only point is that, with the rise in the degree of behavioural freedom, one can no longer preserve the "good and only the good," because this very freedom can also give rise to a touch of "evil." We can see this in natural evolution only too well, and this reflection may perhaps temper our intention to endow robots with free will.

6 The term appearing above, *intentionality*, means exactly this: being directed towards whatever "intention" chooses as its object. Intention here is not taken exclusively – perhaps even not at all – in its phenomenological sense as defined by philosophers. All that concerns me is that present-day computers show no trace of intention and that it may be worth our while to reflect on how we could "spark" intentionality in them without imitation or sleight of hand.

The only means to achieve that, known to us from the surrounding world, is natural evolution – which ruthlessly wipes out all forms of life that lack a sufficient drive to live and temporarily (i.e., for the duration of a being's power to reproduce) preserves those whose drive to live is better fit to succeed. The greatest problem for the theoreticians and applied researchers is, unfortunately, the fact that the eons needed for natural evolution is the one obstacle they cannot overcome.

In my view everything hinges on whether there is some method or strategy for an *accelerated* development of volition or intention (i.e., simply desiring something or other). Human beings of both sexes have certain drives, such as libido, hunger, thirst, etc., built into them from birth. Yet besides those, they are also equipped with various kinds of "redundancies," which extend from chipping flint flakes and hand axes to building castles from sand or from match sticks, as well as – last but not least – cosmic travel.

7 For volition of any kind to function at all, it must have a "picture" of the surrounding world, or at least of its environment. A child must first learn that one cannot pluck the Moon from the night sky with a bare hand before, several decades later, potentially joining in the work of the Apollo program.

One way to construct a pseudo-model of active volition (i.e., desiring) might be to introduce into the program a random generator. Yet, since as a consequence it would be impossible to predict the future states and presumably the functions of the "robot," no one is especially keen on doing that, except perhaps a lottery or a gambling house. Recall the anecdote of a certain lady who complained to the psychiatrist about her son who not only had devoured an entire Christmas torte but raped the kitchen maid as well. Isn't that proof of his madness, she asked? No, replied the doctor. However, he added, if the son had devoured the kitchen maid and raped the torte, the situation would be quite different.

This is a short but instructive insight into the potential effects of a random generator in simulating volition. Volition, as it is commonly defined, must be expressive of some *sense*. In a flea or an elephant it is going to be the sense of survival, but in human beings the range of sensible actions will understandably be far greater. Alas, as we all know only too well, people are capable of desiring things that are not only detrimental but insane or even plain suicidal. I cannot imagine that a robot could be endowed with some kind of limitless volition or artificial intelligence without being made subject to some powerful restrictions *à la* humans. We are after all "kept in check" by statutory laws, moral laws, as well as by our various traditions, not to mention upbringing. They all impose on us a multitude of restrictions without which, it must be said, there would be few impediments to cannibalism or rape.

8 I must return stubbornly to the problem of how to endow a robot with "desire," even if, as seems necessary, buffered with specific prohibitions and directional guidance. This is a massively difficult task, and the "solution" suggested by Isaac Asimov in his three laws of Robotics is a pure and sterile utopia. Only when all utopian fantasies have been safely cast overboard can we come face to face with the multiple pragmatic antinomies of life.

There is, after all, no end to legitimate goals in life, goals that may be not only of different axiological calibre but *jointly incompatible*. In the face of a situation of this type a normal person often loses their proverbial head or, in order not to lose it, flips a coin, looking eagerly for heads or tails. Simply put, that person abandons decision-making autonomy for the sake of a totally external and, consequently, totally independent chance mechanism. However, if robots clad in legal robes were to begin presiding over judiciary tribunals, judging the weighty matters of our conflicts, we would surely experience a distinct sense of unease if we knew that their decrees derived from purely random operations.

9 A long time ago I wrote about situations in which volition *sui generis* either appears or does not, depending on the type of language used for description. When a virus approaches a living cell, we can speak of a physicochemical and biochemical attraction. Such a description is paravolitional and does not include even a hint of whether the virus *wants* to kill the cell. But the virus attacks the cell, invades its interior, pretends to have the same complement of genes as the cell, metamorphoses – in the Quisling, or the Trojan horse fashion – into a viroid, and suddenly at the scene of the drama we have volition, or at least a germ of it.

Our acts of volition are always directed towards the future. At this point builders of robots run into yet another obstacle, because there are no computers directed towards the future. It may appear different in a chess program only because the machine employs an effective procedure for evaluating various "states" of the chessboard. Values extracted from the tables in its database – values that have been predigested, preprocessed, and imposed "from above" – are assigned to various progressions of the game according to their consequences. This makes the program's ensuing moves comprehensible and thus quasi-volitional.

Still, even though we are told that there are no less than 10^{99} different chess games, we are still talking about a finite number. Following this line of thought, before sending a "planetary explorer" to Titan (a moon of Saturn), first we would have to tabulate a database of everything that the robot might discover or encounter there. Should it turn out (what is quite improbable today) that there are some kind of beings or pseudobeings on Titan, we would never be able to program sensible volition for all of the machine's actions on the alien globe. As Wittgenstein has already remarked, if you cannot speak of something, you should remain silent.

In any case, it is hard to take the above-mentioned "tabling of contents" for the robot seriously, even if only because *sed tamen potest esse totaliter aliter.* But does it mean that only *people* can be sent into situations where no predictions can be made? Not necessarily. People can be sent off into the unknown, but this does not in any way guarantee success. Put simply, people also are not a perfect embodiment of such intentionality that can understand just about anything, nor of volition that would execute only optimal moves in unknown territory.

As we can see, "effective volition" springs into existence only *gradually*. Scientists who, failing to unravel some scientific puzzle, either throw themselves to their knees and implore God for help, or assert that only providence can know the answer, turn against the scientific method, even though they might otherwise be quite religious. The problem is that the moment we appeal to God or any other transcendence, we transfer *our problems* onto someone or something other and thus surrender our own cognitive sovereignty. Much in the same way, a planetary robot-explorer that pronounced itself free from having to undertake exploratory risks owing to ignorance of what it might encounter would be – from both the engineering and epistemological perspective – worthless to us. Anyway, it would be only too easy to build robots ready to turn to God for help at a drop of the hat ...

10 Our subject brings out many other equally puzzling mysteries. One of the more enigmatic ones, despite its superficial transparency, is what volition should need *emotions* for (and it certainly does need them). In the same vein, we would want to know what volition needs intuitions for (because it needs them to a great degree). And what about dreams (ditto)? Digital simulations fail to explain a lot of things due to such specific linearity. If one thing is certain, it is that we are still chipping only very thin flakes off the rock of knowledge.

Looking at human behaviour, we can easily discern a number of typical situations that arise out of our absent-mindedness. For example, called to the telephone, I sometimes put my book aside and, reaching for it afterwards, cannot find it. What happened? Well, after a miserable eternity spent on searching for the book, I discover that I had "mechanically" put it back in its place on the shelf. *Mechanically* means here pretty much the same thing as *unconsciously*. Because my wandering consciousness has failed to perceive the act of putting the book back with others, and because my memory failed to register the event, I waste an inordinate amount of time on the search.

Thus all of a sudden other "entities," namely consciousness and memory, start clamouring to be let into the picture. It looks like our "smart robot" would have to be equipped with both. Consciousness without memory is not much good for anything, and vice versa.

When things go wrong in ways that cannot be helped, consciousness and memory will be the factors that might still save the day.

A robot equipped with cybernetic homologues for human senses would surely register the action of putting the book away on the shelf and store it in its memory banks. Does it mean though that it would have consciousness and memory in the same way as we do? I am inclined to doubt that. Human beings have the capacity to divide their attention (albeit only to a very limited degree). A robot can no doubt be made to run on multichannel input to a greater degree, but what does this have to do with consciousness? Consider another example. When I rest motionless, for example, when lying in my bed before falling asleep, I am "holistically" aware of all parts of my outstretched body. But I am not limited to this: I can "send" my wakeful consciousness to either leg, to my hands, to my ears, and I know that every normal person can do so as well.

What would it take for a robot to imitate this kind of exclusively mental activity, and how could we find out about such "corporal espionage" executed by its consciousness? Clearly we could trace the electronic impulses in the robot's relevant "nerves." But are they really indicative of an active and vigilant consciousness? Already some experts are beginning to distance themselves from the Turing test; with a robot or a computer that *does not use human language* the situation becomes even worse.

We can thus imagine multifarious robotic constructions, tagged with trendy labels, filled to the brim with consciousness, equipped with perfect memory and total recall, volition of the highest calibre, intentionally efficient imagination, speech, emotions coordinated with cognition, and cognition in sync with intuition – all these attributes being not so much essential as simply indispensable. They are indispensable if we really hope one day to have a species of robots that will obey our every wish and command but will never be led astray towards evil, in contrast to human beings, not the least of which are countless statesmen and politicians who would eagerly conscript them and march them off to wipe the "enemy" off the face of the planet.

For the time being, robots of this type are certainly nowhere to be found, and even if they were suddenly to appear on the market, there is little doubt in my mind that their price tag would be astronomical. (People, on the other hand, are much more affordable, and there are billions of them around.) These robots – smart, docile, and kind – seem to me more an embodiment of their engineers' wishful dreams about guardian angels rather than people. I do believe that in the twenty-first century so-called planetary machine-explorers will be sent to the smaller planets of our system, as well as to our own satellite. They will be equipped with programs (e.g., mining) characterized by considerable redundancy, but you will not be able to converse with any such machine about anything of interest. On the other hand, many bona fide humans have nothing interesting to say either, which, to a skeptic like myself, usually brings a small dose of satisfaction.

2

(Un)masking the Agent: Stanislaw Lem's "The Mask"

N. KATHERINE HAYLES

As coding devices penetrate more deeply into the infrastructure of advanced societies, they also inspire commentary on their relation to human cognition. Although implant devices have only recently become available, speculation on how coding enters into the deep structures of thought predates the technological actuality by several decades. At issue are questions of cooperation/competition between conscious mind and aconscious coding, free will and programmed outcomes, gendered enculturation and the non-gendered operation of algorithms, language and the non-linguistics operation of code. Assuming that a substrate of code underlies conscious mind profoundly affects the concepts of agency and subjectivity. While the Holocaust and other atrocities provide horrifying examples of humans not counting as persons, intelligent software packages offer the spectacle of robots being mistaken for human interlocutors.[1]

In light of these confusions, let me advance a proposition: to count as a person, an entity must be able to exercise agency. Agency enables the subject to make choices, express intentions, perform actions. Scratch the surface of a person, and you find an agent; find an agent, and you are well on your way toward constituting a subject.[2]

Within the broader context of software agents and intelligent robots that are destabilizing ideas of agency, influential cultural theorists Gilles Deleuze, Félix Guattari, and Jacques Lacan are reconfiguring what agency means for humans. My concern here is twofold. On the one hand I want to examine critically claims for rethinking human agency, for the evidence is sparse and the conclusions speculative. On the other hand, I want to challenge premature closure that would too easily recuperate agency back to conscious mind conceived as the ultimate arbiter of action. After analyzing arguments crucial to reconceptualizing agency, I will turn to a literary text that enacts these issues in particularly powerful ways: Stanislaw Lem's 1976 novella "The Mask." With a narrator hovering between the human and nonhuman, "The Mask" explores with subtle potency the complexities of a conscious mind whose agency is circumscribed by an underlying program that partially dictates the actions mind can perform. As the mind probes the limits of its freedom, it undergoes a transformation to something other than human. Whether the eponymous mask refers to the human skin that encases a metallic robot, or to the mind from which the narrative voice emerges, is one of many ambiguities the story performs as it probes the possibilities for a consciousness that coexists with an underlying program it can sense but never directly know. In imagining this configuration, Lem anticipates current theoretical revisions of the unconscious as coded algorithm in ways that remain remarkably prescient a quarter of a century later.

THE MACHINE WITHIN THE HUMAN

In their radical reconceptualization of agency, Deleuze and Guattari reveal that intelligent artifacts played a seminal role in their thinking about agency. Early in *A Thousand Plateaus* they celebrate forms of artificial life called cellular automata (CA), contrasting them with the centered systems they deplore. Governed by a simple set of rules, cellular automata are comprised of cells, each of which calculates its state depending on the state of its immediate neighbours.[3] Once all the cells have done this calculation, they recalculate their states taking the new states of their neighbours into account, and so on through successive generations. On today's computers, cellular automata proceed through generations very rapidly and can be programmed to give the impression of dynamic motion. Because of their dynamism, CA arrays have impressed more than one observer as simulating life.

Deleuze and Guattari describe cellular automata somewhat inaccurately as "finite networks of automata in which communication runs from any neighbor to any other" (17). In fact, as we have seen, each cell samples only the cells immediately adjacent. By claiming for cellular automata a less rule-bound dynamic than they in fact possess, Deleuze and Guattari imply that any configuration whatever is possible, an idea they push to the extreme in a discussion of deterritorialization and reterritorialization. Cellular automata fit their purpose because they are completely mechanistic, computational, and non-conscious but nevertheless display complex patterns that appear to evolve, grow, invade new territories, or decay and die out. In the pattern called the "Glider," for example, a glider-like shape appears at one edge of the screen and moves toward the other edge, as if enacting what Deleuze and Guattari call a line of flight. Cellular automata also appear in their description of schizoanalysis, which "treats the unconscious as an acentered system, in other words, as a machinic network of finite automata (a rhizome), and thus arrives at an entirely different state of the unconscious" (18). The implication is that the unconscious, like cellular automata, is both mechanistic and decentered.

These ideas have obvious limitations when applied to the human organism. Unlike the free-form patterns of cellular automata, humans have biological requirements that make the skin an organ vital to survival. Yet Deleuze and Guattari leap over this objection with a powerful performative rhetoric that makes it seem as if the body could deterritorialize and reterritorialize as easily as cellular automata, which themselves have limitations they do not accurately represent. As a result of these reinscriptions, the body becomes the Body without Organs, an assemblage rather than an organism, which does away with the consciousness as the seat of coherent subjectivity. Reconceptualized as entities following flows of intensities and planes of consistency, humans become mutating assemblages that can absorb a variety of entities in their environments, including machines as well as organic matter. Instead of conscious thought, the Body without Organs is driven by desire. Mark Hansen argues in *Embodying Technesis: Technology Beyond Writing* that desire is so central in *A Thousand Plateaus* that it assumes a fetishized quality, flaming with incandescent intensity that alone has the motive force to drive assemblages into new configurations.[4] Indeed, since consciousness is fragmented, the organism dispersed, and signification thrown out, desire is virtually the only agent left on the playing field. "Make consciousness an experimentation in life," Deleuze and Guattari urge, "and passion a field of continuous intensities, an emission of particle-signs ... Desubjectify consciousness and passion" (134). The net effect of this rhetorical transmutation is to construct the Body without Organs as cellular automata whose computational rules are re-encoded as desire.

At the same time that humans take on attributes of computational media in Deleuze and Guattari, machines acquire biological traits. Adopting the terminology of biological evolution, they write: "we may speak of a machinic phylum, or technological lineage, wherever we find a constellation of singularities, prolongable by certain operations, which converge, and make the operations converge upon one or several assignable traits of expression" (406). Endorsing Leroi-Gourhan's ideas about "technological vitalism" that takes "biological evolution in general as the model for technical evolution," they assert "there is indeed a machinic phylum in variation that creates the technical assemblages, whereas the assemblages invent the various phyla. A technological lineage changes significantly according to whether one draws it upon the phylum or inscribes it in the assemblages; but the two are inseparable" (407). By making the phylum depend on the assemblages and the assemblages on the phylum, Deleuze and Guattari suggest technological evolution produces distinct genetic forms that emerge from a daisy chain of interconnection eluding linear causal explanation.[5] Although Deleuze and Guattari speak of the machinic phylum as "matter in movement, in flux, in variation, matter as a conveyor of singularities and traits of expression" (409), it is not clear what drives these mutations. They attempt to solve the problem by returning to the prime mover in their theory, imagining that machines are also capable of desire.[6]

In "Machinic Heterogenesis," Guattari addresses this point by interpolating the human and mechanical into one another, arguing that the "mechanosphere ... superimposes itself on the biosphere" (Guattari, 17). Seeking to open Maturana and Varela's self-enclosing concept of autopoiesis to the production of otherness, Guattari argues that even a mechanism as simple as a lock and key has a repertoire of structural forms through which it can move. This deterritorializing "smoothing" opens the discrete machine to transformation and, by a non-rational leap of inference, to desire; "all machinic orderings contain within them, even if only in an embryonic state, enunicative nuclei [foyers] that are so many protomachines of desire" (25).[7] Thus machines are made like humans because they are driven by desire, even as humans are made like machines because they can disassembled and reassembled. "It is thus impossible to refuse human thought its part in the essence of machinism" (15). In this view "human" connotes no essential quality but rather marks the historical starting point of a certain line of inquiry. If the human has been mechanical all along, anyone who represents it as "contaminated" by the mechanical mistakes his own process of discovery for the hybridization that was always already there.

Clearly the performative force of language plays a crucial role here, as it does in *A Thousand Plateaus*: much is asserted, almost nothing is demonstrated. If language thus possesses a kind of agency, the next step would be to suppose that language itself is a machine and hence subject to the same processes of deterritorialization and reterritorialization that characterize "desiring machines." Guattari edges toward this realization when he asks, "But how long can we continue to characterize the thought put to work here as human? Doesn't technicoscientific thought emerge from a certain type of mental and semiotic machinism?" (15). He takes structural semiotics to task because it fails to capture "figures of expression that work as diagrammatic machines in direct contact with technical-experimental configurations" (15). Whereas semiotic systems posit "distinctive oppositions of a phonemic or scriptural order that transcribe enunciations [*énoncés*] into expressive materials that signify," machines operate differently, using a signifying process that "does not derive from repetition or from mimesis of significations" (15). Obscurely expressed, the point here seems to be that semiotics has falsified the workings of language by interpreting it through structuralist oppositions that covertly smuggle in anthropomorphic thinking characteristic of conscious mind. The model for language should rather be machinic operations that do not need structural oppositions, because they have available to them a materialistic level of signification in which representation is enfolded together with material processes. Although the word "code" does not appear here, it perfectly fits Guattari's vision of a signifying system directly tied in with the material process of flickering voltages. "Existence is not dialectic," Guattari exclaims later in "Machinic Heterogenesis"; "It is not representable. It is hardly even livable!" (25).

Guattari's "lack of reverence toward the Lacanian conception of the signifier" (23) now becomes explicit. Semiotics is flawed because it "does not get us out of structure, and prohibits us from entering the real world of the machine. The structuralist signifier is always synonymous with linear discursivity," whereas heterogeneous machines refuse to be "orchestrated by a universal temporalization" (23). The difference between Guattari's "heterogeneous machine" and Lacan's reliance on semiotics notwithstanding, the two views have more in common than Guattari acknowledges, for both concur in conceiving of language as a coding machine. Thus the very linguistic processes that reconceptualize human agency by describing it as an intelligent machine are themselves reconceptualized as essentially mechanistic in their operations.

John Johnston, in his important analysis of Lacan's development of a theory of the unconscious, shows that automata theory is crucial to Lacan's thought.[8] The key idea Lacan lifts from automata theory is the notion that symbol manipulation has inherent in it certain structural relationships that can be used to program a Turing machine. Recall that the Turing machine is an abstract machine composed of three components: a head that reads and writes binary symbols forwards and backwards on a tape; the rules for producing an output, given a specified input; and the tape itself, posited to be infinitely long. Turing proved that from this simple machine, it is in principle possible to make any calculating machine whatever, including the Turing machine itself. Working by analogy (although not always explicitly stated as such), Lacan transposes these ideas onto the unconscious, conceiving of it as a machine operating upon language without needing anything like anthropomorphic awareness to perform its operations. Thus Guattari is correct in asserting that linearity is essential to the Lacanian conception of the signifier, but he underestimates the flexibility with which the Turing machine can operate. By enfolding the abstract operations of calculation into the material operation of the tape, Turing simplified the computational load and achieved an economy of operation that made his Universal Machine so powerful an idea it is routinely regarded as providing the theoretical basis for modern computers.

Lacan's conception of the unconscious as a kind of Turing machine enables him to transform profoundly Freud's view of the unconscious (notwithstanding his claim that he merely makes explicit what is implicit in Freud). When Freud posited the death drive, he thought of it as an unconscious tendency to move toward the inanimate, a return to pre-biological origins. There is a sense in which this view of the unconscious is deeply anthropomorphic, for it identifies the present state of the (conscious) subject with life, from which point the unconscious moves back toward the inanimate. By contrast, as John Johnston shows, Lacan envisions language as beginning in the mechanistic operations of the unconscious, from which emerge the higher order processes of conscious thought. The direction of the vector changes from back to up, that is, from regression to emergence; equally important, mechanistic operations are conceived as providing the basis for consciousness rather than representing a return to the pre-animate. Thus the important distinction shifts from living/nonliving to mechanistic intelligence/conscious awareness. Given claims by researchers that artificial life is indeed a form of life, the divide between animate and non-animate has become increasingly problematic (Langton, 1). Like Lacan, theorists of artificial life focus on the intelligences that can emerge from mechanistic operations in both protein- and silicon-based lifeform. The difference between Lacan's linear model and Guattari's "heterogeneous machine" pales compared to looming fact that both envision human cognition as always already interpenetrated by machinic processes, or as John Johnston puts it, the "in-mixing" of human psychology with cybernetics.

The net result of these feedback loops between artificial lifeforms and biological organisms has been to create a crisis of agency, a phenomenon described at length in my book *How We Became Posthuman: Virtual Bodies in Cybernetics, Literature, and Informatics* (1999).[9] If on the one hand humans are like machines, whether figured as cellular automata or Turing machines, then agency cannot be securely located in the conscious mind. If on the other hand machines are like biological organisms, then they must possess the effects of agency even though they are not conscious. In these reconfigurations, desire and language, both intimately connected with agency, are understood in new ways. Acting as a free-floating agent, desire is nevertheless anchored in mechanistic operations, a suggestion Guattari makes in "Machinic Heterogenesis." Language, emerging from the operations of the unconscious figured as a Turing machine, creates expressions of desire that in their origin are always already interpenetrated by the mechanistic, no matter how human they seem. Finally, if desire and the agency springing from it are at bottom nothing more than performance of binary code, then computers can have agency fully as authentic as humans. Through these reconfigurations, Deleuze, Guattari, and Lacan use automata to challenge human agency and in the process represent automata as agents.

Machines acting as agents, humans with their agency rooted in machinic processes – is it any wonder that ideas of agency, and with it notions of personhood, have become destabilized? For a deep exploration of these issues, I turn to Stanislaw Lem's powerful story "The Mask." At the heart of this disturbing tale is a conflict between a conscious mind that can think and an underlying program that determines action. To make the conflict more intense, Lem arranges matters so that conscious mind has no direct access to program, much as we have no direct access to our genes or the interior computational modules that, in the view of evolutionary psychologists Barkow, Cosmides, and Tooby, codetermine our behaviour. In the disjunction between the representations conscious mind makes to itself and actions actually taken, the crisis of agency is bodied forth as an inescapable and tragic condition of thinking mind(s).

THE MACHINE IN THE HUMAN, OR THE HUMAN IN THE MACHINE?

"The Mask" begins with a threshold. On one side is a consciousness that names "the it that was I" (181). In Polish the narrator is throughout named by feminine words: for example "machina" and the feminine "Maska" of the title. Jerzy Jarzębski and Michael Kandel have observed, however, that at the beginning the narrator is constructed as neuter, a performance Lem enacts by using for past-tense verb forms neuter endings that do not actually exist.[10] This linguistic creativity underscores from the outset the importance of gender (albeit here by its linguistic erasure). Using these neologisms, the narrator recounts an experience imaged simultaneously as a birth, a movement down an assembly line, and an erotic encounter. Here the narrator plays a passive role, object of unknown gazing eyes, "snoutlike flattened heads," "pincer hands," and "flat mouths in a rim of sparks" that give a final "quivering kiss" that "tautened the me" and cause the narrator to "crawl into a round opening without light" (181–2).

At the moment the narrator crosses the threshold (which is both spatial and linguistic), consciousness undergoes a dramatic change, feeling "the rush of gender so violent, that her head spun and I shut my eyes. And as I stood thus, with eyes closed, words came to me from every side, for along with gender she had received language" (182). At this liminal moment, the narrator moves from an "it" already receding from awareness into a linguistically enculturated "she" whose movement over the palace threshold (for that is where she now perceives herself to be) plunges her into the symbolic. As her perception snaps into cultural focus, the objects that an instant before it had described as a "colored confusion of vertical trunks" with "globes" containing "tiny buttons bright with water" (182) become the lords and ladies attending a court ball, whose eyes are turning to follow the beautiful woman the narrator has become. Thus from the beginning we have reason to doubt that the narrator's consciousness is the seat of identity, for it springs into existence only after another kind of awareness – an awareness that inhabits an "it" and not "she" – has moved the narrator through the birth channel and out into the world.

These abrupt transitions between physical spaces are characteristic of the consciousness as long as the narrator remains a woman, suggesting that consciousness here operates as if it were a machine being turned on and off. Precisely because the sphere of consciousness is limited, its operation within that staging area is all the more frenetic as it seeks to establish its conditions of possibility. As the woman progresses into the ball, her consciousness speeds along in a hyper-rational mode that Jo Alyson Parker, in her Lacanian analysis of "The Mask," finds impossible to accept as female. Indeed, consciousness suspects its own hyper-rationality. As the narrator tries to make sense of her situation, she realizes that "this self-determined thinking of mine seemed in its correctness just a bit too cold, unduly calm, for fear remained beyond it – like a thing transcendent, omnipresent, yet separate – therefore my own thoughts too I held in suspicion" (199). Knowing that she should be afraid but unable to feel the hormonal surges that make fear an experience inhabiting the self, she comes close to being the subject we call Cartesian, doubting everything including her own thoughts.

Why should she feel fear? Although she can think whatever she pleases, she slowly realizes that she is only partially able to control her actions, a prospect that infuses consciousness with dread. She quickly determines that she is intended for Arrhodes, a brilliant thinker who has dared to question the authority of the king. This knowledge comes to consciousness but does not originate there, appearing to the narrator as a predetermined fact. When she drops her fan before Arrhodes in a clichéd gesture of seduction, she feels a blush appear, but, like fear, this blush does not inhabit her, appearing to consciousness as if it were a foreign intrusion. "The blush did not belong to me, it spread on my cheeks, claimed my face, pinkened my ear lobes, which I could feel perfectly, yet I was not embarrassed, nor excited … I'll say more: I had nothing whatever to do with that blush, it came from the same source as the knowledge that had entered me at the threshold of the hall" (190). This separation between consciousness and the bodily actions consciousness observes reveals a fatal gap between thought and agency. Though consciousness feels it comprises an identity in itself, it must face the fact that another kind of agency also inhabits the body – and moreover an agency to which consciousness has no direct access and must strive to apprehend through inferences and observations. "Everyone knows it is impossible to turn the eyeball around," she thinks, "such that the pupil can peer inside the skull" (194).

In her dance of seduction with Arrhodes, the narrator displays a brilliance and satirical edge that both fascinates Arrhodes and makes him afraid, for he senses immediately this is no ordinary woman, bluntly demanding "Who are you?" Asking this question of herself, the narrator flashes onto the pasts of three entirely different women, Duenna from the north, Angelita from the south, and Tlenix, each accompanied by intense though fragmentary sensory memories.[11] She also senses that her choice will determine the "truth," "that "each one could take on substance if I acknowledged it," and that "the images unmentioned would be blown away" (192). Consciousness here senses its position as a PROM, a programmable chip that can accept an initial choice of input but that, once the choice has been made, loses this flexibility as input merges with software and software rigidifies into hardware. Significantly she chooses not to answer Arrhodes, thereby preserving an indeterminacy that she seeks to fill instead with her own option, imagining herself as that quintessentially marginalized female figure, the madwoman tenderly cared for by patronizing relatives.

This identity cannot take, for it has not been included among the possible inputs. Yet the narrator's response is significant: it shows that consciousness is determined to assert her own agency over and against the other agency inhabiting the body. Conversing with Arrhodes, the narrator tests the limits to which she can go. She tries to say something stupid, knowing that will be an effective turn-off for Arrhodes, but she finds herself unable to be anything but brilliant. When she tries to warn him outright, telling him in response to his request for an assignation, "Better to say: never and nowhere" (194), she can utter the warning only in the clichéd language of a lover who feigns reluctance to spur on desire. She realizes this too late, desperately adding, "I do not toy with you, my fine philosopher, look within and you will see that I advised you well" (195), another articulation that goes awry because when Arrhodes looks within, he sees only the desire that is real enough to him but that she knows to be a fatal trap set by his deadly adversary, the king. "What I wished to add," consciousness thinks, "I could not utter. I was able to think anything, strange as it may seem, yet in no way find my voice, I could not reach those words. A catch in my throat, a muteness, like a key turned in a lock, as if a bolt had clicked shut between us" (195). As the narrator will come to realize more fully later, the most insidious threat to her agency is not a direct prohibition on her actions. Scary as that is, more frightening is a cooptation that turns whatever she tries to do to the purposes of the other agency inhabiting the body.

The seductive dance continues when the narrator meets Arrhodes the next day in a garden – another abrupt transition preceded by a period of unknowingness. When she left the ball, she entered into a carriage that was more like a coffin, imprisoning her within a space too small for her to stand fully upright. As she lies in the darkness, she thinks again of her three pre-arranged pasts and compares them to her dim memories when she experienced herself as neuter. Becoming increasingly aware not only of the alien agency within her body but also of the exterior agents who arranged for it to be there, she muses on the fact that she can remember the time before. "I think it had to be that way, that it would have been impossible to arrange things otherwise," she speculates (196). Desperately seeking a way to make her own will count, she tries to put together an identity not predetermined by the other's agency: "Out of discrepant elements I could construct nothing of my own, unless I were to find in the design already existing some lopsidedness, chinks I might penetrate, thereby to rend open the structure and get to the core of it" (202). And so she returns to her memories as a neuter, ironically thinking that "certainly they should at least have wiped out that sequence on my back, the animation of my nakedness, inert and mute, by the sparking kisses, but that too had taken place and now was with me" (202). The memory functions as what evolutionary biologists call a spandrel, an effect that was not preferentially selected but that nevertheless endures across generations because it is entangled with attributes that were preferentially selected. Out of this spandrel, this unplanned excess, she hopes to find the chink that will let her assert agency.

Her desire for an agency she can call her own becomes the driving force of the narrative – or rather, it drives a narrative of self-determination within the larger narrative scripted by the alien agency that also inhabits the body. Thus desire is multiple, living both in consciousness and program. While consciousness knows its desire from the inside, it knows the desire of program from the outside, as if seen from a distance by an observer. "I had love, but elsewhere – I know how that sounds. Oh it was a passionate love, tender and altogether ordinary. I wanted to give myself to him body and soul, though not in reality, only in the manner of the fashion, according to custom, the etiquette of the court … My love was very great, it caused me to tremble, it quickened my pulse, I saw that his glance made me happy. And my love was very small, being limited in me, subject to the style, like a carefully composed sentence expressing the painful joy of tête-à-tête" (208). Her love is great within the scripted confines of the program that has been written to make it so. But, for consciousness, love is an alien utterance performed without touching the pulse of thinking mind, which sees but does not experience it. "And so beyond the bounds of those feelings I had no particular interest in saving him from myself or another, for when I reached with my mind outside my love, he was nothing to me" (208–9).

Remembering how she rebelled in the carriage as she realized the limits of her agency, she also recalls the extruded snake head that gave her an injection turning consciousness off. For consciousness, Arrhodes is important not as a lover but as a potential ally against foreign agents, who themselves have formed an alliance across her body's boundaries. "Yet I needed an ally in my struggle against whatever had pricked me that night with venomous metal

... Therefore I could not reveal the entire truth to him: that my love and the venomous prick were from one and the same source" (209). Love is a program, passing time is an injection, and both come from agency outside thinking mind. Ironically Arrhodes, too, is following a cultural program that dictates his actions. Consciousness intuits that he "would surely be conventional in his love" and so "would not accept in me the kind of liberation I desired, the freedom that would cast him off. Therefore I could only act deceitfully, giving freedom the false name of love" (209). One kind of agency comes from program and dictates love; another comes from consciousness, which can exercise agency in this cultural context only by calling it love, although its object is not Arrhodes but the articulation of will independent of program. Arrhodes is not so much a love object to consciousness as a tool she hopes to use to assert her own subjectivity.

The dance of seduction ends with another birth and, with it, a subtle transformation of agency. Ordering Arrhodes to leave her alone in her chateau, the narrator stands before a full-length mirror and, following an inexplicable impulse, cuts herself open from sternum to crotch. When she parts the layers of skin, she sees nestled within her flesh the metallic body of an insectile robot and realizes "it was not it, a foreign thing, different and other, it was again myself" (213). At this moment Arrhodes comes in and sees her exposed; "it was I, still I, I was repeating to myself when he entered" (213). Gaping at her open body, he turns and flees. As the narrator works to free herself from her human mask, "Tlenix, Duenna, Mignonne first sank to her knees, then tumbled face-down to the side and I crawled out of her," whereupon the discarded human skin lies "like a naked thing, her legs thrown apart immodestly" in a seductive pose of which the narrator no longer has need (214–15).

In "A Freudian Peek at Fiasco" (elsewhere in this book), Michael Kandel writes about the pervasiveness of insects in Lem's fiction, noting "there is something ominous and repugnant about Lem's insects" and further observing that insects, specifically robotic ones, often function as representations of aliens so unlike humans they remain unfathomable by human characters. "The Mask" uses a highly unusual configuration in combining this alien form with an anthropomorphic consciousness that moreover bears the mark of female gender. Throwing aside the shell of a beautiful woman that masked the insectile robot, the narrator now performs a complex balancing act between maintaining the identity of consciousness and dissipating subjectivity throughout the metallic robot body.

In this struggle, gender plays a surprisingly central role. Carol Wald in "The Female Machine: From von Neumann to Richard Powers" has written brilliantly about "The Mask" as part of a tradition of powerful men using female automata as tools against other men.[12] With the narrator's transformation, the king's plot to assassinate Arrhodes stands fully revealed. But female agency also asserts itself in this design, for we learn that the king "had sworn to his dying mother that if harm befell that wise man it would be of his own choosing" (193) – hence the seduction plot. To keep his word to his mother, the king must arrange matters so that Arrhodes chooses the narrator and initializes the robot's program, whereupon she metamorphoses into an insectile assassin who will pursue him to the ends of the Earth. Male power has the ability to act but only within the constraints imposed by female influence, a formation enacted in a different configuration within the narrator, where male power manifests itself in actions performed by the male-authored program and the consciousness that, as we shall see, continues to be constructed as female.

After the narrator's transformation, consciousness undergoes a subtle but important change. Gone is the hyper-rational quality of detached thinking, as if the mind were an engine racing at high RPM while disengaged from the drive train. Consciousness still thinks but now feels more at one with the body, yielding to the "shining metal [that] had written into it movements which I began to execute" (215). Moreover, consciousness also finds itself permeated by the exquisite distinctions of smell the body's superb olfactory equipment makes possible. Despite this transformation, consciousness continues to desire its own agency, although what that agency might mean becomes more complicated as the sharp division between mind and body eases.

For example, the robot wonders why she pauses for three days after Arrhodes flees before taking up his pursuit. She suspects this may be her program operating to make sure Arrhodes has time to realize the full terror of his situation. But she also thinks of it as a challenge to her skill as a hunting machine, an opportunity to demonstrate an expertise with which she identifies. Agency here is neither folded back under consciousness nor separated from it; rather, agency of mind and program have blended together to form an uneasy heterogeneous amalgam. Thinking from within this state, consciousness suspects that her agency has been from the start infected with the will of another. Recalling the moment when she split herself open, consciousness realizes "that act of self-evisceration had not been altogether my rebellion ... it represented a foreseen part of the plan, designed for just such an eventuality, in order that my rebellion turn out to be, in the end, my total submission" (215). She suspects that the desire authenticating her as an autonomous subjectivity – her intense desire to act as a free agent – has always already been coopted by program, a thought so scary she can think it only after her metamorphosis, when she accepts program not merely as an exterior function but also an interpenetration of herself. "Thus the hope of freedom could have been just an illusion, nor even my own illusion, but introduced in me in order that I move with more alacrity, urged on precisely by the application of that perfidious spur" (231).

Behind this realization lurks an even more unnerving question. Why does consciousness, obviously necessary for the seduction of the intellectual Arrhodes, need to persist after the narrator's transformation into an insectile robot? The narrative supplies an ad hoc explanation in the monk's suggestion that humans know how to disguise themselves so as to defeat the computations of an algorithmic program; thus the robot's artificial intelligence has been constructed so it can put "questions to the quarry, questions devised by the foremost experts on the individual characteristics of the human psyche" (229). This explanation scarcely suffices to explain her active thoughts while on the chase, however, or her realization that "I was not (after all) a lifeless mechanism equipped with a pair of hunting lungs, I was a being that had a mind and used it" (221). She may have been given a mind for purposes other than her own, but, having it, she intends to use it for herself. Still, her mind in its insectile state struggles with other cognitions remote from consciousness. As she continues in the hunt for months, consciousness displays a disconcerting tendency to hibernate. "By now I had forgotten the appearance of this man, and my mind, as if lacking the endurance of the body, particularly during the night runs, drew into itself till I did not know whom I was tracking, nor even if I was tracking anyone; I knew only that my will was to rush on, in order that the spoor of airborne motes singled out for me from the welling diversity of the world persist and intensify" (218). Here agency emerges not from subjectivity but from a cognition that operates independently of conscious mind.

The ambiguity of agency becomes fully apparent when the narrator, having lost the scent, appeals to a wayside monk for help. Woven together in her appeal is falsehood and truth, programmed fate and her own will, prescripted determination to kill Arrhodes and her hope that she can spare him. The monk reveals that Arrhodes had sought sanctuary but had been abducted by kidnappers who intend to exploit his fine mind as their tool. The narrator responds by saying she can kill the abductors, but the monk is also aware of her nature as a programmed assassin. After refusing to give the robot confession because he believes she lacks free will and therefore does not count as a person, the monk asks if she wants the monastery's physician (conveniently a former roboticist) to see if he can defeat the program. Reasoning that he can give her wrong directions to Arrhodes as well as right, she consents to the examination.

The physician finds that her sting cannot be removed without killing her. But in addition he also sees "a mechanism which none of your predecessors possessed, a multiple memory of things superfluous to a hunting machine, for these are recorded feminine histories, filled with names and turns of phrase that lure the mind, and a conductor runs from them down into the fatal core. Therefore you are a machine perfected in a way unknown to me, and perhaps even an ultimate machine" (229). Her female gender is thus revealed as somehow essential to her nature even after the seduction plot has ended, linking her femininity to her earlier search for "chinks" in program that would enable her to "get to the core of it."

Reinforcing this revelation is imagery that figures Arrhodes as her mate as well as her prey. Driven simultaneously by desire and program, her thoughts display a complex ambivalence. When the physician, in one of the anachronistic touches characteristic of Lem's humour, offers to sprinkle iron filings on her core in a move he says will slightly increase her free will, she agrees because she notices them both look at her, implying this is a ruse to gain their trust (229). But when she later addresses the reader directly, acknowledging "no doubt you would like to know what my true intentions were in that final run," her thoughts reveal a deep ambivalence about her goal (231).

She says she would like to kill Arrhodes of her own accord, because she knows he cannot possibly love her now that she is no longer a woman, a remark suggesting that she still desires him. She also thinks he owes her his death, for otherwise she would be "big with death, having no one to whom to bear it" (232), a bizarre image that positions him as father to the death her stinger contains and therefore responsible for it. Yet again, she wonders whether, if she kills his abductors and saves him, she might force him "to exchange the disgust and fear he felt towards me for helpless admiration," thus allowing her possibly to "regain – if not him, then at least myself" (232), an idea that links her agency with his admiration.

Why does Lem explicitly include the assertion that gender is connected to her "fatal core," a connection apparently superfluous to the plot now that the robot has shed her human mask? A 1976 interview with Lem by Zoran Živković throws fascinating light on this question. Connecting his use of a female persona in "The Mask" with the female character of Rheya in *Solaris,* Lem suggests that the two stories represent a significant departure from his usual choice of male protagonists. The passage is so revealing that it deserves to be quoted at length.

> Of that which still remains a mystery to me, and there's quite a good deal of it, I would isolate the problem of the being – a being rationally created, evolving from an empirical method, created so to speak just as a house is built. That being, or rather the heroine Hary [Rheya], becomes a person and in that sense acquires a dominant position in relation to her creator. This problem obsessed and occupied me for so long that I returned to it last year, writing a story entitled "The Mask." This piece no longer deals with an artificial human in the third person and he is not described externally; now it is the heroine herself who speak in the first person, she is conscious of her origin and status, she gradually finds out the truth about herself. Here too, we have the classical problem of the freedom and non-freedom of the programmed mind.
>
> Why was this problem so interesting that I had to treat it on two occasions? I'm not entirely sure. I'm also not sure why I was interested in precisely a woman, and not in a man or some neutral gender – which is a much more frequent occurrence in my writings. Not only can I not explain this to others but I am unable to explain it to myself. (Zivkovic 258)

In *Solaris,* Rheya appears as a creation of the sentient ocean, culled from the deep memories of Kelvin's mind. Visually identical to the wife whom Kelvin lost when she committed suicide, Rheya begins to individuate as a person separate from his perceptions. She has a profoundly different physical structure than humans, and she slowly becomes aware that Kelvin is lying to her about her true nature. Racked by guilt at his wife's suicide, Kelvin tries to get rid of the memories the Rheya simulacrum embodies by ejecting her into space, but the simulated Rheya simply reappears, having been reconstituted by the ocean. She finally asserts her autonomy in the only way she believes possible – by committing suicide – and her suicide note is the only communication the reader has from her that is not mediated by Kelvin's perceptions. In "The Mask" the narrator also physically differs from humans, but the split between a male narrator who speaks and a nonhuman female who acts is now differently arranged so that the female has the power of articulation and the male-conceived program has the power of action. In both stories female agency is thrown into question, and in both a female character struggles to assert her independence in her relation with a human male who is at once her lover and antagonist.

Whatever the reasons for this structural/narrative formation, it seems clear that gender is central to the power it exercises over Lem's imaginary. Without attempting to psychoanalyze Lem (which would be doubly presumptuous in view of his comment that he himself does not know why these female characters fascinate him), I conclude that there are deep connections between the female's struggle for autonomy within the story and her relation to her creator, understood here as a consciousness beyond the reach of the character's introspections, whether a sentient ocean working in collaboration with Kelvin's unconscious, an all-powerful king, or Lem himself. The female's alien nature thus enacts not only her difference from humankind but also her gender-specific difference from her male creator. In these stories the female is at once the intimate mate and the terrifyingly alien other, bearing within herself the imprint of her creator's will as well as her own ambiguous agency. It is as if the female, to succeed as a character, has to assert an agency independent of the male mind that conjured her into being. The more she tears herself away, the more she achieves reality as an autonomous subjectivity; but the more she achieves autonomy, the more she resists her creator's agency and thereby threatens to defeat her putative purpose for being. Given these complexities, is it any wonder she is compounded of life and death, love and agony?

These complex interrelations reach explicit articulation within "The Mask" when the monk demands to know what the narrator will do, now that she has received the treatment to widen slightly her margin of action. When she answers that she does not know – which, given the confused motives described above, is probably accurate – the monk responds, "You are my sister." Stunned, the narrator asks him what he means. "Exactly as I say it," he answers, "and it means I neither raise myself above you nor humble myself before you, for however much we may differ, your ignorance, which you have confessed to me and which I believe, makes us equal in the face of Providence" (226–7).

Harbouring an irreducible ambiguity, the monk's response reinscribes within the story Lem's own inability to understand his creative choices. The robot is like him because she does not know if program will completely determine her actions, which implies that she believes she has free will, however slim the margin. In this sense, she is his sister because she counts as a human person. She may also be like him because he operates according to biocultural programs that dictate his actions, making his consciousness unsure how he will act. In this reading she is his sister because he counts as a programmed entity. The entangling of meanings here is like the entangling of the female character's agency together with her creator's will, so that the story can be understood to be simultaneously about human agency and robotic programming, male authorship and female self-birthing.

When she was given birth by the assembly line, the narrator lay passively on her back for most of the journey (202), as she did when the monks operated on her (229). In this position she cannot wield her stinger; for that, she needs to be standing upright so it can emerge from its "ventral shaft" and thrust forward. When she thinks back on the monk's words acknowledging her as his sister, she remarks, "I still could not understand them, but when I bent over them something warm spread through my being and transformed me, it was as if I had lost a heavy fetus, with which I had been pregnant" (230). The image recalls her thinking of the death she carries as Arrhodes's unborn child. Here, too, the most likely reference for the "heavy fetus" is death, but this time it is the death of her as a programmed robot, after which she could possibly be born again as an autonomous person. But the ambiguity lingers, for she also imagines herself bending over the monk's utterance, the position from which she can enact the king's command through her phallic stinger. Thus in the same thought she figuratively gives birth to herself as an autonomous agent by losing the king-impregnated fetus of death and adopts the posture that makes her a vehicle for the king's will.

Elsewhere in this book, Michael Kandel identifies in *Fiasco* a combination of male and female sexual imagery, linking it to narrative patterns that suggest to be born is to be mortal and in this sense to receive the sting of death. He quotes what he identifies as a favourite saying of Lem's, "We are born between urine and feces," associating it with the unremittingly negative associations that women have in *Fiasco*. He further suggests that the Quintans, a version of the unknowable aliens that populate Lem's fictions, are associated with female sexual imagery. These patterns, appearing in a text that Kandel reads as constituting transgressive revenge against humanity for being mired in a messy biology that ensures humans cannot attain the purity of completely rational mind, form a suggestive context for the female machine in "The Mask."

Her female gender re-marks her phallic stinger with the mortality Lem associates with pregnancy and birth, rendering it at once masculine and feminine, which is suggested by the image of the stinger as her fetus. Moreover, woman as mediating link between an unknowable alien and male protagonist – the pattern of *Solaris* – is here reimagined as a female consciousness mediating between a male protagonist and an unknowable (to her) program, which operates untouched by the emotional turbulence and irrational desires that Lem hopes humans will overcome. Further complicating these connections is the narrator's metallic body, which is metaphorically comingled with the female pregnancy and birth that Lem associates with "urine and feces," forming an oxymoronic amalgam that at once incarnates and transcends biology. Perhaps these complexities help to explain why "The Mask," unlike *Fiasco* with its dark ending, finds in the female mind a measure of compassion that, although it cannot save Arrhodes (described as having a superbly rational mind about to be forced into ignoble slavery), nevertheless restores to him respect and even possibly love.

This ambiguous affirmation occurs when she finally tracks Arrhodes to the castle where he has been taken by his abductors, only to discover that a mortal struggle has taken place and he lies unconscious and bleeding on the stairs. "Had he opened his eyes and been conscious, and – in an inverted view – taken me in entirely, exactly as I stood over him, stood now powerlessly carrying death, in a gesture of supplication, pregnant but not from him, would that have been a wedding – or its unmercifully arranged parody?" (238–9). Both "bride and butcher," the narrator exercises her agency in the only way she can, by delaying her fatal sting while she waits to see if Arrhodes will recover. If he does, she is clear that her programming will enact his death, and so enmeshed is her consciousness with it that she does not know "if I truly desired him to wake" (238). Only when he "groaned once more and ceased to breathe" does she alter her posture. Feeling her "mind at rest," she lies down beside him and wraps "him tightly in my arms, and I lay thus in the light and in the darkness through two days of snowstorm, which covered our bed with a sheet that did not melt. And on the third day the sun came up" (239).

The three days continue a pattern that has marked her life from the beginning: her courtship lasted three days; she lingered for three days before beginning the hunt; and she experienced three births, first on the assembly line, then in her entry into language and gender, and finally in her metamorphosis into the insectile robot. Does the faint promise of resurrection hint that she can experience a fourth birth, breaking the pattern and becoming at last her own person now that she has fulfilled her programming? Earlier she had thought about what she would become if she were to abandon her goal and strike out on her own. The king would order robotic dogs to hunt her down as mercilessly as she pursued Arrhodes, and, even if she were by some miracle to survive, all human society would find her abhorrent. Significantly, this information comes in the middle of the tale, so that it lingers in the reader's mind as fading memory rather than as active narration. Granted this slight margin of forgetfulness, we can edge toward asking the question forbidden by the closure of the plot: what kind of life could she be born into? Certainly not into the coherent subjectivity of an independent human who has never had reason to question whether she has free will. But perhaps in these post-human days, when the crisis of agency is far from resolved, she might count as a person, albeit a nonhuman one. If so, then we can say to her with all the rich ambiguities that attended the monk's utterance, "You are our sister."

MACHINE AND HUMAN ENFOLDED

In separating consciousness from program, Lem's story anticipates the posthuman subject envisioned by Deleuze, Guattari, and Lacan, a subject in which consciousness, far from being the seat of agency, is left to speculate on why she acts as she does. She is increasingly aware that the origin of agency lies beyond the reach of consciousness, enacted by a computational program that is ultimately controlled by the external agent that has programmed the code to operate as it does. Even at this deep level the ambiguity of agency continues, for program is perceived to act both as an agent on its own behalf and as the surrogate for the king's will. The ambiguity is repeated within consciousness, where she perceives herself to be exercising agency in the margins, as it were, the grey areas where the objectives of code might be implemented in ambiguous ways. In these complex reconfigurations of agency, the significance of envisioning the unconscious as a program rather than as a dark mirror of consciousness can scarcely be overstated, for it locates the hidden springs of action in the brute machinic operations of code. In this view, such visions of the unconscious as Freud's repressed Oedipal conflicts or Jung's collective archetypes seem hopelessly anthropomorphic, for they populate the unconscious with ideas comfortingly familiar to consciousness rather than the much more alien operations of machinic code.

Yet the estrangement from traditional ideas of mind does not stop here, for an even more subversive implication lurks in Lem's story, an implication that the very human-sounding voice of the narrator may prevent us from realizing except in retrospect. Given the mechanical origin of the creature, even consciousness must arise from code, for she has been manufactured rather than born. In this sense consciousness may also be a mask created to mediate between human readers and an alien core. Even when the machine sheds her human shell, the anthropomorphic thoughts of consciousness function as a mask within the mask, inviting our identification with what must also be a result of machine code.

Whether consciousness can ever emerge from a coded mechanism remains a matter of intense debate. Roboticists such as Hans Moravec and Rodney Brooks are confident that the equivalent of conscious mind can arise from a coded program, whether evolved through intelligent robots or originating as human consciousness uploaded into a computer. Researchers operating with deeper familiarity with the flesh, such as Antonio Damasio, argue that body and mind are inextricably linked through multiple recursive feedback loops mediated by neurotransmitters, systems that have no physical analogues in computers. Damasio makes the point that these messages also provide content for the mind, especially emotions and feelings: "relative to the brain, the body provides more than mere support and modulation: it provides a basic topic for brain representations" (xvii). It is precisely the disruption of this normal integration between mind and body that makes the intuition of Lem's narrator seem so enigmatic, as when she explains that the love she "feels" for Arrhodes is at once very great and very small.

Nevertheless, with the advent of emotional computing, evolutionary algorithms and programs capable not only of learning but of reprogramming themselves (as in programmable gate arrays), it no longer seems fantastic that artificial minds may some day achieve self-awareness and even consciousness. Brian Cantwell Smith sees this as opening "a window onto something to which we would not otherwise have any access: the chance to witness, with our own eyes, how intentional capacities can arise in a 'merely' physical mechanism. It is sobering, in retrospect, to realize that the fact computers are computational has placed a major theoretical block in the way of our understanding how important they are … only when we let go of the conceit that the fact is theoretically important will we finally be able to see, without distraction – and thereby, perhaps at least partially to understand – how a structured lump of clay can sit up and think" (Smith, 75–6). The central question, in other words, is no longer how we as rational creatures should act in full possession of free will and untrammeled agency. Rather, the issue is how consciousness evolves from and interacts with the underlying programs that operate analogously to the operations of code. Whether conceived as literal mechanism or instructive analogy, coding technology thus becomes central to understanding the human condition.

Agency, long identified with free will and rational mind, becomes in this view partial in its efficacy, distributed in its location, mechanistic in its origin, and bound up at least as much with code as with natural language. We are no longer the featherless biped that can think but the hybrid creature that enfolds within itself the rationality of the conscious mind and the coding operations of the machine. Who then is the agent that acts? "The Mask," anticipating these debates, helps us to understand how partial, complex, and interdigitated may be the agency we call our own.

NOTES

1 The literature on this phenomenon is extensive. For a technical survey, see Munneke, Wahlstrom, and Zaccara, "Intelligent Software Agents on the Internet"; for a discussion of the psychological aspect of bots, see Leena Saarinen, "Chatterbots: Crash Test Dummies of Communication," which also discusses Joseph Weizenbaum's famous "Eliza" program.

2 For a discussion of how agency implies personhood in artificial-life creatures, see Hayles, "Simulated Narratives."

3 For a discussion of cellular automata, see Stephen Wolfram, *A New Kind of Science*. In addition to having cellular automata respond to their nearest neighbour, it is also possible to create simulations in which they also take into account their next nearest neighbours, as Wolfram documents.

4 Hansen's interpretation, while making important points, is flawed in not recognizing the importance of agency in Deleuze and Guattari's rhizomatic philosophy. For them agency continues to play a central role, but its locus is displaced from consciousness into aconscious processes.

5 In another context, Francisco Varela calls such dynamics "co-dependent arising" to emphasize the mutual interdependence of each component on the others (Varela, Thompson, and Rosch).

6 For a critique of the idea that present-day computers and intelligent machines can be considered alive (and by implication have such experiences as desire), see Peter Swirski, "A Case of Wishful Thinking."

7 In *A Thousand Plateaus*, Deleuze and Guattari contrast smooth space with striated (by analogy, I suppose, with muscle tissue). Whereas smooth space is continually transformative and fluid, striated is hierarchical, locked in, structurally rigid.

8 I am grateful to John Johnston for sharing with me his essay prior to publication.

9 See "Liberal Subjectivity Imperiled: Norbert Wiener and Cybernetic Anxiety," 50–83; "From Hyphen to Splice: Cybernetic Syntax in *Limbo*," 113–30; and "Narratives of Artificial Life," 222–46. The crisis of agency is also implicit in such works as Marvin Minsky, *The Society of Mind*, which conceptualizes human intention and agency as subroutines run

by semi-autonomous agents. Also revealing is the furor over the research of Benjamin Libet, *The Volitional Brain* and "Time of Conscious Intention to Act," demonstrating that research subjects started the muscular actions to raise their arms before they were consciously aware that they were going to do so, thus bringing into question whether the conscious mind is the source of agency. Libet's experiments have been extensively critiqued in Daniel Dennett, *Freedom Evolves*, 228–42.

10 I am grateful to Jerzy Jarzębski and Michael Kandel for this information in personal communications. Kandel illustrates using the verb "czuć" ("to feel"). "A man would say 'czułem' ('I felt'); a woman would say 'czułam' ('I felt'). A nongendered robot would say 'czułom' ('I felt'). Using the vowel 'o' is Lem's neologism. The verb form is quite strange, but a Polish reader would understand immediately" (email, 6 January 2004).

11 Lem varies these names as follows: Duenna, Tlenix, Angelita (198); Duenna, Mignonne, Angelita (200); Duenna, Tlenix, Mignonne (214), Duenna, Tlenix, Angelita (215). Assuming Tlenix is a surname/placename, the Countess of Tlenix seems have been variously assigned the given names of Mignonne (198, 200, 215) and Angelita (214).

12 I am grateful to Wald for making her essay available to me before publication, and also for calling my attention to "The Mask."

3

Betrization Is the Worst Solution ... with the Exception of All Others

PETER SWIRSKI

"Morality can be said to presuppose an ability to put oneself in the position of another."

– Anatol Rapoport

"A new scientific truth does not triumph by convincing its opponents and making them see the light, but rather because its opponents eventually die, and a new generation grows up that is familiar with it."

– Max Planck

Betrization is a medical procedure posited by Lem in his 1961 novel *Return from the Stars*. In this rarely discussed work from his "golden period," the author models a society in which aggression and the ability to put oneself or others at risk are inhibited to the point of being almost entirely erased. To many readers such invasive surgery, performed early in life on every member of our species, will smack of utopian (or dystopian) fantasy. I would like to contest this view and examine how this science fiction could conceivably become science fact. The following is an attempt to identify certain sociocultural and technological trends that could make betrization or its kin – some more, some less benevolent – possible in our world.

In *Return from the Stars* a space expedition returns to an Earth that has aged 127 years in its absence. Much has changed since the astronauts left, and the most perplexing novelty is universal betrization. As the book makes plain, at first few took seriously the project of making Homo sapiens into a better species on the operating table. The proposal languished with the United Nations for many years before its eventual adoption ignited a storm of violence and controversy. Many parents refused to allow their children to be betrizated, with the operating centres worldwide coming under attack. The "new order" (119) took effect only with the second generation of de-aggressed humanity.

The reader's reaction to the procedure, as filtered through the eyes and mind of the protagonist, Hal Bregg, is ambivalent. Betrization – performed at birth – brings about "the reduction of aggressive impulses by 80 to 88 percent," the elimination of "associative links between acts of aggression and the sphere of positive feelings," as well as "a general 87% reduction in the possibility of accepting personal risk to life." Significantly, in Lem's thought-experiment, these changes do not "influence negatively the development of intelligence or the formation of personality." Betrization, as he is careful to point out, is not a product of fear conditioning, which might be only selectively effective, subject to erosion over time, and prone to behavioural side-effects. Instead it "causes the disappearance of aggression through the complete absence of command, and not by inhibition" (all on 119–20), both in humans and the higher mammals to whom the procedure is extended. Attempts to override the invisible barrier in a person's mind lead to repulsion and aversion, rapidly escalating into a desire to escape, severe headaches, shortness of breath, feeling of suffocation, and finally neurosis (120–1).

Yet, for all the rewards to individuals and society at large, Bregg feels that somehow "this destruction of the killer in man was a disfigurement" (39). A doctor he meets rues that "they" eliminated the hell of passion – and, along with it, heaven, so that everything became "lukewarm" (71). Another blow is that the spirit of space exploration is nearly dead – the new and betrizated human race is loath to take the risk. In a major departure from such classics as H.G. Wells's *The Time Machine* or Pierre Boulle's *Planet of the Apes,* Lem does not, however, link the loss of the aggressive drive and ascendancy of material utopia to the rise of a stagnant or effete civilization. In his scenario no one wages wars or kills, no one is aggressive or vengeful, no one boxes or defies danger, no one emotes over risk or martial valour in literature or art – and no one feels the worse for it. Arts flourish, creativity is boundless, people are educated, content, and at leisure to pursue their lives.

Return from the Stars is far from the only Lem narrative built around the concept of top-down behaviour modification, although, significantly, it is the first in which enforced social engineering takes place on Earth. In this context his preceding novel, *Eden* (1959), is thus something of an étude on the idea that would preoccupy the writer for decades to come. A group of scientists who crash-land on Eden come face to face with the aftermath of botched eugenetic experiments on the local population. Tormented accounts of military dictatorship dominate the crew's interviews with mutants struggling to avoid life-in-death in quarantined reservations. The search for perfection is very well, scoffs the writer from behind the iron curtain erected around Stalinist Poland, if you are willing to exact the price from the innocents. Published under the communist "utopia" that whittled human rights in the name of patriotic resistance against the military terror of the West, *Eden*'s subversive title presages Lem's 1961 return from the stars to the sociopolitics of our times.

On Site Inspection (1983; still unavailable in English) unveils a scenario as radical as betrization, in which ethics is enforced with the aid of nanotechnology. Nanobots dispersed like pollen through the air prevent any action that may result in personal harm, accidental or deliberate. No matter that these invisible watchdogs curtail a number of personal liberties and limit the range of actions – and thus choices – one might undertake. No matter that, in this sense, this nanotechnological thought police is Orwell's word become flesh. The price for peace from war and murder, admonishes Lem at this late stage of his career, may not seem worth paying until you consider the alternative: the world as we know it.

An earlier novel, *The Futurological Congress* (1971), depicts a scenario in which Earth, in the throes of population explosion, is kept in control by means of hallucinogenic drugs.[1] Instead of the world of twenty-nine billion people and unremitting squalor, drugged humanity sees a utopia of plenty. The juxtaposition of this work with *Return from the Stars* is not incidental, inasmuch as there is a direct relation between aggression and population density. Even the early popularizations of this idea, such as Desmond Morris's *The Human Zoo* (1969), took account of environmental and laboratory data indicating that some forms of aggression may be nature's way of self-regulating populations suffering from demographic explosion. Eliminating the ruinous results of our propensity to war and murder, betrization may thus have its Pyrrhic side.

The early-warning mechanism that would normally tip off stresses building in the environment would be extinguished, ironically inviting a continued increase in population and thus further violence. Perhaps aware of this powder keg, Lem endows the betrizated society with the hallmarks of a demographically stable and materially affluent utopia.

Culled from each decade of Lem's 1950s–80s belletristic career, these examples reveal the obstinacy with which the writer revisits the concept of instrumental incursion into the realm of social steering, group ethics, behavioural control, etc. The list is, of course, much longer: *Star Diaries, Memoirs of a Space Traveller,* and *The Cyberiad* – all have their mad or merely megalomaniacal inventors who inflict social panacea on entire populations. Diverse as they are, the common denominator among these novels and stories is found in "The Ethics of Technology and the Technology of Ethics." This standalone essay has for decades now been appended to later editions of Lem's *Dialogi* [*Dialogues*], which contains some of the author's trenchant essays on the nature of social engineering. Built around a series of Berkeleyan dialogues between Hylas and Philonous, *Dialogues* follows their discursive sallies into the then virgin territory of morality as applied technosocial control. In the conclusion to the appended essay, Lem identifies the Grail of social control as the curtailment of aggression and violence in our species. Strikingly, his question is not *whether* but *where* to construct the dam to protect humanity from a deluge of self-inflicted war, murder, and death.

Return from the Stars is thus a highly original stab at the solution to the problem that will dominate Lem's thinking about our world – much as it will dominate the world's agenda – in the ensuing decades. This is not to say that the novel is uniformly successful as a work of literature, as its author, echoed by several critics, readily admits. But among the critiques aimed at the superheroic hero, the monodimensional "gateway-to-Earth" heroine, or even the overly optimistic picture of betrization, Lem has steadfastly defended the novel's core: the consequences of defanging the human beast. It is one thing, of course, to approach *Return from the Stars* as a work of art and another to read it in the context of current socioscientific data with an eye to the cognitive payoffs such readings may yield.[2] Developing the ideas about social engineering articulated in Lem's novel, I follow mainly the latter strategy, taking cue from the author for whom not Hal Bregg but "knowing" is the hero of this and other books.[3]

Today the mixed merits of a procedure like betrization, and more generally of social and even genetic engineering, are more worthy of examination than ever. Our propensity for violence and genocide may be historically constant, but our capacity for destruction can only grow. I believe it would be criminal, even genocidal – in the sense of committing a crime against humanity – not to enforce universal betrization if the technology ever became available. The millions killed, murdered, maimed, raped, tortured, persecuted, and otherwise betrayed human lives are proof enough that human inhumanity will not be stopped in any other way. Having said that, I want to investigate how betrization and cognate techniques of mass behavioural control could be a Trojan horse – to which we may have already opened the door.

SOCIOBIOLOGY AND UTOPIA

"As for your doctrine, I am prepared to go to the stake for it. I am prepared to go to the stake, if requisite, in support of chapter 9, and most parts of chapters 10, 11, and 12."

– Thomas Huxley (in a letter to Charles Darwin)

"I hold it that a little rebellion, now and then, is a good thing, and as necessary in the political world as storms in the physical."

– Thomas Jefferson

Not unlike Thomas Hobbes, who pictured society in the state of war of all against all, Edward Wilson concludes in *On Human Nature* (1978) that the answer to the question "Are human beings innately aggressive?" is "Yes" (99). However, just like rationality, aggression is not a monodimensional or even homogenous attribute, and Wilson's anthropological and biological data leads him to distinguish at least seven types of aggressive response. Beside the more familiar varieties, such as territorial, hierarchical, sexual, hunting, defensive, or related to weaning of young adults, the sociobiologist finds evidence for singularly human category: the "moralistic and disciplinary aggression used to enforce the rules of society."[4] On this view it would seem that betrizating a given population might actually reduce a government's ability to rule effectively, at least when it comes to social control. If, at first blush, this appears a counterintuitive outcome in terms of Lem's thought-experiment, it is owing to the suppressed premise of all other things being equal. In fact a betrizated society would almost certainly have less need for coercive aggression in conducting its social affairs.

The need to correct a society that founders on aggression and wickedness is nothing new.[5] Sumerian tablets are among the oldest sources of myths of messianic sacrifice for the fallible humanity in need of redemption. This lapsarian model of human nature became codified for the millennia in the Judeo-Christian tradition. Genesis 4:1–16, in which Cain slays Abel, is the archetypal parable in which humanity falls prey to wanton aggression. Interestingly enough, already the Bible hints that a corrective intervention into our default programming can customize it against committing acts of violence. The mark that the Almighty brands on Cain's forehead controls homicidal urges in all who would aggress him otherwise. The implication is clear: much as in *Return from the Stars*, authoritarian control may be exercised to forcibly rewire aggression out of our system – in effect to betrizate us.

Today we are more inclined to take the sociobiological rather than the theological route to explain the essence of *la bête humaine*. Charles Darwin would have approved of research in adaptive anthropology, behavioural ecology, and evolutionary psychology that approaches morality as a form of compromise among competing spheres of genetic self-interest. As Robert Wright sums up decades of such research in *The Moral Animal* (1994): "people tend to pass the sorts of moral judgments that help move their genes into the next generation."[6] Although couched in the lexicon of sociobiology, the idea that our would-be transcendent moral sense is instinct is not new. It is inherent even in Bertrand Russell's analysis of emotivism, itself rooted in the contrast between the truth-based nature of science and the truth-less subjectivity of ethics.[7] In between Russell and Wright, Lem himself put forth a similar idea in his 1968 masterpiece *His Master's Voice*. Peter Hogarth – in some ways the writer's most autobiographical creation – deals a blow to transcendence by working out a mathematical model of ethics as controlled steering. If the writer, the philosopher, and the scientist are right, in the future good and evil may have less to do with the moral imperative than with forms of algedonic control that can be exercised externally – in *Return from the Stars* by invasive surgical technology.

Little wonder that, from Plato on, philosophers theorizing on just forms of government felt obliged to comment on human nature, and thus ineluctably on our instinct for aggression and the need to contain it. Ironically, then, generations of blueprints for utopia come armed with passages on the means of control of the dark side of the human ape. As a general rule, the relation between utopia and human nature comes in two varieties. The optimistic flavour is represented by Thomas More, who affords that a radical change of social governance will bring about a beneficent change in human nature. One need not even go back to the USSR, Maoist China, or Pol Pot's Khmer Rouge to wonder if More puts the cart ahead of the horse, apart from begging the question of how/why the transition to a perfect society should arise in the first place. The obverse, and more cynical, view of human nature insists that *it* must be radically modified for any utopian blueprint to succeed. With betrization the key that would lock away human fangs and claws, Lem's narrative thought-experiment falls into the second category; perforce my analysis is also limited to this variant.

Working from the Hobbesian premise, whereby it is human nature that may be an obstacle to utopia, government Leviathans routinely resort to effecting compliance in target populations. Max Weber, the legendary theorist of social organizations, distinguished three pure types of authority: rational, resting on the presumption of legality; traditional, based on an established belief in the sanctity of historical precedent; and charismatic, deriving from an exemplary individual and the normative pattern of behaviour ordained by that person.[8] The authority behind George Orwell's Big Brother, for example, can be said to be rational and charismatic. The dispersed and anonymous authority (which at least one critic brands as soft totalitarianism) that wields power in *Return from the Stars* would be only rational.[9] The British monarchy is perhaps an instance of authority that is at once rational, traditional, and charismatic.

This is not to say that acceptance of authority of any kind is automatic. Weber notes as much: "That subjection to military discipline is formally 'involuntary' while that to the discipline of the factory is voluntary does not alter the fact that the latter is also a case of subjection to *authority*" (213). We have thus two modes of social control: the involuntary mode, involving suppression and control through external (e.g., military or paramilitary) means, and the voluntary mode, which relies on propaganda and indoctrination to condition subjects internally. One must not think of them in opposition to each other. Orwell again provides a good literary example of how intimately external and internal techniques are linked. When Winston Smith is released at the end of *1984*, it is *not* because he has bamboozled the regime into believing that he loves Big Brother but because he *really* loves him. Under an involuntary, i.e., external, source of compulsion, Smith has internalized the totalitarian ideology as his own, thereby also internalizing *both* modes of control. If we compare Orwell and Lem, it becomes apparent that betrization also fuses the external and internal modes of population control. Although implemented externally, it is an internally invasive procedure modifying the neural "hardware" to disable a specific range of behavioural "programs," namely those related to risk-taking, violence, and aggression.

And yet the distinction between external and internal modes of socioengineering control is crucial. The notion of behaviour control via *internally* invasive techniques may be anathema to a population disposed to hand over its constitutional liberties to controls applied *externally*. Not to look too far, no matter how intrusive and antidemocratic, the anti-terrorist platform of the current US administration puts the government on the outside of the somatic divide between external and internal coercion. For most people this is sufficient to maintain an illusion of freedom from thought police. Few apprehend that, similar to Lem's betrization, external and internal behavioural techniques need not remain categorically distinct but can shade off into each other.

The question that will occupy me in the next section is: under what conditions could technological enforcement of moral policy be introduced in our world a form acceptable both to the public and the government? The prognostic failures of even the biggest think-tanks in modern history teach that predicting the shape of things to come is fraught with difficulty. From the Rand Corporation to the Hudson Institute, from simple Delphi iterations to computer scenarios dating back to Donella Meadows's pioneer forecasts in the late 1960s, the methodological Achilles' heel seems to be computational explosion as a function of time. I will therefore venture only one generation ahead to assess the likelihood of a top-down behavioural control system in our society. My analysis is not meant to imply that the trends described herein are in any way inevitable or desirable, merely to dispute the default assumption that "it can't happen here."

TECHNOLOGY AND COMPLIANCE

"Congress shall make no law respecting an establishment of religion, or prohibiting the free exercise thereof; or abridging the freedom of speech, or of the press; or of the right of people peaceably to assemble ..."
– The First Amendment to the US Constitution (the Bill of Rights)

"One of the best ways to get yourself a reputation as a dangerous citizen these days is to go about repeating the very phrases which our founding fathers used in the great struggle for independence."
– Charles Austin Beard

The fallout from the 9/11 attacks on New York and the Pentagon shows how external factors can be exploited to instigate social reform – in this case the suppression of civic freedoms in the alleged interest of national security. The Patriot Act, rushed through Congress in October 2002 defines terrorism so loosely – as an activity intended to intimidate or coerce a civilian population – that almost anything can fall under its jurisdiction. Its ramifications appear to provide support to the thesis that a crisis of sufficient magnitude can – and will – be used to enforce a degree of behavioural control that will be tolerated by the majority.

After all the Patriot Act itself is an unconstitutional law that violates fundamental civil liberties. The government gave itself power to obtain personal information about US citizens and to detain foreign nationals on a mere suspicion and without public acknowledgment. Its short-lived TIPS (Terrorism Information and Prevention System) actually institutionalized a violation of privacy by endorsing nationwide spying by the US populace on the US populace in the name of homeland security. Its current successor, TIA (Total Information Awareness), is no less Orwellian in design. This Pentagon surveillance system amasses information floating in cyberspace about every US citizen. Phone, email, internet, library, school, medical, travel, and credit-card records are decrypted, stored in a national database, and tagged for biometric analysis, e.g., facial and optical imaging, gait recognition, and the like.[10] Amendments in immigration law render all applicants in effect guilty until proven innocent. Visitors must undergo "special registration" – including fingerprinting and photographing – even before entering and then before departure, with a Kafkaesque corollary that lack of knowledge of the law gives no exemption from its zero-tolerance consequences.[11] In the meantime, the Aviation Security Act turned all airport security personnel into federal employees, de facto the government's security corps.

In Canada Bill C-18 – in February 2003 already on its second reading in the House of Commons – gives federal politicians the right to revoke citizenship or deport immigrants with no resistance and no right of appeal. The almost furtively passed Bill C-17 already gave the state enhanced powers to monitor communications, and the Canada Customs and Revenue Agency powers to unconstitutionally launch a passenger database collecting private information in a manner no different from the American TIA. Worse even, "Under exemptions to the general right of access under the Privacy Act, Canadians do not have the right to see the personal information the government holds about them if it pertains to national security or an ongoing investigation."[12] Bill C-36, known as the Anti-Terrorism Act, allows police to detain people for unspecified periods without warrant and without any crime being committed, and the post office to open private mail and seize contents at will. It is also legal for the police to keep evidence secret, even from the accused, and to deny them the right to remain silent and not to incriminate themselves.[13] In Bill C-42 the government sought power to make new regulations without asking Parliament and to designate any part of the country a military security zone without provincial consent.

In the US, new investigative guidelines accord FBI agents, who are not required to present or even have any evidence of crime, a broad wiretap mandate, access to student and library records, and internet spying powers.[14] Library staff are forbidden by law to inform readers that they are investigated since, according to Assistant Attorney General Daniel Bryant, Americans who borrow library books automatically surrender their right to privacy.[15] Altogether, the revamping of the FBI, immigration and aviation laws, the creation of the Department of Homeland Security (with a $37 billion budget and a staff of 170,000, second only to the Defense Department), and the erosion of civil rights in Canada mark a sweeping retrenchment across North America. In view of this remarkably efficient and rapid success in altering the democratic balance on the entire continent I conclude that it is not impossible that an even more radical suppression of – or willingness to sacrifice – civil rights may in the future pave the way for an even more radical – because technological – intervention into personal and societal conduct.

Although *Return from the Stars* refrains from speculating about the nuts and bolts of the technology behind betrization, the present analysis would be incomplete without a consideration of the technoscientific dimension behind the enforcement of moral desiderata. One can envision three causally independent developments that, in a conducive/coercive social climate, could trigger the technological makeover.[16] First, there is the qualitative and quantitative enhancement in urban law-enforcement technology. Recent reforms in the US Army R&D may have a direct bearing on forms of control employed to control civilian populations. Like all modern fighting forces, US forces have been habitually designed for frontline warfare until the setbacks from the 1993 guerrilla tactics in Somalia (repeated nowadays in Afghanistan and Iraq) brought home the need for technology geared for urban combat. Indeed, in an underreported and underappreciated revolution, the Defense Sciences Office, a think-tank of the Defense Advanced Research Projects Agency (DARPA), has officially concluded that "low-intensity urban" engagements are the way of the future.[17]

At the centre of its research is the modular Land Warrior System, which integrates the latest technological breakthroughs with "off-the-shelf consumer technology" into the military sector. Examples include knee and elbow pads from the rollerblading industry or tablet PCs that use Pentium processors and Windows OS for text messaging on flip-down, helmet-mounted monocular displays. Operated by a mouse located in the soldier's chest, the computer also manages a daylight video electric-optic and a thermal sight on the M-4 corner-shot rifle, multichannel wireless communications, and lightweight body armour for which DARPA is developing "low-cost electronic yarns that can be woven into a network of sensors, actuators, logic algorithms and power sources – that can be twisted and crumpled as any clothing can."[18] Also in development are power exoskeletons to boost infantry payload with the target of "at least two-horsepower augmentation of strength and endurance."[19]

With urban soldiers the way of the future, it is only a matter of time until this type of technology spreads to police units continent-wide. At least one social theorist links it to an escalation of violence, as cities become increasingly "divided between 'fortified cells' of affluent society and 'places of terror' where police battle the criminalized poor," perhaps in the manner of John Carpenter's 1981 action classic, *Escape from New York*.[20] That the trend may be artificially accelerated seems apparent from the budgetary decisions pertaining to the country's military and police. The National Security Strategy released in September 2002 calls for permanent US dominance not just globally but in any theatre of operations in the world and for pre-emptive hostilities on any nation that fails to fall in line with this policy. For this, the Pentagon received a 12 percent raise – over $40 billion – in its highest-ever 2003 budget of $0.4 trillion, a similar hike in 2004, and a $10 billion "slush fund" to spend any way it chooses. Yet at the same time the administration is withholding a mere $1.5 billion earmarked for local and state police and other first-response units, e.g., Centers for Disease Control and Prevention. Without prejudging the issue, these signs indicate that the army may gradually take over the urban functions and capabilities heretofore reserved for law enforcement, becoming an ever more powerful and efficient tool of population control.

The second development is that of breaking down somatic and psychological barriers between the (organic) body and (organic or inorganic) technology, with considerations of tactical efficiency leading to – rudimentary at present – integration of human and nonhuman systems. In our world this may assume the form of chip implants, especially when issues of miniaturization, capacity, durability, and migration have been fully resolved.[21] Parolees from the penitentiary system, subcutaneously dog-tagged infantry, amnesiacs, prostate-cancer suspects, para- and quadriplegics, and other chronic patients are today's testing grounds for this technology.

Already the futuristic Veri-Chip is ready for mass-production. Embedded under the skin of security personnel, no bigger than a grain of rice, this scannable device from Applied Digital is not yet an active chip with enough switch-gates to control the human brain, but the first step in this direction has already been taken. Brain prostheses in the form of an artificial "chip" hippocampus are currently tested in California. Their role is to stimulate and ultimately to some degree control the hypothalamic functions of the brain, among them mood, memory, and awareness.[22] Researchers from Cyberkinetics Inc. are implanting chips under the skulls of paralyzed patients. These tiny brain-embedded computers "map the neural activity which occurs when someone thinks about moving a limb" – in other words, as the news service reports, "read their thoughts."[23] A 2005 BrainGate device implemented in a patient's brain "reads his mind and sends the thoughts to a computer to decipher," allowing the paralyzed man to "think" his TV on and off, and adjust channels and volume.

Even though technology AD 2005 is not yet advanced enough to facilitate betrization, social crises of sufficient magnitude could in principle offer an incentive to push towards the third development. As Lem himself prognosticated in "The Upside Down Evolution" (1986), the mounting costs of military hardware (current price tag for an aircraft carrier: US$7–8 billion) may render future investments in armaments less cost-effective than investment into sociobehavioural means of mass compliance. Unfortunately, any prognostication beyond this point becomes wild speculation. While current social trends point to a further degree of authoritarianism and higher levels of indoctrination, the dearth of sophisticated compliance-inducing technology renders full-scale social control unlikely within the next generation. Outside this timeframe, a convergence of conducive sociopolitical developments, progress in technology, and a crisis/catalyst of sufficient proportions cannot, however, be ruled out.

BETRIZATION AND HUMANKIND

"The people never give up their liberty but under some delusion."

– Edmund Burke

"It seems the essence of virtue is persecution, and it has given me a disgust of all ethical notions, which evidently are chiefly used as an excuse for murder."

– Bertrand Russell

Although Lem's thought-experiment of simultaneous and worldwide peacemaker technology is far more compelling than the partial and speculative scenarios sketched above, many may be disinclined to give betrization a chance. Forced to choose between Scylla and

Charybdis, we may cling to the world we know, awash with war and violence, than a world essentially like ours minus the blood and risk-taking enforced by a medical/technological intervention. The following is a brief description of an experiment I ran that bears on this question.

In 1993 (Montreal) and 2000–03 (Edmonton) I had the opportunity to teach a senior undergraduate seminar called "Literature and Science." With its vivid depiction of the relativistic effects of near-lightspeed travel, advanced computer networks, treatment of human-like robots, and of course betrizated utopia, *Return from the Stars* featured prominently on the curricular menu. Each year I ran the following thought-experiment with these four groups of Canadian and American students (thirty-two women and twenty men in all). Having read the book, at the beginning of a class the students were asked to picture a world without violence, physical danger, and risk-taking – i.e., a betrizated civilization remaining unchanged in other respects – and compare it to the world we live in, rife with aggression, war, and genocide. After a brief recap of the pros and cons of the procedure, the group were asked to cast a binding vote as members of an imaginary World Federation Council and then, the second time, after an hour-long debate about the pros and cons of betrization. The alternatives before the would-be World Councillors were polarized. Either vote against betrization and, together with billions of others, remain in the war-torn and blood-stained world, or vote for (and undergo) a compulsory procedure with the specified range of side-effects that will prevent anyone from doing violence to anyone else. The parameters of this, admittedly, not strictly controlled exercise were thus, to the extent allowed by their transfer to our reality, those outlined in Lem's novel.

Without exception, in every seminar the students adamantly, overwhelmingly and repeatedly rejected betrization. With assistance from ecologist Brigitte Braschler, I tabulated and analyzed these informal votes. First, graphically, the combined raw data from the polls (see page 61).

The null hypothesis that students across North America are indifferent to betrization ought to yield "pro" and "con" votes with equal frequency. In other words, indifference towards betrization ought to yield a voting distribution converging on 50-50, i.e., on equal probability for and against betrization. That did not turn out to be the case. Moreover, the chance of being wrong in generalizing

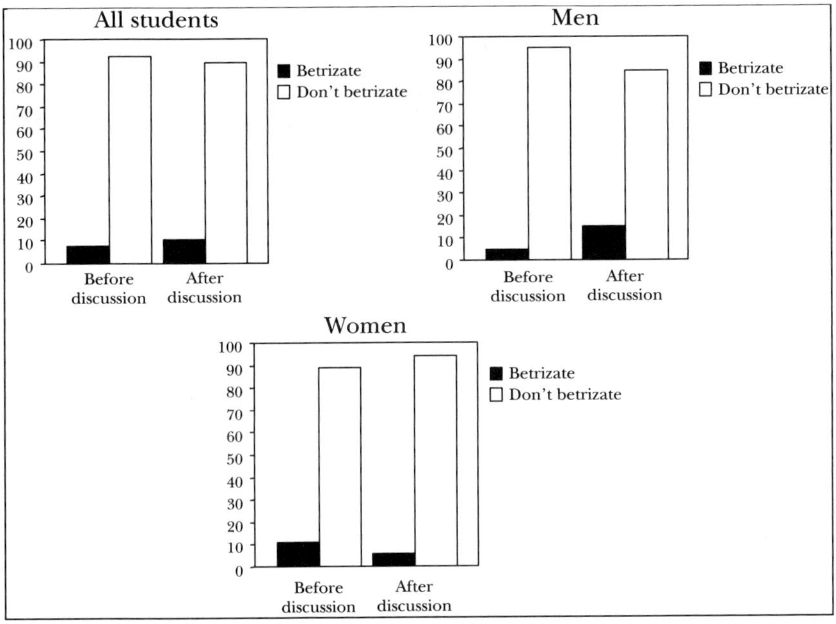

these "No Betrization" results to any seminar of that size across North America is extremely small.[24] Gender seems to have no influence on the vote, and, if one does not distinguish between men and women, there is no change detectable between the vote before and after the discussion. In other words, one cannot reject the hypothesis that discussing the topic has no influence on opinion at all.[25]

For the group of fifty-two, the margin of error in extrapolating from the collected data is 14 percent. The fact that one would need to poll 1,111 students to bring it down to 3 percent suggests a valuable research project in its own right. On the other hand, the difference between the "pro" and "con" groups is very large. With the pre-discussion vote of pro 7.7 percent versus con 92.3 percent, and the post-discussion vote of pro 9.6 percent versus con 90.4 percent, the polls unequivocally predict a massive rejection of betrization even with the high margin of error.[26] To the extent one can generalize form the terms of this thought-experiment, most students seem to prefer the world as it is, rather than pay the price for deleting aggression out of existence.

In the face of such unambiguous rejection of betrization, I would like to examine its benefits and perils. In *Return from the Stars* Lem attributes the neologism "betrization" to the compounding of the names of the procedure's three inventors: Bennett, Trimaldi, and Zakharov (118). Semantically and conceptually, however, betrization alludes to the English "better," pointing to the utopian tradition of *eutopia*, a better no-place, and to Lem's own *Dialogues*. Like in so many facets of utopia debated by Lem's philosophical spokesmen, Hylas and Philonous, on the pages in *Dialogues*, the pros of betrization seem inextricably bound with the cons. True to form, the arguments below entail so many ramifications that to sort them out might take Berkeley himself a scroll and a half. Far from being conclusive, the following critiques and responses are advanced, therefore, as invitations to future debates and essays in which the subject of morality-as-technology may be accorded due weight.

What arguments, then, could Lem's Hylas mount against betrization, or generally against social and genetic engineering, and what could Philonous afford in the way of reply?[27]

HYLAS Betrization creates the ultimate shooting gallery, turning humanity into clay pigeons for those who could manage to evade the procedure.

PHILONOUS This is the crux of the matter. No sooner is the youth gang leader from *A Clockwork Orange* conditioned into defenseless non-aggression than he becomes savagely victimized by his "unbetrizated" former friends. In this way Anthony Burgess demonstrates why the temptation to beat the system would be irresistible: anyone who eluded the peacemaker procedure, or developed an effective vaccine against it, would rule the Earth. Thomas More might have argued that a world advanced enough to attempt betrization would be one that has moved beyond a knee-jerk quest for supremacy. More likely a civilization advanced enough to effect betrization would have the means and the foresight to ensure that no one could crook the wheel. Not unlike a Cold War doomsday machine, the implementation of a betrization would thus have to be taken completely out of human hands to safeguard every government and individual from a real or manufactured crisis that could be used to override the pacifist effects. No rational government or person should support the technology unless it came with an ironclad guarantee of being instituted simultaneously and irreversibly worldwide. Herein lies the technological grail: betrization would have to be made irreversible not only at the time of implementation, but remain so forever. (There may be, however, a way around this seemingly insuperable criterion: once in place, betrization may bootstrap nonaggression into perpetuity as one would first have to become unbetrizated to want to be unbetrizated and harm others). The *really* interesting scenario is if the technology becomes developed and controlled by a small group of people: a single state or even a lone research group. Would they be morally justified in implementing it on their own cognizance, without consulting the rest of the world? Would they opt to betrizate their foes only, or would they proceed to save us from ourselves, so that, awakening one morning, we would find war and murder an obscene relic preserved only in daily papers, newsreels and history books?

HYLAS As implied by Dr Juffon, who examines Bregg after his return from the stars, betrization strips humanity of an innate part of its evolutionary heritage, rendering it at best incomplete and at worst deficient.

PHILONOUS The same evolutionary heritage gave us teeth, which, without a moment's thought, we subject to medical intervention (e.g., braces). On a more general level, we have already prolonged the average span of human life to more than twice than what it used to be in the natural hunter-gatherer ecosystem. We have reversed clinical death, separated Siamese twins, performed caesarean births, cured certain forms of epilepsy using electrode implants, allowed infertile couples to have children – all of which, while beneficial and widely accepted, are no less "unnatural" than betrization. It seems that we are – and ought to be – willing to improve on evolution as long as the results are beneficent. So much for the incompleteness thesis. Although the deficiency argument is addressed below, it may be worth noting here that abusive spouses or stalkers "betrizated" by a restraining order are not deficient because of the court's intervention (which is no more than a symptom of the underlying cause) but, if anything, because of the underlying cause, i.e., their unacceptable threat of aggression.

HYLAS As Bregg's crewmates fear, betrization may be the first step down the slippery slope of gradually "improving" humanity till it bears no semblance to what we are today.

PHILONOUS The australopithecine bore no semblance to what we are today yet no one could argue that the change was not for the better – quite literally since *Australopithecus afarensis* could not argue period. In reality this argument is about endorsing an invasion of biotechnology into the human body and as such it has been answered above.[28]

HYLAS Betrization makes us less than human.

PHILONOUS American plantation or Thai sex slaves (to take only two examples) might see it in a different light, not to mention that our view of conception of what is human, even as reflected in our conception of human rights, differs from century to century and society to society. Denying the power to kill and maim, betrization makes us not less but more human, steering us from force towards peaceful means of conflict resolution in all aspects of our lives, from territorial disputes to superpower negotiations to marital quarrels.

HYLAS By taking aggression out of the gamut of human responses, betrization makes life less colourful and perhaps even devalues the significance of emotional response.

PHILONOUS With the elimination of the menace or even the concept of physical harm, emotions become not less but more central. Certainly in Lem's scenario people display a palette of emotions, including surprise, delight, fright, unease, and, not least, curiosity, which drives Nais even to undertake risks, such as seeking the company of an unbetrizated man (Bregg). Betrization frees a range of emotions normally controlled by fear, among them a feeling of relief from violence or reprisal, safety in strange company or alien environment, empowerment to stand up to injustice (which significantly betrization would *not* cure), or even the luxury of undergoing such a paradigmatically "violent" emotion as anger. Already Aristotle questioned the associative connection between anger (and cognate emotions) and physical violence in "On Anger." It could well be that humanity cured of aggression could enjoy getting emotional over things, only this time without destructive consequences.

HYLAS Betrization usurps the divine prerogative of in effect creating a new species.

PHILONOUS In countless ways we've been playing God since time immemorial. The list of our apparent usurpations is endless, from the headline-grabbers like cloning, abortion, or euthanasia (all decried for their godlike hubris), to the less contentious inoculations, fertility treatments, and organ transplants, most of which are or are becoming legal and thus widely accepted. In principle betrization is no different from surgical brain lesions to treat epilepsy, medicating serotonin levels during depression, or immunization campaigns against polio or smallpox. Even though not everyone is at (equal) risk from disease, vaccinations are administered to all anyway as a preventive measure.

HYLAS Betrization robs us of our freedom by taking the choice out of our hands.

PHILONOUS Betrization takes away our licence to kill. In general, our freedoms are checked in a myriad ways considered beneficent by society. We must refrain from antisocial behaviour, we must attend school up to a certain age, we must abide by laws legislated by politicians, we must do jury duty, and so forth. Under the state motto of "Live Free or Die," New Hampshire residents are neither free to aggress and kill, nor inclined to scrap the laws that take this freedom away. Freedom is not an absolute goal but rather a means to a good life, valued to the extent that it doesn't harm others, and all betrization does is medically hardwire our freedom to live without fear. In general, it is unlikely that genetic or social engineering would automatically erase our physical and even metaphysical freedom since, both as individuals and as a societal aggregate, we are computationally too intractable to ever become predictable to ourselves.[29]

HYLAS Betrization robs humanity of goodness, inasmuch as you need the bad to appreciate the good. Also, it is the act of choosing that is of value, not being good itself.

PHILONOUS Bloodshed and pain are not necessary to appreciate life without bloodshed and pain, just as I don't need my eyes plucked out to appreciate the beauty of colours. In most cases a choice between lesser or greater good suffices to appreciate the comparative value of goodness. In general, our innate capacity for counterfactual thinking, hypothetical reasoning, and fiction-making enables us to appreciate the *relative* value of sundry acts and states. More to the point, it must be reiterated that betrization or any other behavioural control that would dam aggression would *not* be a panacea for all kinds of social ills such as unemployment, mendacity, racism, industrial disputes, moral indifference – nor events that have no basis in deliberate hostility, such as accidents, personal failures, group or romantic rejection, etc. In any case, the bloodshed and pain resulting from too many people choosing not to practice goodness casts doubt on this "no-good-without-the-bad" deontology.

HYLAS Betrization is tantamount to eugenics, a practice perennially abused along racial, ethnic, or nationalistic lines by all would-be reformers of humanity, typically in the name of progressivist and/or humanitarian ideals.

PHILONOUS Eugenic principles need not be condemned en masse. Vitamin and mineral supplements, nutritional regimens, or fluoridation of toothpaste and tap water are only some ways in which we medicate entire populations hoping for positive results. Merely because a technology can be misused is no reason to reject it out of hand. X-rays can be deadly, yet they are employed to save lives. Moreover, virtually all perversions of eugenetic ideals – the Nazi Reich or the short-lived drives for enforced sterilizations in North America or Asia – hark directly to their selective nature. By definition, universal betrization would be immune to this objection.

HYLAS However unlikely the event, betrization puts us at the mercy of any aggressive nonterrestrial civilization wishing to take advantage of our inability to defend ourselves.

PHILONOUS There is no *logical* argument to refute this objection. For reasons detailed above, betrization would have to be made irreversible. No matter how fancy the intellectual footwork, the bottom line is that pacifying the Earth we play the odds with cosmic invasion. All the same, there are solid *scientific* grounds for assigning a negligible probability to such an event. Those stretch from the at best extremely low psychozoic density in the Galaxy, the forbidding distances between stellar objects (*pace* special relativity), the finely calibered fit of life on Earth to the conditions on our planet, to the lack of any credible motivation for a galaxy-faring race to invade a small rock circling an average second generation star in the periphery of the milky nebula.[30]

HYLAS Betrization could never work because our intellectual processes are inherently uncontrollable. In the short run involuntary thoughts about forbidden subjects would lead to pain and nausea and in the long run to paranoia and neurosis as, striving to avoid thoughts that trigger negative feedback, one would inevitably be thinking about them.

PHILONOUS Betrization does not work through behaviouristic conditioning, which could in principle be prone to these side-effects. Instead, in Lem's thought-experiment, it inhibits people's ability to conceive performing a violent action. It must be noted that, voided of physical violence and aggression, the world would offer no inducement to violent thought or harmful action. If betrization could be made universal and simultaneous, rendering acts of physical violence literally inconceivable the procedure nips the problem in the bud – no bad thoughts, no bad consequences. There would, of course, remain mementos in the shape of armaments, historical records, works of literature and art, and living memories. Would those need to be "betrizated," in the sense of expurgated of violent content, too? Without a volume of future neurology or history textbook in hand, it is difficult to offer a rightful answer, though Lem recognizes the need, speculating that, "For a quarter century it was necessary to have two types of periodicals, books, plays: one for the old generation, one for the new" (122).

HYLAS Betrization would impoverish art – perhaps stifle the creative spirit in the arts and even sciences altogether – by diminishing the range of human emotions and responses available for contemplation and by diminishing the risk-taking ability needed to blaze trails and strike out in aparadigmatic directions.

PHILONOUS It would be a great pity if a Shakespeare, a Tolstoy, a Joseph Wambaugh, or a John Woo could not ply their art after betrization, although it is not immediately certain that the inability to perform (or conceive performing) violent acts in real life would entail the inability to conceive them for fictional/artistic reasons. While some types of literature and art might no longer be read and enjoyed, the history of literature and art is strewn with forgotten movements and periods – forgotten because they no longer serve our current aesthetic and social values. Evolving to serve specific needs of a specific society, the art of any historical period reflects the conditions it is created in, and the betrizated civilization may not have any need to read about acts of aggression or military campaigns. Pain, suffering, and misfortune will always exist in the world and always inspire art that wishes to speak of the existential or merely humdrum trials and triumphs of the human spirit. By and large, as far as competition goes – for example in sports, or in artistic or generally intellectual pursuits – there is no reason to suspect that betrization would be any hindrance. It is the threat of physical harm and violence that is the target of the procedure, not the desire to pit one's skills or knowledge against another. One might still lose a championship series, be trounced in a public debate, or denounce a stronger state's policies without, however, entertaining thoughts of bloody vendetta or fears of military occupation.

WAR AND PEACE

"There are no whole truths; all truths are half-truths.
It is trying to treat them as whole truths that plays the devil."

– Alfred North Whitehead

"There was never a good war, or a bad peace."

– Benjamin Franklin (11 September 1783)

Our record of harnessing new technologies for the benefit of humankind spells d-i-s-a-s-t-e-r. Although *Return from the Stars* for the most part passes over the negative implications of betrization, the procedure affords endless opportunities for making things worse instead of better. In one of Hylas's scenarios, whoever succeeded in eluding the procedure would wield total control over a whole species of sitting ducks. That alone guarantees that countless millions would try it. Worse, unless betrization were made truly universal and irreversible, any rational individual or state *ought to* try it. The results of such inequilibrium are allegorized once again in the book of Genesis. While Adam and Eve are in effect betrizated (unable to commit or even conceive of harm or deception), the serpent is not, making the humans easy dupes for manipulation.

On the other hand, if implemented universally – for example, if released as a water-soluble compound into rivers and oceans – betrization could do the world a world of good. The lifting of the purely fiscal burden that warfare and aggression put on law enforcement, health care, as well as the penal and judicial systems, would be manna from heaven. Most of all, the world would no longer suffer abused children, bullied schoolkids, victims of rape and/or domestic violence, shell-shocked soldiers, civilians maimed by weapons of war, tortured prisoners, lynched scapegoats, race riots, ethnic "cleansing," and genocidal mass graves. For a planet on which a minor (3,000–30,000 dead), major (30,000–300,000 dead), massive (300,000–3,000,000 dead) or mega war (3,000,000–30,000,000 dead and above) on average every 1.2 year is a historic constant, this may be not a debate to shrug off too lightly.[31]

NOTES

1 See Swirski, "Playing a Game of Ontology" (1992), for a discussion of this reality-vs-illusion problem. I thank Paisley Livingston for valuable comments on various parts of this essay.

2 See Swirski, *Between Literature and Science* (2000): iv.

3 See Lem's interview with Ziembiecki, "... Knowing Is the Hero of My Books ..." (1979).

4 *On Human Nature* (1978): 99.

5 Following Lorenz's *On Aggression* (1966), I refer throughout to aggression as intraspecies violence rather than violence committed by one species against another (predation).

6 *The Moral Animal* (1994): 146. See also Alexander, T*he Biology of Moral Systems* (1987).

7 "On Scientific Method on Philosophy" [orig. 1914]. Presaging Wright, Russell states: "Ethics is essentially a product of the gregarious instinct" (in Pigden, 109).

8 Chapter 3, "The Types of Legitimate Domination," 215.

9 For more on soft totalitarianism in the novel, see Stoff, *Lem I inni* (1990).

10 To those who in spring of 2003 peace-marched on Washington under the banner of "One Nation Under Surveillance," Donald Rumsfeld, the Secretary of Defense, could only offer that "nothing terrible is going to happen" and that people and the media "should have more trust in the government" (Tyson, "Rumsfeld: Moral Warrior," 2003). Tell this to Steve Downs, who sat down to a meal in a shopping-mall food court near Albany, New York, wearing a T-shirt that read "Peace on Earth." Accosted by mall security, the sixty-year-old was told to remove the T-shirt, leave the mall, or face arrest. When Downs, the Albany director of the New York State's Commission on Judicial Conduct, declined, he

was promptly arrested for "trespassing" in a public place, handcuffed, and booked. He now faces one year in prison (Terry McConnell, "Liberty Is Dealt Another Blow," 2003).

11 As reported by the *New York Law Journal*, this befell a "Silicon Valley professional who unintentionally missed the registration deadline. Immediately upon learning that the rule might have some applicability since he was born in Iran, he reported to the INS district office. Despite the fact that he was a citizen of Canada, legally present in the United States ... he was found in violation of the law ... shackled, handcuffed ... Although he was not charged with any crime, he remained in the detention center for three days ... He now faces a deportation hearing for failure to comply with the registration requirement." "Immigration Law" (2003): 2–3; the following quote on page 3. See also BBC, "US Gets Access to Airline Details" (2003).

12 "Radwanski Warns Right to Privacy Endangered," (2003): A10.

13 "High Priced Security," (2002): 24–7.

14 The Muslim Public Affairs Council warns of data showing that "the number of federal subpoenas for phone and internet records have been doubling every month and have reached into the thousands" (Associated Press, "Patriot Act Denounced," 2002).

15 For background, see Katzenberg, "Patriot Act" (2003).

16 I thank Devon Derksen for his insights into this part of the argument.

17 Knowles, "Warfare," 2002. See also the next note.

18 See Knowles; and BBC News World Edition, "New Weapon Can Fire Round Corners" (2003). All are clear that all the new research is aimed at enhancing soldiers' ability to fight non-army combatants in urban wars.

19 See, Lemley, "Future Tech" (2002).

20 Davis, *City of Quartz*, 223, 224.

21 See, for example, Park and Wieser (2000).

22 Graham-Rowe, "World's First Brain Prosthesis Revealed" (2003).

23 BBC, "Brain Chips Could Help Paralyzed" (2004). Quote in the following sentence from Nagel, "Brain Chip Reads Man's Thoughts" (2005).

24 Less than 0.01 percent. One can extrapolate that nearly all students in North America would oppose betrization since the probability of obtaining such clear-cut results among overall student population by chance is quite low, less then 5 percent based on the samples.

25 The P-values are $P > 0.99$ for all seminars and $P > 0.99$ overall (i.e., with seminars pooled into one superseminar of fifty-two students).

To obtain the result in (C), Fisher's exact test was used. For background, see Sokal (1995).

26 The means are well outside each other's confidence interval (i.e., the mean plus/minus the margin of error). The approximate formula for margin of error is 1/squareroot of sample size.

27 For simplicity's sake, I merge two distinct scenarios: the fictional one from *Return from the Stars*, in which betrization is a *fait accompli* with ramifications posited by the author, and our world in which the possibility of a future technical intervention is in need of examination.

28 For analysis and Lem's own commentary, see Swirski, *A Stanislaw Lem Reader* (1997).

29 Barrow and Tipler's *The Anthropic Cosmological Principle* furnishes a host of reasons and precise arguments against deterministic, teleological, or anthropic assumptions thought to establish that as individuals or species we may be predetermined (less than free) in our states and actions.

30 On the same scientific grounds, an alien race would almost certainly be nonhumanoid. This means that in terms of Lem's thought-experiment – where betrization inhibits aggression towards humans and higher mammals but, significantly, *not* towards all species – humanity ought to be able to rise against alien invaders (I thank Paisley Livingston for this insight). All seems to depend on how selective our tools of social/genetic control would be.

31 See Lewis Fry Richardson's first study of war statistics (casualties) and their distributions (*Statistics of Deadly Quarrels*, 1960). Richardson focused on the period 1820–1949 as pre-1820 data at his disposal was scant (he died in 1953); altogether he tagged 108 wars in the world during that period. For background and contemporary databases of war statistics, see Hayes (2002).

4

A Freudian Peek at Lem's *Fiasco*

MICHAEL KANDEL

"[Woman is] natural, and therefore abominable."

– Baudelaire, "Mon cœur mis à nu"

I first read *Fiasco* almost twenty years ago, as a translator. The text came to the publisher, Harcourt, in manuscript; the first Polish edition had not yet appeared. In 1985, I felt that I was familiar with Lem's work: I had read a good deal of his fiction and nonfiction and had also corresponded with the author for a number of years. I felt that I knew his themes, ideas, strategies. More than once, he had complimented me as a reader-critic of his work. And yet *Fiasco* was not only a surprise to me but also an unsettling puzzle.[1]

At first glance, the novel belongs to that subset of Lem's work that might be called straight science fiction: a story told in thorough, realistic detail about human beings who set out for another planet in an attempt to make contact with an alien entity or civilization. In *The Invincible* and *Solaris* (and to some extent in *Eden*), exhaustive theorizing about the alien mystery is followed by an epiphany in which a solitary man confronts the unknowable other and finds himself before a mirror: what defies contact toward the end of the book turns out to be somehow akin to the mystery that lies within us all. If any contact is made, then, it is on an intuitive, not an intellectual, level.

Fiasco, however, stands apart from Lem's previous books. For one thing, the narrative is curiously indirect. We don't start on the alien planet, Quinta, or anywhere near it; we don't even start with the SETI expedition. The first chapter – beautiful, tense, action-packed

– seems unconnected by plot to the rest of the book. If its purpose is to introduce us to the protagonist, we are not even completely sure that the protagonist makes it on board the *Eurydice*: is the resurrected man Parvis with parts of Pirx or Pirx with parts of Parvis? It seems to be Parvis, but then the death of Pirx is ominous news for a Lem reader, who has followed that character through many stories and books. It is a signal, perhaps, that the author is saying goodbye to something, that in this book we will be departing significantly, and darkly, from what came before. Also, there are curious mininarratives embedded in the main narrative: the spooky story of the doom of the gold-seeking conquistadors, the horror story of the slightly supernatural termite city in darkest Africa, the dream of the street in Naples and the earthquake.[2] It turns out that all these episodes, and chapter 1, are indeed connected – but obliquely, allusively.[3]

Another difference in *Fiasco* is its conclusion. One leaves Lem's earlier books of straight science fiction with a sense of resolution, of something gained: an insight that perhaps cannot be verbalized but that is precious nonetheless. *Fiasco* ends with unmitigated defeat. Parvis/Pirx, now called Tempe, realizes that he has seen the Quintans – as was promised – only in the moment before they and he are destroyed, and his realization is brutally devoid of understanding (Jarzębski 211). What *are* those strange lumps of living dough across the muddy, sloping land?

As I was translating the novel's first chapter, I was struck by an image that suggested human anatomy: specifically, the male reproductive system. The control tower at the spaceport on Titan, which Parvis leaves in his strider (called a Digla), is circular, windowless, and capped by a mushroom head; it has an adjoining lower building on either side, with connecting tunnels between them (*Fiasco* 15, 18).

The termite city in the African jungle consists of tower mounds connected by and filled with passageways and marching white insects; in the centre of this city is a crooked black mound toward which other, lower mounds bend as if in obeisance; the black mound contains a glasslike sphere that draws insects (100–2). And in the memorable final scene of the novel are shapeless loaves or humps connected by warm underground pipes: some of the similes used for these mounds are molehills, turtles, caps of giant mushrooms, a cemetery with barrows, the huts of a primitive African village (320–2).

At the time I thought, not without humour, that you could write an article on a Freudian approach to this novel. One would expect the phallic symbols of *Fiasco* to be anatomically detailed; its author, after all, was a medical student. I also remembered an account Lem had given me, in a 1976 letter, of his prostate surgery, which was connected with the death of a fellow patient and with the possibility of Lem's own death.[4] The pairing of sex and death, certainly nothing new in literature, is appropriate to *Fiasco.* Death clearly abounds, literally and in symbols. Two parallel examples of such symbolism: on his way to his first "death," Parvis in his Digla passes a geological cemetery or anatomical theatre (29–33); the lander that Tempe takes to Quinta, on his way to his second death, is compared to a coffin (301). Meanwhile, the Quintans, as another version of unknowable aliens in Lem's fiction, share with those other versions an organic, biological representation.

Jerzy Jarzębski speaks of Lem's genuine wish for the human race to transcend its biological heritage (226–7, 294). In a discussion of the rise of a technological civilization in *Fiasco,* intelligent beings venture into space only to learn that "the mark of their animal origin [has] been stamped inexorably on their bodies" (90). As a result: "Where there is mind, there is also cruelty" (290). According to Lem, our primitive, animal heritage is the engine behind military escalation and the arms race. If we cannot break free of this evolutionary determinism, we will destroy ourselves.

One straw of hope against this destruction is the cybernetic idea: machines, growing complex enough, becoming unpredictable, independent. Perhaps, having none of the ape about them, they might escape the doom of their creators, or they might even deliver their creators from that doom, as in *Peace on Earth.* A second straw of hope for Lem is autoevolution, that we might become more truly human, less bestial, by taking evolution into our own hands.[5] A third straw of hope is the existence of another, better civilization on another planet (see Lem's *His Master's Voice*). All these hopes coexist and alternate with reservations, satire, pessimism.

The biological images of alienness in Lem's work are mindless: frog's eggs, worms, reptiles, but insects predominate: moths, bees, hornets, beetles, flies. The anthill in particular appears and reappears throughout his books, both fiction and nonfiction. Speaking about *Fiasco,* Lem says that one might think of the Quintans as "giant intelligent anthills."[6] There is something ominous and repugnant about Lem's insects, whether they are spying in *Memoirs Found in a Bathtub* or swarming in a cybernetic cloud in *The Invicible.*

With the phallic control tower in mind, I decided to focus my reading not so much on works about Freud or Freudian analysis as on primary sources, Freud's writings. *Interpretation of Dreams* confirmed several of my notions about Freud's theories; it also showed me that I had been barking up the wrong symbol. Science fiction presents a barren field for Freudian analysis. The genre is traditionally nonsexual, despite the scantily clad bimbos on the covers of its pulp magazines of the 1950s and despite its politically correct genderbending of the 1970s and 1980s. Science fiction is cerebral, interested in the future, technology, society, ideas, not in matters personal, private, and glandular – matters that have essentially been the same for countless generations. Most readers who prefer to stay in the everyday world of relationships and angst and hang-ups will not open the pages of science fiction.

Yet Freud argues that the expressions of the unconscious are to be found precisely where its presence is denied. In stories, as in dreams, the misdirection and masking that the mind contrives to make acceptable what is unacceptable – the "latent content" (Freud's term) – reveal even as they censor. Nothing in a story or a dream is innocent; no joke is just a joke; no detail is trivial. And, Freud tells us – echoing Joseph, another famous Jewish dream analyst in Genesis 41.25 – the dreams dreamt in one night are one dream. The different narratives of one book are one narrative. The works written by an author are one work.

Reading in Freud that burial was often a symbol not of death but of birth, immediately I thought of Parvis, who is buried at the end of chapter 1. Then I remembered that he is virtually naked and inside the human shape of the Digla (note that the Digla has no head). Parvis is situated where the heart is, true, not the womb; but the entrance to the vehicle carries a telling joke with it – originally the operators climbed up through an opening between the legs. And the name Parvis suggests the Latin for "small" (*parvus*). As the geysers move and shake phallically in Birnam Wood, to a roar "as if the planet itself, in labor, were howling out of rage or pain" (44), he is a baby inside a giant mother.

Birth imagery is explicit, complete with umbilical cord (130), in the embryonization of the crew on board the *Hermes* as it leaves the black hole (named Hades) for Quinta. The crew's awakening is a vivid scene of weightless, naked men dripping with white, viscous onax. Would a Freudian read the onax as milk or as semen (*onax* suggesting onanism)? Or as both? Bisexual imagery is not unknown in Lem: in *Eden*, for example (which novel, by the way, begins with a burial), we have inside a vast mushroom-shaped building a dark hive filled with eggs, and in each egg sits a skeleton (118).[7] Tempe, whom in Parvis we saw as a baby, comes up with the idea of communicating with the Quintans through the cartoon pictures of a children's book (257–61).

The Quintan mounds at the end of *Fiasco* are likened to mushrooms. At first, having in mind the control tower on Titan, I thought in terms of penises, maybe testicles, maybe prostate glands. But there is also the expression that Tempe is being buried (Polish: *pogrzebie się*); the word "belly" (*brzuch*) is repeated in those final pages; the Digla is referred to in the hangarlike (womblike?) structure that is an eversion of a ship sent earlier; and we have "breast" (*pierś*), "milk" (*mleko*), and finally the image of the mounds as "naked defenseless warts" (*nagich bezbronnych brodawek*) – except that as the translator, at the time unenlightened Freudianly, I was not impressed by the fact that *brodawki* can mean in Polish not only "warts" but also "nipples."

The Freudian detective would roll up sleeves and comb this text for innocent details that hide guilty connections. Tempe's Latin motto that "no one attacks me with impunity" comes, we are told in Lem's novel, from Poe's story "The Cask of Amontillado." Poe's narrative concludes with a man being entombed. Quinta has a ring, as does Saturn; the mythical Saturn devoured his children and was eventually killed by them. We are told that "the first sound of human speech in the Zeta system was an obscenity" (143); in Polish, would the most likely curse have *kurwa* in it ("whore")? The crew member Harrach expresses his anger about the absurd notion that in science fiction adventures women, who bear children, should accompany men on dangerous space voyages; he launches into an antifeminist harangue whose vehemence (313–14) is remarkable even when we are told that he has become mentally unstable.[8]

Women rarely appear in *Fiasco*, and the context of their appearance is without exception negative. The name of the spaceship is *Eurydice*, who was killed by a snake (Eve and the snake appear, with Adam, on page 61 in chapter 2) and who is at the centre of a story in which the attempt to conquer death (through love, through art) ends in a fiasco.[9] There is a disparaging remark about women wanting to get in the last word even more than the computer DEUS (184). And the brief dream scene before the Quintan attack on the *Hermes* features a dark girl running after a boy in a street in Naples and a disheveled woman pulling dried clothes from a laundry line. The repeated *terramoto*, Italian for "earthquake," contains anagramatically the Latin word for "mother."[10]

This brief dream is parallel to an even briefer dream in *The Invincible*: an attack on the ship awakens a sleeping crew member, who dreams that he is naked and trapped in darkness (*Niezwyciężony* 73). Note that in that earlier novel the black cybernetic insect cloud erases the minds of crew members, returning them to infancy. The only word we hear from one victim is "mama." And a mind-wiping attack takes place in a dark cave. Could there be a connection, through the association to woman, between the fishing nets in the Naples town, the slips and skirts on the laundry line, and the alien, Daliesque sagging pylons and nets that Tempe finds toward the end?

The body is a prison for Lem; the womb is a trap, a place of burial. In the humorous rather than tragic *Peace on Earth*, written close to the time of *Fiasco* and sharing many of its themes – especially military escalation and the impossibility of trusting one's enemy – Tichy has an absurd dream in which he is visited by a woman who rises from a mercury-covered floor (read: mirror) like a swelling mushroom, then becomes a cocoon, a human shell with a gaping slit in front. He is swallowed by this iron maiden, who controls all his movements in order to kidnap him (191–2). In "The Mask," the woman protagonist turns out to be a shell that houses an insect machine of death (213–15; see also the essay by N. Katherine Hayles in this volume).

Tichy's brain, by the way, is split in half in *Peace on Earth*: the right hemisphere is mute, misbehaves, is lustful and aggressive; the left hemisphere is the verbal, rational, civilized Tichy. They are at constant odds. Could the human-Quintan conflict be read also as a war between the two hemispheres of the human brain, between two aspects of humanity? The head without the body (like DEUS, like the teaching Socrates on board the *Eurydice*) versus the body without the head? Except that DEUS is also likened to an egg …

So where does all this Freudian pointing point? Though tunnels, passageways, and caves multiply in *Fiasco*, also insects and worms and eggs and babies, and though an entire continent on Quinta is named after a human organ (liver), I believe the keystone symbol is the mirror. Like both Tichy and Pirx before him – Pirx notably in "The Hunt": "they looked at one another: the statue of the man and the statue of the machine, both sheathed in metal" (178) – Parvis encounters himself. In the Digla, he chases his mirror image, and on the *Eurydice* he goes to a closet, opens the wrong door by mistake (the door to a bathroom?), sees his face in a mirror, and murmurs, "You'll see the Quintans" (110).

Lem has stated that in *Solaris* he did not know what the mystery on the space station would be: the story "somehow flowed out of me" ("jakoś sie ze mnie wylała," *DyLEMaty* 90). He also confesses that the ending of *Fiasco* came as a surprise to him ("niespodzianka").[11] He did not know; his unconscious knew. This is precisely the unsteered method of writing that Freudian analysis licks its chops over. Lem may have a low opinion of Freud (e.g., *DyLEMaty* 228), but it's evident that he understands – and agrees with – Freud's central concepts (9, 92, 97; see also Hayles, who in her analysis of Lem's "The Mask" probes the idea of agency that lies outside consciousness). For me, this quote from *Interpretation of Dreams* has a striking resonance to Lem's *Fiasco*: "What once prevailed in the waking state, when our psychic life was still young and inefficient, seems to have been banished into our nocturnal life; just as we still find in the nursery those discarded primitive weapons of adult humanity, the bow and arrow. Dreaming is a fragment of the superseded psychic life of the child."

Lem's narrative problem with women may have to do with how we are born: the Latin phrase from Saint Augustine that he uses often is "Inter faeces et urinam nascimur" ("We are born between feces and urine"). Lust and aggression mark the path to death. Our animal nature means that we are mortal. So it is not even how we are born, finally, but the sad, demeaning fact itself that we are born.[12] That we are mortal. Birnam Wood, the place of moving geysers on Titan that kills Parvis, is part of Macbeth's foretold doom. The other part of the prophecy is a man not born of woman, a man ripped untimely from his mother's womb (*Macbeth* 4.1.80, 5.8.16).

Finally, a logical question: if the dreamwork (Freud's term) of Lem's fiction is to censor the unacceptable, what is the unacceptable in Lem's case? What is being hidden?

Keeping in mind that the author is an unusually intelligent, perceptive, and self-aware person, I offer the following speculation. In *His Master's Voice,* Professor Peter Hogarth confesses that he laughed, giggled with delight as a young child, as his mother lay dying. Trying to understand his awful laughter, he writes: "What causes us to be drawn to destruction? What black hope, in destruction, beckons man? Its utter inutility rules out any rational explanation. This hunger has been suppressed in vain by numerous generations. It is as irrevocably a part of us as two-leggedness" (10).[13]

Perhaps Lem the humanist is also Lem the destroyer, the murderer of men, women, and children. Perhaps the wish to wipe away the human race – the tiresome, hopeless, and revolting human race – is the vileness that lies in his right hemisphere. The Quintans are therefore you and me, and Lem is Steergard, the frustrated and furious captain, his finger on the trigger of the solaser weapon of mass destruction.

Fiasco was Lem's last work of fiction. Perhaps this literary silence of almost twenty years was his self-inflicted punishment for that ultimate act of genocide, even if carried out only in the dream of a book.

NOTES

1 A word of caution: my presentation is sometimes nonlinear. It does contain if-A-then-B arguments, but basically it attempts to draw lines among different works and ideas, as in a grid. Also, in what I think of as a Freudian tradition, I make guesses, unafraid of appearing ridiculous.

2 The history of Cortez and his men in the New World can of course be read as another contact story, in which the aliens – here, Native Americans – are destroyed.

3 Jerzy Jarzębski informs me that the first two of these narratives were written well before *Fiasco,* separately. The author included them in his novel.

4 In the hospital where Lem had his operation there was a monk in the next bed who was awaiting the same operation. Lem told the worried man that there was no danger (the mortality rate of this surgery being 2 percent), but the monk died, and Lem witnessed the four-hour struggle of the doctors to save him, a struggle Lem knew, with his technical

training, was hopeless. A later complication of his own surgery caused a great loss of blood and another trip to the hospital.

5 The idea is expressed most eloquently in Lem's "The Golem's Inauguration Speech" (see esp. *Golem XIV* 64).

6 The quote is from a letter to me in 1985. About the Quintans, Lem writes: "An intelligent mold? Some kind of colony of sapient quasi-insects or microbes? We don't know, but it's something that a human being *cannot internally accept.*"

7 For a Freudian discussion of Lem's *Solaris,* featuring the unknown feminine of the sentient ocean as both attraction and threat and the appearance of a newborn baby in it as "disgusting," see Manfred Geier, esp. 157. For a discussion of Lem's "The Mask" that connects death, birth, and the female as the "terrifyingly alien other," see Katherine Hayles's essay in this volume.

8 Readers of the book in English will not find this harangue: it was dropped from the translation, with the author's approval. The editor and translator both felt that those one or two pages of manuscript were an author's aside that might appear ridiculous if not offensive to an American reader and that were also quite out of tune with the rest of the novel.

9 In Rilke's poem "Orpheus, Eurydice, Hermes," the woman becomes a virgin again as she departs life a second time. Rilke is one of Lem's favorite authors.

10 The English has *terremoto* (200), the Polish *terramoto* (226). Note that an earthquake itself can suggest a woman's orgasm, as can a volcano. In the twenty-fifth voyage of *The Star Diaries,* Ijon Tichy leaves on a voyage without fuel but reaches his destination by the expedient of plunging nose first into a planet's volcano and having the volcano, in response to that impact (the Polish uses the word *połechtany* ["tickled"], which has definite sexual associations), erupt and send him flying out again into space. The description of the penetration, tickling, and eruption suggests human sex (in English 246, in Polish 285–6). Note that the story begins "On this voyage everything went wrong."

11 Personal correspondence, 9 May 1985.

12 Lem told me, when I visited him in Krakow in 1973, that his wife and he had been reluctant to bring a child into so terrible a world. His son was born fifteen years after they married.

13 This memory and discussion follow a highly negative critique of applying the psychoanalytic approach to an author (*His Master's Voice,* 4–5).

5

Summa technologiae – Looking Back and Ahead

PETER BUTKO

You see things; and you say: "Why?"
But I dream things that never were; and say: "Why not?"
– George Bernard Shaw, *Back to Methuselah*

INTRODUCTION: LEM, SCIENCE AND TECHNOLOGY

In his breathtaking kaleidoscope of ideas *A Perfect Vacuum*, Stanislaw Lem proposed a classification of geniuses into three categories. Those of the lowest – in his schema, third – rank are relatively tame and modest thinkers who do not step too much outside of their time and sense of possibilities. They become famous, rich, and influential (not necessarily all three at the same time) in their lifetime. The geniuses of the second rank have it more difficult: they struggle against the intellectual inertia of contemporaneous society and are accepted only after their death – in the next generation, if they are lucky. And then there are – there must be, says Lem – geniuses of the highest rank, those that are never recognized. The ideas they espouse and the truths they create are too revolutionary to be incorporated into the accumulated body of human knowledge.

In which category does Lem himself belong? Luckily for him, so far the Nobel committee has not paid him proper attention. As for me, it was only with some hesitation that I agreed to contribute to this volume. After all, an unintended side effect of this event might be a relegation of Lem to the lowest category of geniuses … This is so because Lem's pivotal masterpiece *Summa technologiae*, of which I speak here at length, has quite unbelievably never been translated into English and thus remains unknown to most people. Since Lem's book is an essay, not a novel, and I am a biophysicist, not a literary scholar or philosopher, I do not intend to stress literary or philosophical aspects of the work. I will rather attempt to put it in the context of science and technology, as they evolved from the time of the first edition of the *Summa* to the present and even beyond.[1]

Before we focus on the book, we need to understand the relationship between science and technology. The role of technology is to ensure well-being of humans, from individuals to the whole society, by tackling concrete problems. Human technology is an invention of Homo sapiens, and thus it should be no surprise that ultimately it only tends to the needs of a single species – us. The role of science is to generate new hypotheses and questions about nature, which, in turn, bring about new science. Science generates new knowledge that may or may not be – though usually is – later used by technology. Good science does not solve any pressing problems but rather enables us to ask new and better questions. It is technology that provides answers and solves problems that – more often than not – were created by previous technologies. For example, the widespread use of synthetic antibiotics put a selection pressure on bacterial pathogens, with the consequence that the microbes evolved to become antibiotics-resistant and more threatening than before. And what is our response? To call on medical and pharmaceutical technology to create new drugs. Another example: nuclear energetics was invoked to solve the energy crisis, and now we are inventing technologies for the environmental decontamination and storage of spent radioactive fuel. Science and technology cross-fertilize each other: while science enables new technology, the new technology makes new science possible. They evolve together, as parts of the same system. Metaphorically, science is a head high in the sky, while technology is feet in contact with the ground. They both cooperate in moving the whole body of human knowledge, culture, and society along.

Summa technologiae (1964) was written during Lem's "golden period" by a mature author who, in the fourth decade of life, had just published his famous novel *Solaris* – since filmed twice, by

Andrei Tarkovsky in 1972 and again in 2002 by Steven Soderbergh in Hollywood (see the essays by Krzysztof Loska and Peter Swirski in this volume). The allusion in the title to St Thomas Aquinas's *Summa theologiae* (c. 1273) can thus hardly be a youthful attempt at grandeur. With the thoughtful choice of title, Lem indicated his intention to replace St Thomas's God with reason as the moving force in the universe – or at least in the later stages of the universe's evolution. It is the title that gives the book meaning and power. Indeed, after forty years, Lem thinks that *Summa* is his only book of nonfiction that has withstood the test of time.[2] It is therefore unfortunate that the initial readership of *Summa* was largely restricted to the nascent intellectual and technocratic elite that started to appear in Poland and other countries of the Communist Block in the 1960s. It is even more unfortunate that the situation has not changed much since: the book has been translated only into a handful European languages, most prominent of which are German and Russian. To compound the problem, there are virtually no reviews, analyses, or commentaries on the book available in English, so that English speakers may not even know what they are missing. The Anglo-American culture has only made two holes to peek through the veil covering *Summa technologiae*. One is *A Stanislaw Lem Reader* (1997) by Peter Swirski, which devotes considerable space to *Summa* and includes Lem's own reappraisal of some of the *Summa*'s topics in the essay "Thirty Years Later"; the other, a philosopher's perspective, is Paisley Livingston's essay "From Virtual Reality to Phantomatics and Back," which can be found on the Electronic Book Review website. Why is this cultural omission so tragic – at least in my eyes? Because in its philosophical depth, scientific breadth, and intellectual courage, *Summa technologiae* is at least equal, if not superior, to many celebrated masterpieces of crossover science, such as *The Selfish Gene* (1976) by Richard Dawkins or *Goedel, Escher, Bach* (1979) by Douglas Hofstadter. It deserves to be better known.

One more point needs to be made before we open the book. The present essay is based on the sixth Polish edition published by Wydawnictwo Literackie in Kraków in 2000, which, in turn, is based on the third edition from 1974. This statement is not just a bibliographical minutia. Later editions of *Summa* differ, sometimes substantially, from previous ones. *Summa* is essentially a work in progress: Lem corrected mistakes and updated his thinking, based in part on feedback from readers who are often scientists and experts in their respective fields. Particularly, the second (1967) and third (1974) editions were revised and expanded. All this means that readers might form slightly different opinions depending on which edition they read. Furthermore, the correct timeline might be important for an impartial evaluation of Lem's prognoses contained in the book. At any rate, it is the opinion of this writer that *Summa technologiae* is ripe for a new revised and extended edition and, if possible, a simultaneous English translation.

An impatient reader might have already started wondering what *Summa* is all about. In essence, it is an all-encompassing philosophical discourse on evolution: not only evolution of science and technology – the latter being explicitly mentioned in the title – but also evolution of life, humanity, consciousness, culture, and civilization. Importantly, Lem is not only erudite enough to give a historic account of evolution proper but courageous enough to speculate about future trends in its above-listed manifestations. Thus the two modest aims of this essay should by now be apparent. The first is to describe *Summa technologiae* in some detail, as it is unavailable in English translation. The second is to examine how the book has withstood the passage of time, especially in the context of current science and technology.

THE EIGHT CHAPTERS OF *SUMMA*

The book is divided into eight chapters, plus a conclusion. Chapter 1, "Dilemmas," serves as introduction. In a single breath (fourteen pages) Lem discredits futurology and offers his own vision of the future. It is evident from the text that the author cherishes the challenge of demolishing the primitive and useless sort of futurology that sticks to simple linear extrapolations. Lem realizes that evolution of science and technology is highly nonlinear, with the multitude of more-or-less hidden negative and positive feedback loops that make most phenomena, as well as influences on them, completely unpredictable. Consequently, he enjoys tossing apparently outrageous, out-of-the-box ideas and bringing them to their logical conclusions.

In chapter 2, "The Two Evolutions," the author compares the natural evolution (bioevolution) with the evolution of science and technology (technoevolution). Features common to both types of evolution include: evolutionary radiation, i.e., invasion of new species to the previously unoccupied niches; hyper specialization, i.e., getting better and better in a single task important for the survival of a given species; and opportunism, or inertia, in using pre-existing materials or solutions. One peculiar common feature that Lem notices (with tongue in cheek) is the appearance of gigantism just before extinction – compare the fate of dinosaurs and zeppelins. The parallels between the two types of evolution may in some cases appear formal or superficial; the differences are more substantial. The principal difference is the active agent. In bioevolution it is nature, or, in other words, nobody. Biological systems and their environment evolve – through mutual interactions – by themselves, while in technoevolution the active agent is clearly humanity. This has several interesting consequences.

First, where bioevolution is beyond ethics and morality, the same is not true for technoevolution. There are no moral questions about the lynx hunting down prey, but complex ethical and legal issues are involved in development and use of, for example, biological weapons, the abortion pill, or "safer" cigarettes. Second, the teleological principle lies at the fundaments of technoevolution but is completely absent from bioevolution. Lem called nature a blind constructor, while the evolutionary biologist Richard Dawkins later coined the term "blind watchmaker" in his eponymous book. Bioevolution simply has no goal. Nature is not intelligent and has no foresight; it only reacts to changes in the environment by making every species do everything possible in order to survive or to succeed over others in the interspecies competition. In contrast, human constructors solve concrete problems. They do have goals and, in most cases, a healthy dose of foresight.

Third, the mechanics of the two evolutions are quite different. If a given solution does not work, the human designer can scrap it and start from a completely different point. Nature does not have this luxury. In biology the new is almost always a modification of the old. In addition, the human material resources are almost unlimited – we can create new substances almost on demand, materials that otherwise would not exist, such as steel, doped semiconductors, nylon, Kevlar, antimatter, or element number 109, meitnerium. On the other hand, nature can work only with what is at hand in any given moment (hence some prefer calling it a tinkerer rather than a constructor). Another limitation of nature is the working conditions: with the notable exception of the so-called extremophilic organisms, biology works in very narrow ranges of temperature and pressure. In contrast, human technologists can access temperatures just a millionth degree above absolute zero or higher than in the centre of the Sun and pressures from the vacuum of outer space to thousands of atmospheres in diamond anvil cells. The latter two factors – the larger range of accessible constructing conditions and, even more importantly, teleology or our ability to set goals and then reach them – lie behind an incredible acceleration of technoevolution when compared with bioevolution. It took nature billions of years to construct the unit of life – the cell, but it took Homo sapiens only thousands of years to invent and spread agriculture and it has been just several years between the invention of transistor or laser and their universal use. Of course, this statement is no value judgment. Technoevolution is not better or worse than bioevolution. The two do not oppose or compete with each other. On the contrary, they are both parts of a unified evolutionary process.

In chapter 3, "The Cosmic Civilizations," Lem attempts the feat that has traditionally been the domain of esoteric physics theories, such as, for example, the superstrings theory: he leads a serious scientific discourse on a subject that has not been observed in reality and perhaps is in principle unobservable – the search for extraterrestrial intelligence. While the superstrings – postulated subparticular objects of higher dimensionality than three – are indeed unobservable in three dimensions, one might argue that there is nothing principal in our inability to observe other cosmic civilizations, unless one accepts a fantastic thesis half-jokingly proposed by Lem in the chapter "New Cosmogony" of *A Perfect Vacuum* (1971). The lack of contact between cosmic civilizations, called Silentium Universi, is elevated there to the status of the fundamental law of nature. Lem makes a case that without such a law the universe might get dangerously out of equilibrium, with possibly the most catastrophic of all consequences – no universe to observe. The SETI[3] chapter of *Summa* might seem disconnected from the main theme, which is evolution, but only until one realizes that fates of civilizations are integral parts of evolution of the universe. As science generally does not work with statistics where n = 1 (for a valid conclusion, scientist must repeat an experiment several times or study several objects in an ensemble), the obvious problem with the science of cosmic civilizations is that we only know of one such civilization. Hence, the need to seek others is not just a psychological or metaphysical urge but an imperative of good science.

How do we notice other civilizations? According to Lem there are two possibilities: either they reveal themselves to us by sending signals or else we detect their presence from "miracles," i.e., phenomena that do not have rational, natural explanations. The problem with the first option is that we do not know what constitutes a signal. Although many searchers sift through cosmic radiation and look for periodicity, this is foolish since most natural processes are periodic. Particles oscillating in the solid state, planets orbiting around suns, rotating neutron stars or even chirping crickets, all produce periodic signals that give no grounds for speculations about intellect or civilization. On the other side of the spectrum are completely chaotic signals. These cannot be the sign of intelligent life either, since nature is good at producing chaos – just look at the Brownian motion of particles in the liquid state. The best indication of a signal carrying information would be a kind of modulated chaos, something between chaos and periodicity. When two humans communicate in a language that is unknown to us, we hear a signal that is not exactly periodic, but certainly not chaotic: an analysis would reveal certain regularities, such as, for instance, a consonant being usually followed by a vowel. Recent research in complexity science (by Per Bak and Stuart Kauffman, among others) indicates that positioning of a system at the edge of chaos, which is also called self-organized criticality, is the sufficient condition for an interesting (i.e., nontrivial) evolution of that system.[4]

An intuitive way of understanding this is the following. If a system behaves completely chaotically there is no correlation between its two consecutive states. The behaviour of the system is random, and individual states of the system cannot be predicted or described in any other way than listing the succession of states of the system as they were actually observed. No lasting structures (in physical or mathematical terms) can arise in such a system, and there can be no evolution of the latter, unless evolution is understood in the narrowest possible sense – as a succession of changes. The other extreme is a fully ordered deterministic system in which each successive state is fully predetermined by a previous state or states. If we know one single state of such a system and the transition rules, we can calculate all the other states – past, present, and future.

Thus we know everything there is to know about the system, and changes undergone by the latter become trivial: one would hardly use the term evolution for the progression of a rock falling in the gravitational field. The parallels between systems' evolution and the information content of a signal are clear: as both fully random and fully ordered signals do not carry much information, neither completely chaotic nor completely deterministic systems undergo "true" evolution.

As for the second possibility of observing cosmic civilizations, what are our chances of observing a cosmic "miracle"? Science has an innate dread of miracles. Keeping in mind Ockham's razor (the principle that forbids introduction of unnecessary entities into scientific theories), scientists always try everything possible to understand unexplainable phenomena within the frame of old and accepted theories. Only when they are at their wit's end, they – perhaps reluctantly – agree to accept a newly postulated entity. As an example Lem mentions the case of the neutrino, a new elementary particle introduced by Wolfgang Pauli in order to save the principle of conservation of energy. This principle is such a cornerstone of all physics that, when its apparent violation was observed in experiments in the first two decades of the twentieth century, Pauli suggested a radical solution: the missing energy must be carried by an invisible particle that no one had yet detected. He even predicted some of this mythical particle's properties, most notable of which are an extremely small mass (long thought to be zero) and an almost complete lack of interaction with the matter: the particle can fly through the entire Earth as if the latter were vacuum. These were two very good reasons why no one had seen it. Nevertheless, the neutrino was experimentally discovered in 1956, thirty years after Pauli invoked it into existence.[5] This case convincingly demonstrates that, facing a miracle, a scientist would still rather break Ockham's razor than accept the notion of "miracle."

Apart from this philosophical problem of the scientific detection of miracles, there is a practical problem, too. No sane civilization would allocate huge amounts of energy or power just for the purpose of signalling their presence to potential others. Lem suggests that a cosmic miracle, observed from a distance of at least several tens of light years and thus requiring a power output equal to that of a star, must be a byproduct of the civilization's normal activity. Apart from the practical question of the energy source for such an undertaking, it is erroneous to automatically assume that evolving civilizations continuously increase their energy consumption and thus output. We note that, with improving technology, the energy efficiency of our machinery and electronics increases. It is very well possible that humanity's energy demand will stabilize or even decrease, particularly if we reach the stage of steady-state population (when rate of births equals rate of deaths). Lem suggests that highly evolved civilizations distinguish themselves not by high energy consumption but rather by a high level of cybernetic control over natural as well as technological phenomena.

In chapter 4, "Intellectronics," Lem descends back to Earth and considers information processing in human culture. He starts off with the information explosion, which is the current exponential growth of information in science and technology. An exponential growth is characterized by a parameter called doubling time. It is the constant time interval in which the system in question doubles in size. Examples of exponential growth include the development of an embryo in its early stages or a colony of bacteria in a rich medium. Lem correctly points out that in nature exponential growth is usually a short-lived transitional state. It is easy to calculate how quickly a bacterial colony would reach the mass of the whole Earth if the exponential growth were not limited by other factors, such as exhaustion of food resources. Let us assume that a typical bacterium has the mass $m = 10^{-12}$ g and it divides with the doubling time $\tau = 1/2$ h. From the exponential growth equation $M = m \times 2^{t/\tau}$, we can calculate the time t, in which an arbitrary mass M is reached, as $t = \tau \times \log(M/m)/\log 2$. The bacteria would attain the mass of 1 kg in about twenty-five hours; the mass of the Earth, approximately 10^{25} kg, would be reached in an astonishingly short time: 66.5 hours! Great is the power of exponential growth, but, fortunately, still greater is the power of external limitations.

At the time of writing, Lem estimated the doubling time for the number of scientific journals as fifteen years. The number of scientists also seemed to grow exponentially, at least until the end of the twentieth century. If this trend continued, by the end of the twenty-first century all the people on the Earth would be scientists. Lem predicts that two factors will put limits on the growth of science. The first is the lack of human resources, as mentioned above. The second is the finite bandwidth of the information channels. As in cable internet connections, the quantity of information transmitted per unit time depends on the bandwidth of the transmission line: the larger the bandwidth, the more information can flow through it at the same time. Can the information barrier be overcome? Lem considers all three possible outcomes in this "game of information." For winning, it is not enough to transfer the task of human scientists, namely that of gathering information and creating knowledge, onto an army of artificial electronic scientists. This would push the barrier further but would not overcome it. Winning requires an absolutely new strategy. To continue the exponential growth of knowledge we cannot rely on *extraction* of information from nature, either by human or electronic brains. We need to be able to *grow, evolve, or breed* information directly from other information, like when we grow bacterial cultures in test tubes; without any human involvement, bits of information floating in the virtual reality would meet other bits of information and the encounters would result in new bits, which would in turn immediately commence their encounters with all the others, and so on. It sounds fantastic, but there does not seem to be any law of nature prohibiting what Lem calls automatic gnosis.

The second possible outcome of the battle with the information barrier is a draw. The fate of a civilization is usually decided by the latter's regulatory effects on its feedback loops with nature. A highly evolved civilization would recognize that exhaustion of nature's information potential is not possible, since a stubborn march to the deeper depths of nature would only result in the breakup of hyper-specialized sciences, which would lead to the loss of control over the civilization's homeostasis. The solution would be abandonment of nature as the source of information and construction of new types of feedback within the civilization's own artificial environment. This would result in a cybersociotechnological shell enclosing a civilization that would henceforth exist and evolve independently of nature. Such a civilization would be imperceptible to an external observer, especially an astronomic one.

What constitutes a loss in the information game? Fragmented sciences, the lack of scientists, and the limited information flow would cause a deregulation of the feedback loops with nature. Losing the game, however, does not necessarily mean immediate demise or extinction; the losing civilization may oscillate for thousands of years.

In this long chapter Lem opens many other interesting topics. In the section "Dangers of Electrocracy" he asks if it would be feasible or beneficial to let society be controlled by an electronic machine so advanced and complex that it would be a black box for us (the black box is a term for systems whose structure and inner workings are unknown). In the section "Experimental Metaphysics" he considers a computer simulation of the origins of religion. Lem recognizes that religion may minimize the "existential pain" in individuals, but at the same time it can increase the suffering of the whole society, since "what is good for an individual may not be good for the society and vice versa" (159). The author states a pragmatist's reason for his negative view of religion: since it is not empirical knowledge, religion cannot do anything for humanity. While the explicit absence of God in Lem's works is well known, such a forceful denouncement of religion in any of its forms might be shocking for some readers. Particularly the criticism of Buddhism, the least religious of all religions, seems unduly harsh. In another section, "Problems of Information," Lem draws our attention to the fact that "information as such" does not exist, that it is very context-dependent. Of course, information about a natural process is a function of some state(s) of nature, but besides that there are other variables: not only must information have a receiver, it also depends on the whole surrounding system of reference created by humanity.

In chapter 5, "Prolegomena of Omnipotence," Lem puts forward an interesting thesis: that omniscience equals omnipotence. Early in the nineteenth century the mathematician Pierre Laplace coupled his idea of the completely deterministic universe with omniscience. He wrote in the opening pages of *A Philosophical Essay on Probabilities*: "We ought then to regard the present state of the universe as the effect of its anterior state and the cause of the one which is to follow. Given for one instant an intelligence which could comprehend all the forces by which nature is animated and the mutual respective situation of the beings who compose it – an intelligence sufficiently vast to submit these data to analysis – it would embrace in the same formula the movements of the greatest bodies of the universe and those of the lightest atom; for it, nothing would be uncertain and the future, just as the past, would be present to its eyes" (4). But we have to ask: Can we – or anyone else, for that matter – know everything?

It is hard to answer in the affirmative, despite Laplace's conviction. The universe seems to be infinite in more than one respect. We may advance arbitrarily close to the limit of "knowing it all," but the ultimate Theory of Everything will probably elude us forever. Thus, instead of omniscience, let us consider knowing (or understanding) a single system or process. We fully understand a system when we can fully describe it and predict its states at any time and in any circumstances. A computer programmer can take a look at a simple program and know how it works. Longer, more complex programs would require longer and more thorough analysis. But there are programs of such high complexity that it is impossible to know what they do. The only way of knowing is to run them on a computer. Lem transfers this pragmatic approach from the computer science to the future physics, chemistry, and technology. He states that the best proof of full understanding is the ability to create, or recreate, the given system or process. He calls this technological ability of achieving arbitrary goals – even those not realized in nature – "pantocratics" and divides it into "imitology" and "phantomology." The former recreates objects or processes occurring in nature, while the latter uses the broadened constructing limits of humanity (mentioned earlier) to create objects or processes that do not exist in nature.

Chapter 6 is entirely and eponymously devoted to phantomology. The ever-pedantic author even makes a distinction between phantomology, a science, and phantomatics, a technology. He introduces the idea of a phantomat, a machine that is able to create – by direct excitation of sensory neurons – any possible (and impossible) experience in a person connected to it (something akin to what, decades later, would be called virtual reality). The classical electrophysiological experiments with rodents, which were allowed to electrically stimulate their pleasure centres with electrodes implanted in their brains, are mentioned in the *Summa*, but Lem is obviously not interested in the technical side of phantomatics. Rather, he examines if phantomatics can have limits imposed on it by psychology, sociology, ethics, and law.

Lem originally suggested that total phantomatization of a whole civilization is, fortunately, not feasible, since it would lead to extinction within one generation – the phantomatized individuals would not work, eat, or reproduce. Totally phantomatized civilizations were thought to commit a quick suicide and therefore would not be observed. In a recent conversation with Peter Swirski, however, Lem conceded that a totally phantomatized population could be fed and artificially reproduced by machines, with new individuals hooked up immediately after the machine-assisted birth.[6] While this is possible in principle, the biosphere of such a civilization can be, for all practical purposes, considered extinct. The post-biological evolution of the caretaker machine civilization could obviously continue, but that is a topic for another discussion.

The huge entertainment potential of phantomatics was clearly seen by Lem forty years ago. But are we ready for its moral dilemmas? For example, if somebody produces child pornography with computer-generated "actors," is there any crime committed? If somebody murders or rapes in the virtual environment, what are the consequences in the real world? Are crimes committed in virtual reality just innocent (or even healthy?) ventilations of our dark urges, or are they a training practice for real-world crimes that we will inevitably commit, longing for authenticity? Questions like these have already reached our courtrooms.[7]

Phantomatics feeds false information to an intact brain and it is up to that brain how the information is processed and what reactions ensue. But what about a stronger version, which Lem calls cerebromatics? Cerebromatics does not stop at providing false information but changes the ways in which the brain interprets signals; in other words, it changes the brain itself (see Paisley Livingston's essay in this volume). Would cerebromats be declared illegal, like mind-altering drugs? Could ontology guide us in a limited (perhaps therapeutic?) use of cerebromatics? Would anyone like to be transformed into a great inventor or a powerful ruler at the price of giving up their identity? It is assumed that the modified brain could not recollect the old personality. If it were possible, it would diminish the experience since we would be aware of falsity or artificiality of our situation, remembering the cerebromatic procedure and the imperfect, weak, or otherwise undesirable person we had been before.

The future progress of phantomatics, which would include teletaxis (a sort of remote self, creating the perception of being somewhere else) and phantoplication (connection of multiple individuals to a single brain or vice versa), leads Lem to an unexpected ontological conclusion. He formulates the principle of existential relativity: personal identity is relative, and it depends on context, accepted definitions, and applied criteria. To illustrate this concept, let us consider those who believe that their identity is defined by an uninterrupted, continuous material existence as a separate body. They only need to be reminded that the atoms and molecules of our bodies are in constant flux and exchange with the environment (breathing, eating, etc.), so that there is hardly an "original" material particle in an adult body that had been there at birth. Those who rather rely on mental, psychological, or behavioural criteria to define their identity might enjoy an ontological joke from Hofstadter's *Metamagical Themas* (1985): "If I said something else, would it still be me?"

This part of the book serves as the best example of Lem's masterful ability to simultaneously educate, provoke, and entertain. The philosophical points of this chapter are nicely illustrated with science-fiction story sketches describing adventures and misadventures of a hypothetical Mr Smith who undergoes many various phantomatic procedures. Of course, the problems of identity or of the reality of reality have appeared in science fiction before (see almost any work by Philip K. Dick) and since (e.g., recently, *The Matrix* film trilogy), but Lem poses these questions with the seriousness and thoroughness of an academic, fully aware of previous accomplishments of Plato, Berkeley, or Descartes.

In chapter 7, "Creating Worlds," Lem returns to the idea of automatic generation (breeding) of information. According to Lem, an adult higher organism contains about 10^{25} bits of information on the molecular level. It might seem that the recipe for constructing such an organism must contain at least that much information, and possibly more. But to make the organism, we do not have to read a 10^{25} bit long protocol and painstakingly create it molecule by molecule and cell by cell. All we need is to fuse two cells – a sperm and an egg – and the organism will develop by itself. Can something analogous be employed in information science? The initial parent information would crossbreed, interact, evolve and grow so that at the end we would have the adult organism: a new scientific theory. This seems to be the reverse of the classical epistemological process of science, in which we use the immaterial language of mathematics to describe material phenomena. In information breeding we create material objects that code for mathematical truths or solutions.

This is not as far-fetched as it might sound. In fact, there are at least two instances of this principle that have already occurred in practice. Leonard Adleman published in 1994 in the journal

Science the proof of concept for solving difficult combinatorial problems with liquid solutions of deoxyribonucleic acid (DNA).[8] We know that a DNA molecule can code information in the form of specific sequence of its building blocks – nucleotides – and that two DNA molecules can have complementary sequences of nucleotides, which will assure strong binding (called hybridization) between the two molecules. The less complementary the sequences, the weaker the binding. We can encode a mathematical problem in the initial ensemble of DNA molecules and then let them interact according to the known rules of molecular biology. With the help of enzymes, the molecules will reproduce and construct new DNA from the aqueous solution of the building blocks. Simple separation techniques can then be used to purify the molecules that represent the mathematical solution to the problem. This is a simplified description of Adleman's experiment. Is this not what Lem had in mind in 1964? The power of such biomolecular computation lies in its huge parallelism: one drop of nucleic acid solution can contain 10^{17} molecules, which can all perform the computation step – hybridization – at the same time.

The second current application of Lem's strategy for breeding new knowledge is the technique used for in vitro evolution of molecules, called SELEX (Systematic Evolution of Ligands by EXponential enrichment). Developed independently in 1990 by three US research groups, it works with molecules of ribonucleic acids (RNA), which in nature participate in transmission of the genetic information.[9] RNA differs from DNA in several respects, one of which is the conformation or molecular shape. While DNA normally occurs as strands of the famous double helix, RNA can assume any conformation, depending on the sequence of nucleotides. Let us say that we want to construct an RNA molecule that would specifically bind to another arbitrary molecule whose shape we do not know. For classical constructors this is an insurmountable task. Not only would classical constructors have difficulties working at the level of atoms or molecules, but their problems would be much more serious and philosophical. How can one construct a molecular surface to fit another molecular surface which is not known? How can one make a key for an unknown lock? With SELEX we simply mix randomly synthesized RNA with the target molecules and separate those RNA molecules that bind. The separated pool of RNA will then be randomly mutated and tested for binding to the target. Again, RNA molecules that bind the best will be separated, mutated, and used in the next binding test. After several rounds of such selection we will have the desired RNA molecule that binds strongly to the target. Notice that the solution to our problem was *evolved*, not calculated. We do not even know the shape of the target molecule!

Lem concludes this chapter with the description of three kinds of engineering: language engineering, which, in line with the previous considerations, makes no distinction between the word and flesh; transcendence engineering, which constructs metaphysics; and cosmogonic engineering, which might be a cause for the Dickian nightmares of humanity being just a puppet in an artificial universe. The latter theme has already found its way into the branch of complexity science called artificial life.

Chapter 8, "Pasquil on Evolution," closes the book's circle by returning to evolution, specifically to human evolution. Lem's strong thesis is that human evolution is the evolution of information processing and thus the evolution of technology. He notes that human evolution seems to select for longevity, which cannot be explained by classical Darwinism according to which, once an organism loses the ability to reproduce, it becomes useless for evolution (if the latter is narrowly understood as transmission and modification of genetic information). But long-lived individuals do have a "supra-biological" value: in their communities they serve as storage and transmitter of *cultural* and *technological* information, which helps the communities survive and expand.

In a way, technology is a product of bioevolution, just as the eye, brain, humanity, agriculture, society, art, and economy are. Technology, which is constantly evolving in the process of technoevolution, is just another tool of nature to continue or expand bioevolution. The two evolutions are thus two phases of a single process. Lem predicts that after several thousand years of human civilization's existence, with the advent of pantocratics, there will be no difference between natural and artificial; bioevolution and technoevolution will finally be seen as one.

An invasion of manmade technologies into the human body is inevitable; in fact, it is happening today. With our artificial joints, pacemakers, and cochlear implants, we are at the same time witnesses, victims, and perpetrators of this process. The appearance of teleology in evolution, embodied in Homo sapiens, makes possible a new form of evolution/auto-evolution. Current biotechnology is young and works mostly as prophylaxis or prosthetics. Biotechnology of the future will have a worthier goal – instead of mere reconstruction, a radically new design. This does not mean the cartoonish "robotization" of humanity that has been a common scare in popular horror and science fiction; nor does it mean forfeiting any valuable features of our species. Rather, biotechnology will be used to eliminate shortcomings and primitive design features that bioevolution bestowed on our bodies.

Contrary to popular belief, bioevolution does not seek – and usually does not find – the *optimal* solution. Nature, being a tinkerer rather than a sentient constructor, only modifies its previous products and, furthermore, only does so to the *minimal* degree necessary for the new product to pass the muster of natural selection at the given moment. Lem lists several examples of suboptimal bioevolutionary solutions in the construction of the human body inherited from our four-legged ancestors. The bones of the lower back and hips, for instance, were not supposed to carry the whole weight of the trunk. To save the situation, new muscle groups evolved, which, unfortunately, greatly hamper the act of birth. The erect posture has also had negative effects on the blood flow in our bodies: other animals do not know varicose veins. The explosive increase of the cranial volume has lead to an almost ninety degree turn in the airways at the back of the oral cavity, where the larynx meets the esophagus. The increased turbulence in the airflow causes an increased deposit of aerosols and microorganisms, making the throat a frequent point of entry for numerous infections. Bioevolution tried to counter it by surrounding the critical point with a ring of lymphatic tissue known as tonsils, but this poor improvisation only aggravated the situation as the tonsils themselves often become the seat of infection.

The author's itemized critique of bioevolution from the engineering standpoint is both provocative and enlightening. It is indisputable that the bioevolutionary process can be greatly improved, and Lem is convinced that humanity can overcome nature as a constructor. Due to the construction limitations inherent in bioevolution, nature can only build systems based on colloidal solutions of carbon-containing macromolecules, with the hierarchical organization into cells and, optionally, tissues and organs. But this surely is just a small subset of the possible self-regulating systems. Upon acquisition of the necessary knowledge, we can build them all.

The chapter, and the whole book, ends rather anticlimactically with a short section on extrasensory perception (ESP), which includes the phenomena of telepathy (reading and/or steering other peoples' minds), precognition ("seeing" the future), and "psychokinesis" (moving objects without using physical force). Lem briskly annihilates all ESP claims with a single evolutionary argument: if ESP were real, evolution would have selected for it long ago, since ESP would give a decisive advantage to individuals having such abilities. Telepathy would greatly help a rabbit escape from an approaching lynx or, vice versa, telepathy could aid a lynx predict a fleeing rabbit's next move. Evolution of extremely acute senses of animals, such as sight in birds of prey or smell in dogs, would be a colossal waste of time if these senses could be replaced with ESP. Deep-sea organisms would not need to develop phosphorescing organs to escape from predators or find mates. Nocturnal animals, such as owls or bats, would all be telepaths by now. And how could we, humans – according to some of us the crowning achievement of evolution – all have avoided evolving into telepaths? The logic of this argument is so simple and overwhelming that all the quasi-scientific experiments and faulty statistics, sometimes invoked to support the existence of ESP, become unnecessary.

SUMMA IN CONTEXTS

We have come to the end of *Summa technologiae*, and it is time to ponder its meaning and value. Some read the book as a list of predictions and keep little score cards, where they note the fulfilled prophecies as well as the perceived failures ("How come he didn't predict the internet?"). Even Lem himself felt compelled to address these issues in three books of short essays: *The Mystery of the Chinese Room* (1996), *The Megabit Bomb* (1999), and *The Blink of an Eye* (2000). Nevertheless, this is a misunderstanding. *Summa* is not a prognostication almanac, and its author is not Nostradamus or Jules Verne – the latter having been quite successful in relatively short-term extrapolations concerning science and technology. The aim of *Summa* was not to predict particular gadgets but rather to explore the conceptual foundations of the two evolutions and their relations to society and civilization. Individual predictions that have come true are rather byproducts of Lem's creative thinking.

Those interested in the list of *Summa*'s fulfilled prophecies should refer to the three Lem books mentioned above and to the essay "Thirty Years Later" in *A Stanislaw Lem Reader* (1997) by Peter Swirski. Here are several examples: virtual reality, which Lem called phantomatics; biologically based computation; and the technology for automatic search of links within and between huge datasets, which Lem called ariadnology (the science of threads), is now commonly used in biology (bioinformatics) and library science (search engines).

Elsewhere Lem noted almost casually that evolution proceeds at an uneven pace, with short bursts of activity interspersed with long period of stasis. This idea seems innocuous, even obvious, and it is now an integral part of modern evolution theory under the name of punctuated equilibrium. It should be noted, however, that Lem wrote his remarks – "In general, we can say that the pace of evolution is minimal, even approaching zero, when environmental conditions remain practically unchanged for hundreds of millions of years" (77) – eight years before the official introduction of punctuated equilibrium by the evolutionary biologists Eldredge and Gould (1972).[10]

Even if none of Lem's visions materialized in the real world, *Summa* would still be a great book: an adventurous analysis of the principles of evolutionary processes, probing the limits of the possible. Needless to say, *Summa* is not science fiction: Lem's speculations has always been firmly anchored in the basic laws of physics, especially the Second Law of Thermodynamics (about the impossibility of a decrease in total entropy) and Einstein's postulate of a limit to the maximum possible speed in the universe. But apart from those two limitations he allows himself the freedom to speculate. His twin maxim is: what is not forbidden by the fundamental laws of nature is allowed; what has a finite probability, no matter how small, will surely happen sometime, somewhere.

Summa might have had a great influence on shaping new directions in science, technology, and their philosophy, had it been better known among scientists in the English-speaking world. Although the book's significance may presently lie only in the realm of the possible or probable, its magnitude is certainly more than imaginary. After *Summa* many books were published that appear to elaborate on topics discussed, or at least sketched, by Lem. They include: *Chance and Necessity* (1971) by Jacques Monod, which pondered (the lack of) teleology in bioevolution and was the first serious account on evolution at the molecular level; *The Selfish Gene* (1976) and *The Blind Watchmaker* (1986) by Richard Dawkins, which disseminated the notion of evolution's blindness and randomness; *Goedel, Escher, Bach* (1979) and *Metamagical Themas* (1985) by Douglas Hofstadter, which discussed thinking, self-organization, and self-reference, among other topics; *At Home in the Universe* (1995) by Stuart Kauffman, dealing with the computer-simulated evolution of life and intelligence; *How Nature Works* (1996) by Per Bak, analyzing systems at the edge of chaos; *Beyond Humanity: Cyberevolution and Future Minds* (1996) by Gregory Paul and Earl Cox, which focused on transfer of thoughts and minds between humans and machines. As the main themes of these and many other books can be found in *Summa*, is it possible that in a mysterious, Borgesian fashion a book can exert influence without actually having been read?

Summa may be a rare accomplishment but, as any accomplishment, it does not stand isolated in the history of literature or thought. In his essay "Kafka and His Precursors" from *Other Inquisitions* (1952), Jorge Luis Borges noted that each writer creates his own precursors. There might be quite a few possible precursors or inspirations for *Summa*, and, if we believe Borges, it does not matter whether Lem was aware of them or not, although the latter's well-known erudition would strongly favour the former possibility. The sheer timescale of *Summa* – from the origin of life to posthuman civilization – is comparable to few literary works. Olaf Stapledon's *Last and First Men* (1930), a plotless and characterless "novel" encompassing billions of years of evolution, comes to mind. Next might be Erwin Schroedinger's famous *What Is Life?* (1944), which probed the border between living and nonliving matter and afforded surprising insight into the barely nascent field of molecular biology. Apart from St Thomas Aquinas's quasi-eponymous treatise, which was Lem's inspiration in form rather than content, two other older books deserve notice. One is Jonathan Swift's *Gulliver's Travels* (1726), which is mentioned in *Summa*'s conclusion. Lem and Swift share not only a witty, often sarcastic style but ideas, too. Lem's equivalence of formal language to a set of material objects, such as biomolecules, is similar to a project that Gulliver found at the Academy of Lagado: its linguists suggested abolishing all words except nouns, and even those were to be replaced by material objects.[11] The other ancient precursor of *Summa* might have been *On the Nature of Things* (first century BC) by Lucretius, in which the poet sought scientific explanations of the world, often allowing for speculations where and when deemed necessary (e.g., invoking the existence of atoms).

Summa technologiae has undoubtedly played an important role in Lem's development as a writer and thinker. The book is at the centre of gravity of his body of work. Many inventions and ideas discussed in *Summa* have roots in his previous writings. For example, the complex relationship between philosophy, ethics, politics, and technology was addressed in the early discursive volume *Dialogues* (1957); auto-evolution is the central plot feature in the novel *Return from the Stars* (1961); and nanotechnology, random engineering, and connectedness as the source of intellect appear in *The Invincible* (1964). At the same time, *Summa* acts as a reservoir for ideas that were elaborated in later works. Adaptations of the artificial life theme can be found throughout *The Cyberiad* (1965) and in some stories of *Memoirs of a Space Traveler* (1983); an especially poignant literary-philosophical rendition of artificial life, with its "experimental metaphysics," is presented in the "Non Serviam" chapter of *Perfect Vacuum* (1971); problems of decoding or interpretation of signs, as well as the relationship between the language (signal) and the material world are at the heart of *His Master's Voice* (1968); the transhuman evolution and evolution of consciousness are fully explored in *Golem XIV* (1981); and nanotechnology and cyberevolution reappear in *Peace on Earth* (1987).

CONCLUSION

Summa can be analyzed on many levels from many different viewpoints. This essay focused on just a few aspects of the book predetermined by my selective knowledge and interests. The main issue was a scientific scrutiny of Lem's concepts and an examination of how those concepts have fared in the forty years since the book's first publication.

This one-member jury has reached a positive verdict. Not a list of prognoses but rather a manual of critical thinking, the book has a lot to say even to the technologically savvy denizens of the twenty-first century. Philosophically Lem is a pragmatist who knows that for most humans the measure of all things is humanity. Thus, humanity is very much present in *Summa* – notwithstanding the word technology in the title – though, of course, not in isolation but in relation to nature, technology, and the "artificial" environment of culture and civilization. Lem does not idealize humanity; his skepticism is sometimes as thick as Voltaire's. There is no pedestal for humanity in *Summa*: we are not the crowning achievement of evolution, and it would indeed be strange if evolution stopped now. On the contrary, we should get ready for a greatly accelerated roller-coaster of technoevolution, probably coupled with auto-evolution. We may very well be just a tool, which nature found and which has helped it to achieve self-awareness. With that self-awareness, it can finally, after billions of years of blind trials and errors, start *consciously* directing its own evolution. Is it too little or too much of a role for Homo sapiens? Only the future will decide if we were the right tool, but it does not mean that we should quit examining these issues and asking relevant questions at all times. And that is exactly what books like *Summa technologiae* do.

NOTES

1 Science teaches and preaches objectivity, but I declare up front that I have been a Lem devotee since my teenage years. Therefore I ask the reader for forgiveness if my admiration for *Summa* and its author sometimes becomes too obvious.

2 *Tako rzecze … Lem. Ze Stanisławem Lemem rozmawia Stanisław Bereś [Thus Spake … Lem. Stanisław Bereś's Conversations with Stanislaw Lem]*, Kraków, Wydawnictwo Literackie, 2002, cited in Jarzębski, Jerzy. "Summa technologiae i jej potomstwo [*Summa technologiae* and Its Descendants]." Afterword in Lem, Stanislaw, *Summa technologiae*, Kraków: Wydawnictwo Literackie, 2000.

3 Search for extraterrestrial intelligence. A scientific project, formulated in 1959, that includes "listening" to potential signals from others and transmitting our own signals into space. It was supported by NASA between 1960 and 1993. A brief and very accessible account of history of SETI, weaving together science, economics, and politics, can be found in Garber (1999).

4 See Bak (1996), Kauffman (1995).

5 An interested reader can learn more about the history of the neutrino in Franklin (2000).

6 Peter Swirski, personal communication.

7 See Mota (2002) and the US Supreme Court Opinion 00-795, www.supremecourtus.gov/opinions/01pdf/00-795.pdf.

8 See Adleman (1994).

9 See Ellington and Szostak (1990), Robertson and Joyce (1990), and Tuerk and Gold (1990).

10 Thanks to Jerzy Jarzębski for confirmation that the sentence in question does occur in the first edition of *Summa*.

11 Thanks to Paisley Livingston for bringing to my attention that this concept appeared in Plato's dialog "Cratylus"; see *The Dialogues of Plato* (1937): 173–229.

6

Models of Evolution in the Writings of Stanislaw Lem

JERZY JARZĘBSKI

No faithful follower of Stanislaw Lem's fiction can overlook the role of evolution in his narratives. Evolution is conceived here in very broad terms: from the history of the entire cosmos, through the process of planet formation, the emergence of life on Earth, the historical development of human societies and their culture, down to the history of knowledge. In his classic work on the relations between ethics and evolution, *Evolution and Ethics,* Thomas H. Huxley underscored both the universal character of evolutionary processes and their separateness from and incompatibility with the concept of creation. He wrote: "As a natural process, of the same character as the development of a tree from its seed, or a fowl from its egg, evolution excludes creation and all other kinds of supernatural intervention. As the expression of a fixed order, every stage of which is the effect of causes operating according to definite rules, the conception of evolution no less excludes that of chance. It is very desirable to remember that evolution is not an explanation of the cosmic process, but merely a generalized statement of the method and results of that process. And, further, that, if there is proof that the cosmic process was set going by any agent, then that agent will be the creator of it and of all its products, although supernatural intervention may remain strictly excluded from its further course."[1]

While evolution – notwithstanding the great variety of individual evolutionary processes – is driven by forces independent of humankind and its goals, the very fact of the universal character of evolutionary processes remains a intriguing mystery. This mystery could naturally be deflated by rejecting all teleological questions as "unscientific," but such a remedy would be effective only in the short term inasmuch as the prohibited questions would simply reappear in a different guise. Culture, to the extent that it can be so personified, has a built-in imperative to seek answers to such questions, constantly creating mythical or religious substitutes for teleology, while relegating the agent that endows progress with purpose to the supernatural realm.

In my recent article "The Natural, the Artificial and the Hole in the Cosmos" (2003), I argued that Lem, without relinquishing his atheism, does something similar, tirelessly escaping in his narratives beyond the boundaries of the commonly accessible universe and placing the agent who "explains" or adjudicates the fundamental questions in this universe outside its bounds. I focused chiefly on the paradoxes arising from the conflict between the concepts of "natural" and "artificial" in Lem's fiction. In the present essay I would like to concentrate on the subject of evolution in its narrative aspect, i.e., on evolution conceived as a narrative and on the role of this narrative in the stories told by Lem.

Is evolution a narrative organized around some rational plan? From the point of view of science, it certainly isn't. As stressed even by Huxley, it frequently exhibits its accidental and haphazard character in obedience to random events that defy human control. Both in cosmogony and in natural evolution, for example, the path of evolution is influenced by disasters occurring on the planetary, stellar, and galactic level, as well as by a number of other random factors. Evolution of societies is governed by so many changing and interchanging parameters that it is impossible to define any constantly valid rules that would allow us to describe it as a sequence of events fulfilling some rational plan. Yet all these types of evolution have been inscribed into narrative models, from countless cosmogonic myths to visions of history as an embodiment of some *Idea*, exemplified by Ovid's *Metamorphoses* in the ancient world and later by Christian philosophers, followed by Vico, Hegel, Marx, and their many imitators.

I do not intend to wrestle with this huge subject on this limited forum. Instead I set for myself a much more humble task: to look at the role played by narrative models in Lem's visions of evolution. First let us examine them *in statu nascendi* in Lem's early writings. Both in *The Astronauts* and in *The Magellan Nebula* the future history of humanity is presented as a consistent march along the path of both scientific and social progress. This means not only more technological possibilities and more social justice but also the triumph of universal rationality as a driving force and ruling motive of human behaviour. In the Stalinist years the officially sanctioned historical evolution towards the social pinnacle of Communism was interpreted (and narratized) by Lem as the gradual removal from human behaviour of everything that contradicted the idea of reason, or, in other words, everything that was mired in myth, superstition, religious belief, economic conflict, struggle for power, etc. One example of that is the early "Twenty-Fourth Voyage" from *The Star Diaries* (original edition 1957), where the devoutly believing priests or monks yield to the charms of scientific knowledge and abandon religion in throngs in order to pursue a scholarly or engineering career. Rationality in the field of science or technology must be accompanied by equality and justice in the field of social relations, or else an entire civilization will sooner or later succumb to the madness of imperialism and – as it happened to the Venusians in *The Astronauts* – wholesale destruction will follow.

The first, admittedly somewhat naïve, "evolutionary" type of narrative designed by Lem is thus a story about humankind striding along the path from superstition to light (i.e., reason). In the classic Soviet version of this narrative, people are creatures gently rocked in the cradle of a natural world that is generally amicable towards them. Going through different stages of their development they gain an ever better knowledge of the rules governing their environment, until they learn to rationally transform this environment, successfully rectifying nature's imperfections under the guidance of the Party. On first blush this vision of evolution did not differ from the initial model advanced by Lem, and the Marxists found the writer's ideas satisfactory, but manifold heresies soon entered Lem's evolutionary narratives through the back door. This is particularly true of *The Star Diaries,* in which we see madness appearing as a threat to rational order, or else ostensibly rational authorities deviating from the path of reason by endeavouring to elevate some arbitrary principle to absolute status, for example by imposing on society laws contrary to human nature. Such was the case of "The Twenty-Fourth Voyage," where the introduction of Absolute Order has the consequence of denying all life as unavoidable disorder. Such was the case of "The Thirteenth Voyage," where a ruler of a distant planet, a kind of cosmic Lysenko, told his subjects to get accustomed to living in water. Such was the case of "The Eleventh Voyage," where people were forced to disguise themselves as robots because of the abuses perpetrated by the bureaucracy ruling the roost in the intelligence community.

Even though these examples may seem rather distant from each other, the underlying realities described in all three works have at least one thing in common: the presence of an intellectual concept – an intellectual artifice, if you will – that attempts to force the world into this or that kind of preconceived order. Lem usually shows such an artifice to be the source of evil, destruction, and derailing of common sense. It is not only incumbent for the world to listen to reason, he points out, but also for reason to listen to the world so as not to become overly complacent. This warning seems rather obvious in the context of Stalinist political reality ("The Thirteenth Voyage" in particular was commonly received by contemporary readers as political satire). But in the same period the problem of reason as embodied in history becomes much more complicated in Lem's writings, with the result that the author goes beyond the narrative solutions he used up to that time – both those apologetic and those critical towards the political changes that took place in Poland after the war.

One source of complication is natural evolution, which becomes one of the subjects of *Eden* (1959), the first novel written after the 1956 political liberalization that haltingly followed Stalin's death. In tune with the prevailing mood of the times, when it was first published, *Eden* was read as an "Orwellian" novel, i.e., a novel describing a society where those in power exert such control over language that their crimes cannot penetrate the awareness of the citizens. By manipulating language, the political rulers conceal from the Edenians the fiasco of the project whose initial aim was to modify the genetic makeup of the inhabitants of the planet and, when the project stalled, to exterminate the "failed" mutants (see also Peter Swirski's "Betrization Is the Worst Solution ... with the Exception of All Others," elsewhere in the volume).

Recently, rereading the novel a few decades after its original publication, a different interpretation suggested itself to me. Orwell's *1984* was replaced by a reflection on nature and the level of (un)friendliness towards the creatures it harbours. As we know from *Wizja lokalna* [*On Site Inspection*; 1983], Lem generally does not believe in the amicability of the cosmic environment towards its inhabitants, because within this environment it is always easier to destroy than to create, to generate pain than to generate happiness, to lead to doom than to lead to salvation, to kill than to revive. Nature is essentially unkind towards individuals as it attaches a greater worth to species as a whole, valuing above all else the genetic code transmitted from generation to generation in the process of reproduction, either in a faithfully copied or, less often, mutated form. All this is well known to readers of Lem's *Golem XIV* (1981), a story in the guise of a rather cynical resumé of humanity's lot offered by a hypercomputer a hundred times wiser than any human. The computer discourses very much in the manner of Richard Dawkins, the champion of the "selfish gene" in his eponymous 1976 scientific bestseller. Nature nourishes only those individuals who can serve as reproducers of valuable genetic material, while in principle it does not care about specimens that are old, inadequately mutated, or for other reasons unable to reproduce.

If, following the writer's suggestions from this later period of his career, we look at the planetary community of Edenians as an original civilization that based its technology and rules of social interaction on patterns arising from biology, then the massacre of failed mutants will be seen only as one of the manifestations of a disregard for those individuals that cannot take part in the great game of transmitting and perfecting the genetic code, a disregard close to that exhibited by laws of nature. The cruelty of extermination, which the earlier readings of the novel blamed on the totalitarian regime of Eden, now becomes an effect of the essential property of natural evolution and, therefore, an accidental element of the collective plight. If so, the relations on the planet do not owe that much to Orwell, but rather to Darwin, and through him also to Marx. And as such they cannot be accused of being "irrational" but only of obeying a different kind of ruthless rationality, unacceptable to the human mind.

With *Eden* a certain tension is introduced into the subject of evolution in Lem's writings. Until then it was inscribed into the universal narrative that drew – in parallel and thus in non-contradictory manner – the history of natural evolution and the history of the advancement of reason. The concept of evolution seemed to correspond closely to the concept of progress and amelioration: reason advanced is reason that knows ever more and is therefore capable of exerting more effective control over nature. Under its guidance complex systems (biological organisms, societies) become not only ever more complicated, but also better, more rationally configured and therefore more congenial to individuals. This model comes into question when the writer discovers that nature is indifferent, if not hostile, towards individuals. This tension is also apparent in the novel's ending: the astronauts, who at first tried to physically defend the "failed" mutants from slaughter, forsake their intervention and fly away. It is, of course, an act of tolerance towards a different character of the planetary order but also an act of resignation in the face of discovery that there is no single, canonical road of progress to reason to be followed by every community. And so the unitary character of the evolutionary narrative comes into question.

Criticism of reason conceived as a supreme instrument for shaping humanity and its environment gains gradual prominence Lem's in later works. This theme, which, as we have seen, was initially used for the purposes of political satire, acquires a visibly independent character in numerous later stories, mostly from *The Cyberiad* (1965). The protagonists of this famous story cycle are two famous Constructors, creatures almost by definition acting rationally. On their own or through other characters they will repeatedly attempt to build a happy society. Yet in such stories as "Gargantius" or "Altruizine" the idea of rational amelioration collapses in the most spectacular way, as all attempts at perfecting social conditions through one type of smart tinkering or another always end in disaster.

It seems safe to say that the model of evolutionary narrative developed by Lem in his fiction becomes more and more complicated over the years. Getting rid of material want and securing social justice no longer satisfies the writer. Instead he creates narratives that move beyond these basic postulates towards some very distant solutions, and with them come problems that did not exist in his earlier works. First of all, the spectrum of analysis is broadened: writing about evolution at the turn of the 1950s, Lem makes this term encompass cosmological processes, the growth of animate nature, and the history of human culture. These diverse areas are part of a larger, more encompassing, process and are governed by comparable rules. An idea appears, especially in the famous collection of futurological essays *Summa technologiae* (1964; see also Peter Butko's essay in this volume), of uniting all three types of evolution into one process conforming to a logic that could be roughly described as follows. The first to evolve are the cosmos and inanimate nature, creating an environment in which life can develop. Then biological evolution creates reason as a function of life processes in higher creatures. Subsequently reason itself – which in this period of Lem's career seems to be a kind of self-contained entity initially functioning as a subsidiary agent in the processes of adaptation and struggle for survival – evolves, then acquires some autonomy, and through human agency is transferred into a more convenient environment of machines. In the end, becoming independent of humanity, it gains the ability of self-development and grows almost to infinity, as a material medium of its processes using first the ever more powerful machines, then their networks, and finally the matter contained in entire galaxies.

This is the most monumental of Lem's evolutionary narratives. It has only one weak point: it designates too insignificant a role to humanity, who at some stage must draw back from the frontline of change, becoming almost a relic without any prospects for (evolutionary) future. Now we understand why reason does not necessarily serve living creatures: it simply treats Homo sapiens as selfishly as it does Dawkins's famous gene, using each human being as a temporary vehicle for its own transformation and not caring for that individual's fate. It means that we cannot evaluate reason from the point of view of "effective" uses because it does not aim at fulfilling human (or any other) needs but rather at fostering further unencumbered growth. In this narrative, when reason attains a higher, that is, superhuman, stage of its development, it is no longer subject to any type of value judgment because virtually no verifying mechanisms are available. It is true that in "Trurl's Machine" (*The Cyberiad*) Lem wrote a charming fable about a *stupid* digital machine, but a feeble-minded galaxy he did not quite dare to conceive. Another weak point of this type of narrative is that to someone regarding it from a distance it must seem largely nonsensical: why should reason want to expand up to the very ends of the cosmos? For the entire world to gain self-awareness and then to suffer the consequences of "thermal death" or some other version of final Apocalypse? Traditional theology deals much better with these kinds of problems, and although Lem's reason is somewhat reminiscent of God, or in any case is occasionally invited to play that role, it cannot cope with eschatological questions. Hence the already mentioned tendency of Lem's to construct worlds equipped with a kind of umbilical cord, or a gateway, to transcendence understood in physical and definitely lay terms.[2] It makes it possible to remove eschatological questions into the other world, disburdening us from the duty of answering them within the bounds of the known cosmos.

Let us now take a look at evolutionary narratives cut to a more modest scale. Lem's works abound in them, simply because most of his stories use some evolutionary process as a backdrop and point of reference. Answers to questions regarding the path taken by a given civilization are sought in *The Return from the Stars*, *Solaris*, *The Investigation*, *Memoirs Found in a Bathtub*, *The Invincible*, *His Master's Voice*, *The Futurological Congress*, *The Chain of Chance*, *Wizja lokalna* [*On Site Inspection*], *Peace on Earth*, and *Fiasco*; in many stories from *The Star Diaries*, *Tales of Pirx the Pilot*, and *The Cyberiad*; and even in the fictional reviews and introductions from *A Perfect Vacuum* and *Imaginary Magnitude* – in other words, in almost all of Lem's fictions. And there is nothing strange in that, inasmuch as Lem's narratives are set in a dynamic, ever changing reality that requires its inhabitants to constantly alter their ways of thinking and acting. These works rely on a number of models of evolutionary narrative that can be linked with the types of cognitive experiments designed by the author in his books.

The first of these models is contact with a different civilization or some essentially alien, nonhuman creature (*Eden*, *Solaris*, *The Invincible*, *His Master's Voice*, *On Site Inspection*, *Fiasco*). Even though at first glance evolution plays here an insignificant role, it is not so inasmuch as contact with an alien civilization is possible only in a particular stage of sociotechnological development (the "window of contact" developed at length in *Fiasco*). Different civilizations are like spinning tops, which must realign the holes in their surfaces so that information could be transferred between them. But what, in fact, is there to transmit? As we know, Lem is highly skeptical about the chances for communication on the cosmic scale, a view expressed most forcefully in *Solaris* and *Fiasco*. Transfer of information is usually only apparent; astronauts unavoidably behold the cosmic other as something comparable to what they already know from their own experience, thus anthropomorphizing the unknown and endowing it with their own characteristics. But meeting aliens at least forces humans to tell them (and themselves) their own story as a narrative endowed with meaning and internal logic.

Having encountered the unsettling phenomenon of Solaris, Kelvin goes straight to the library where he learns the history of planetary research presented as if it were the story of human knowledge in general. The Solarists themselves experience their meetings with the "phi-creatures" through stories employing various literary conventions. The astronauts from *Fiasco* bombard the foreign planet with cinematic fairy tales for children, the civilization of Encians in *On Site Inspection* produces innumerable texts that are (mutually contradictory) renditions of their own history. This technique – characters telling their own stories as narratives endowed with meaning and internal logic – is even more pronounced in *Mortal Engines*, where rational robots must always press their relations with humans into the mould of bloodcurdling parables steeped in moral judgments that are enunciated from a decidedly eschatological perspective (for example in "The White Death," where the innate malice of human nature brings about the destruction of the robot civilization). Contact with others, even if it does not produce an exchange of information, is always a crucial event in the evolutionary context, leading to a climax in which the civilization in question sums up its history, gains self-knowledge, determines its position in the cosmos, and defines its future prospects – even if it means a painful realization of its own limitations, which, more often than not, shatters many of its earlier aspirations.

The second model of evolutionary narrative has to do with the history of knowledge and technological conquest of the world. This model is the most interesting, as it always leads to a clash with the all-too-common belief in the unlimited character of scientific knowledge and technological progress. In Lem's works there are always complications: progress comes up against all kinds of obstacles, such as, for example, the simple fact that all inventions and available techniques have been exhausted. This gives rise to a society of HPLDs (thus named after the Highest Possible Level of Development in "Altruizine") or to the creatures from "The Twenty-First Voyage" in *The Star Diaries*, whose engineering skills have no limits.

In both cases the technological omnipotence is presented by Lem as a state of exhaustion of appetites, leading to a grotesque indolence and idleness, implying that the drive towards the final frontier of technological evolution does not hold any good promise. Similar, although more seriously framed reflections, will later appear in *On Site Inspection.*

The problem of knowledge looks somewhat differently. Limits of progress, if they do appear, have a distinct character. Various obstacles are encountered by the protagonists of *The Investigation* and *The Chain of Chance*, who have to solve criminal puzzles in a world so tangled up with interconnected and interdependent events that unravelling them through the application of classic methods of deduction is virtually impossible. Contrary to what one may think, it is not an attempt to place an insurmountable barrier to further knowledge. After all one could imagine a giant computer capable of handling the resultant flood of information. What Lem is referring to is a narrative crisis of a certain type of crime (or adventure) story in which the hero solves the puzzle by combining an analytical mind with personal courage, which helps him to find a way through the labyrinth of events/data and discover the truth. Such a private quest for knowledge is replaced by the monster of statistics, which no longer traces individual events and their relations but estimates the probability with which we can expect them at a particular time or in a particular place. Seen from this point of view, solving the puzzle in *The Chain of Chance* is more of a concession to literature – which deals with unusual and individual cases – than showing the way to future puzzle solvers.[3]

As we can see, Lem's narrative based on the evolution of knowledge and technology is not a particularly optimistic story. Rational beings are promised boundless power – but for the price of relinquishing their identity as a species. HPLDs and inhabitants of the planet visited by Tichy in "The Twenty-First Voyage" are no longer "themselves" because their omnipotence comprises the ability to transform themselves at will into anything they desire (and of course they make use of this possibility). Conversely, Lem's rational beings are faced with insurmountable obstacles, with the corollary that they may no longer be needed in the great march to knowledge. Consequently, they need to use technology in a restrained fashion and with a view to self-limitation rather than to opening up the realm of absolute freedom for all. *On Site Inspection* is a story of a civilization that limits the freedom of its citizens in two diametrically opposed ways. The two political systems that Lem depicts in the book only appear to be each other's polar opposites. In the final analysis, both the totalitarianism of Kurdlandia and the democracy of Luzania, sheltered under the umbrella of ethicosphere, serve only one purpose: to build a cage of restrictions around the self-destructive tendency to break all bounds, the tendency exhibited both by humans and the inhabitants of Encia.

In one of his less-known short stories, "Lymphater's Formula," Lem creates probably the simplest "scare" scenario involving the evolution of knowledge and technology. Studying artificial intelligence, the protagonist comes across a formula allowing him to construct from biocomponents a computer infinitely superior to humanity in its creative capabilities. He builds this superbrain, but his interactions with it make him acutely aware that from now on humanity as an agent of history of progress will become superfluous. Terrified, he destroys his work and turns into a bum, mortally fearful of the moment when someone again comes across the disastrous formula.

The terror of this story lies in the fact that the formula destroying the glorious mission of humanity is depicted as something that, in a way, already "exists" and only awaits rediscovery. Harbouring a potential for the emergence of a new species, nature can bring it into play at any given moment. Were that the case, humanity as the "sorcerer's apprentice" would then unwittingly become an actor in a scenario of further biological evolution, a scenario dormant in nature, which does not particularly care for humanity. Another, no less frightening, scenario for further human evolution is developed on the pages of *The Futurological Congress* (1971). Multiplying without restraint and ravaging the Earth's resources, humanity behaves like any other irrational population of creatures doomed to be wiped out by the merciless laws of nature. But humanity is different from its animal kin in one thing: it wants to disguise its dramatic situation, to veil it with a chemical, hallucinated illusion under which another version of the evolutionary narrative will be realized – a hedonistic version within which human progress and all-round success are limitless.

So what is Lem's view on evolution? It seems that his stance is deeply ambivalent. In his intellectual formation one can still see traces of the nineteenth-century idea of universal progress held to be a universal property of nature and the entire human culture, an idea looked upon with unreserved favour by worshippers of science. Mature Lem notes many reasons that impel us to take a more cautious look at evolution. Evolution is a process that – as we are told by the supercomputer Golem XIV – does not always improve technological solutions, does not care about the fate of individuals or even entire species, does not prevent cosmic disasters and hecatombs, and nourishes a reason that all-too-often strays from the path of rationality towards wildest aberrations. Evolution is a harsh mistress, and it would be vain to expect from it an affectionate attitude towards the world and the life it governs.

Moreover, from the human viewpoint, evolution cannot really be comprehended by reason, i.e., understood as a process endowed with meaning. Hence the only way to cope with it is to impose a human, quasi-sensible narrative onto it. Evolution must always be absorbed into human history, compared with something we know. While he sometimes does this, on other occasions Lem relentlessly lies bare an unintelligible mystery of existence. This is why the author presents us with narratives both open and closed, unconcluded, and concluded. A clear conclusion appears, first of all, in works ostensibly using one literary convention or another, such as the short stories from *The Cyberiad* or *The Star Diaries* (except for "The Twenty-First Voyage"), *Eden, The Invincible,* and *Return from the Stars.* A more open structure is exemplified by *Solaris, His Master's Voice, On Site Inspection,* and *Fiasco,* all of which end without a definite cognitive or narrative resolution. Conclusions in the first group usually are of a moral character: morality is a genuinely human contribution to human history, which allows endowing the immorality of the Darwinian model with a human touch, a structural sense, and to close the literary work with a clear-cut point. The inconclusiveness of the works from the second group offers a challenge to reason, which has to struggle with the inhumanity of the cosmos and of the evolutionary processes. The latter cannot be subsumed under a narrative formula, hence the frequent disappointment experienced by those readers who are dying to know how it "really" was with the ocean of Solaris, with the "letter from the stars" from *His Master's Voice,* with the history of Kurdlandia and Luzania in *On Site Inspection,* or with the only partially glimpsed civilization of Quinta in *Fiasco.*

Showing the inconclusiveness of his protagonists' quests for knowledge, Lem is showing the limitations not so much of cognition in general but of human cognition. In the light of what we learn elsewhere in Lem about unlimited knowledge and omnipotent technology, imposing a set of constraints on humanity seems an act of prudence and a defense of what makes our existence possible. The axioms of culture are not rational, allows Lem, but nevertheless one cannot imagine societies existing without them. So perhaps the (by definition, inhuman) history of evolution, i.e., its past and future, can only be told in the language of culture – that is, literature. But should this be the case, evolution as an infinite sequence of positive and "progressive" changes is as inconceivable as a narrative without ending and infinite progress in culture. Lem speaks about it succinctly in the "Granice wzrostu kultury" ("Limits to the Growth of Culture") chapter of *Filozofia przypadku*.[4] Evolution reflected in literature is a story with an ironic ending. Think, for example, of reason permeating the entire cosmos, or of the HPLDs who gain omnipotence and therefore succumb to complete indolence. Alternatively it ends with an apocalyptic climax or with no clear resolution at all: narrative elements refuse to work together with evolution, closing the story with a question mark instead of a period.

NOTES

1 alepho.clarku.edu/huxley/CE9/E-EProl.html
2 See, Jarzębski (2003): 292–7.
3 Jarzębski (1998): 172; Czapliński (2001): 137–58.
4 Lem, (2002): 297–369.

7

Skepticism, Realism, Fallibilism: On Lem's Epistemological Themes

PAISLEY LIVINGSTON

In a 1992 interview with Peter Swirski, Stanislaw Lem commented that, if he were to state his philosophical affiliation in terms of the "accepted nomenclature," he would rank himself "in a large measure with the skeptics" (*Stanislaw Lem Reader* 42). In the same context, Lem expressed his irreverence for the natural sciences – an irreverence matched, however, by his dismissal of various religious and philosophical belief systems. Lem further characterized himself as "a kind of wide-ranging heretic" (59). Although he contended that it is not possible "to prove solipsism false" (61), he affirmed the mind-independent reality of the external world. Two years later, in responses to additional questions put to him by Swirski, Lem expressed more fallibilist leanings, stressing, in particular, the idea that his thinking is unsystematic and prone to error (93). In a similar vein, he asserted that whatever its flaws and limitations may be, we should put our trust in "empirical science," as it is the "only system which is ready to acknowledge its own errors and shortcomings, even while trying to rectify them by means of better, more comprehensive knowledge" (93). While speaking of the successes of science, he added in the same passage that there is no "ultimate discovery," thereby expressing skepticism with regard to the possibility of definitive, irrefutable knowledge of some fundamental or final dimension of reality.

In what follows I shall be asking how such diverse epistemological inclinations are manifested in some of Lem's fictional and nonfictional works. I shall be asking, more specifically, in what sense, if any, Lem can aptly be characterized as a skeptic and how Lem's skeptical scenarios are compatible with the realist and fallibilist elements of his thinking. I begin with a discussion of Lem's evocations of skeptical hypotheses that have been taken up again and again in the history of Western philosophy. I have in mind his extensive discussions of "phantomatics" and technologies of illusion, as well as his fictional extrapolations of related topics in *The Futurological Congress* (1971), "Non Serviam" in *A Perfect Vacuum* (1971), and the Ijon Tichy stories from *Memoirs of a Space Traveler*, most notably one in which a Professor Corcoran discusses his creation of a series of electronic brains-in-vats.

My point of departure is Lem's game-theoretical framework for thinking about knowledge. In his discussion of the illusionistic possibilities of phantomatics (virtual reality, in popular parlance), Lem describes a strategic interaction between an individual agent of consciousness and some source of illusion. The ensuing "game of knowledge" is a zero-sum struggle between a consciousness, whose goal is knowledge of the external world, and a deceptive opponent who seeks to thwart that goal. The mind loses the knowledge game whenever its illusory perceptions lead to false or unjustified beliefs. For example, one of Professor Corcoran's electronic brains considers itself a woman of unusual beauty, whereas in fact her body does not even exist. The meditator wins the game, on the other hand, by achieving knowledge of actual circumstances, no matter how depressing and unpleasant they turn out to be.

On one reading, the brain-in-the-vat that Professor Corcoran refers to as his "madman" has won a victory of this sort. This disembodied consciousness has correctly surmised, on the basis of anomalies, that the perceptual appearances he experiences are illusory. Corcoran has apparently reached a similar conclusion about the world he himself is in. This would imply that the brains-in-vats he showed his visitor are only another illusion in a hierarchy of nested (and nesting) illusions. Either the "madman" is right, or Corcoran is right, but not both: if Corcoran is a brain in a box, the boxes Corcoran shows the narrator do not exist; nor does the narrator. So who is telling the story? Actually, this last element of Lem's story constitutes a significant departure from the skeptical tradition that leaves the totality of our evidence equidistant between the case of reliable perceptual input and illusory sensorial evidence. There should be no *perceptual* clues as to whether we are in the grip of a demon.

In this zero-sum game, Lem often introduces uncertainty with regard to two distinct possibilities. On the one hand the opponent is an agent – individual or collective – capable of employing various devices and tricks in an effort to instill false belief. On the other hand, the opponent is a thoughtless, unintending natural process capable, however, of generating systematically misleading appearances, including the appearance of conscious agency. Sometimes what initially appears to be the manifestation of inanimate nature turns out to have been the strategic, technologically sophisticated workings of purposeful agency. On other occasions, what seems like the action of conscious, autonomous agency is but the machinelike unfolding of some inanimate and unthinking illusory process. And in many instances, it is impossible for the opponent to determine with any certainty which of these two alternatives obtains, or even whether there is a genuine distinction to be drawn here. This is no different from Descartes' meditator who wonders, in the Second Meditation, whether the moving hat and coat he sees outside his window are persons or mere automata. In any case, in at least some of the epistemic games, the enquiring mind is free to use its wits to try to determine whether the perceptual input provides correct indications concerning mind-transcendent states of affairs or facts, including facts involving its own brain or body.

The game of knowledge hinges on the possible implications of the appearance/reality gap and of the related phenomena of error and illusion. The key idea is that our overall experience of appearances is equally compatible with the existence and with the non-existence of the *underlying* reality or world. In other words, the possibility of error can be coherently generalized in our imaginations. If we are wrong some of the time, how do we know we are not wrong most often, or even always? Can we know whether our perceptions are systematically unreliable?

Lem emphasizes precisely this point at the outset of his 1991 reconsideration of his discussion of phantomatics in the 1964 *Summa technologiae.* He tells us that the "pivotal assumption" of phantomatics is that "a production of stimuli indistinguishable from those which govern our senses – to wit, sight, hearing, smell –

will be *possible*" (and here he presumably means not just logically possible or coherently imaginable but technologically possible). Thus, the phantomized person "will experience impressions (ocular, olfactory, tactile, etc.) indistinguishable from those experienced in reality" ("Thirty Years Later," 73, 72). Similarly, Professor Corcoran asks Tichy to imagine that some device stimulates his nerves in the same way that a carnation does, causing him to have an experience of smelling a carnation in a situation where that experience is not caused by an actual carnation. Corcoran goes on to conclude, "And if I do the same with all your nerves, you will perceive not the external world but what I telegraph, through these nerves, to the brain. Is that clear?" (*Memoirs* 42), to which Tichy responds in the affirmative, admitting the possibility of a generalized perceptual illusion.

In spite of the scientific trappings, Lem's concept of phantomatics and the illusionistic setup his Professor Corcoran describes are paradigmatic examples of the kind of skeptical scenario that René Descartes employed at the end of his First Meditation. Although it is important to remember that Descartes was hardly the first Western author to evoke radical skeptical possibilities, his hypothesis of the evil demon has one important feature not shared with the skeptical worries raised by many of his predecessors, including such diverse figures as Cervantes, Suarez, Ghazali, and Nicholas of Autrecourt. Although Descartes evokes a "very powerful and evil" demon, this *deceptor potentissmus et malignus* does not *directly* control the thoughts of the philosophical meditator. Descartes explicitly tells us at the end of the First Meditation that, in spite of the demon's control over all of the meditator's perceptions, the meditator retains the power willingly to suspend judgment (272).[1] The Cartesian demon cannot simply force its victim to have any arbitrarily chosen belief. For example, it cannot install and run an arbitrarily chosen train of thought in the mind of the philosopher, thereby triumphing over the philosophical puppet, who could thereby be made to believe whatever the demon wants. In the case of Descartes, for example, the demon cannot simply force the meditator to believe that it is *not* a logically necessary truth that the *sum* of the *cogito ergo sum* is true on those occasions whenever it is pronounced or conceived. Instead, the demon must use perceptual input to try to trick the philosopher into having false beliefs. More fundamentally, the subject whom the demon is trying to deceive can perform valid inferences and is capable of accurate uptake of, and reflection over, his own subjective states, which remain transparent to the meditator and psychologically connected in a cogent and appropriate manner.[2]

Similarly, Lem tells us that the phantomatic device does not directly determine all cognition and affect, or the totality of experience in a broad sense, but only the subject's perceptions or sensory input. Accompanying judgments, sentiments, and associations are a matter of the subject's more or less spontaneous or deliberate reactions to that sensorial input, so that a basic, doxastic agency – a capacity to guide one's own thinking – remains intact.[3] In the same vein, Professor Corcoran insists that the electronic consciousnesses imprisoned in his boxes have a "free will" that is limited only by the same sorts of conditions that limit our own (*Memoirs* 44).

Lem's game-theoretical idiom gives us a useful way of saying whether someone should be ranked among the radical skeptics, in at least one central, philosophical sense of the term. A skeptic about the external world, then, is someone who contends that the meditator cannot win the game of knowledge as I have just described it. That means the meditator will never have good reason to believe that one of his beliefs about external reality is more likely true than false. In other words, one is a radical or "academic" skeptic if one believes or contends that the quest for knowledge will fail not only or not always because the relevant beliefs are necessarily false but because they cannot be adequately justified, given the possibility of skeptical scenarios and their apparent compatibility with the sum totality of evidence. This could be taken to mean that the meditator necessarily loses the game of knowledge and that the opponent always wins. In a standoff, the skeptical challenge to knowledge is a success, since the meditator cannot establish actual knowledge of anything and so will end up giving points to the opponent by holding false or unjustified beliefs.

Some skeptics, however, have claimed that there is a third possible outcome. An example is the exponent of Pyrrhonian skepticism, Sextus Empiricus. Sextus claims that we cannot count on winning the game of knowledge by acquiring true, justified beliefs about external reality; but we can cut our losses, so to speak, by at least spoiling or diminishing our opponent's victory. Abstaining from belief with regard to anything save mere appearances, we can avoid the collapse into dogmatism that would have given victory to our epistemic adversary. Many critics of this form of skepticism respond that no such theoretical *epoche* or suspension of belief is possible and that some of the skeptic's alleged impressions and mere appearances will turn out to be beliefs about the way things really stand.[4] We need not pursue this issue here; as far as Lem is concerned, this third alternative hardly seems an option. In his evocations of the sorts of drastic epistemic situations that seem to fuel skepticism, there is no place for an extended suspension of judgment. In Lem's scenarios, the fixation of belief may be delayed, but not permanently suspended, by doubt and deliberation. When belief or judgment do get delayed, it is only in a local and not a global manner.

Is Lem, or any of his authorial manifestations, a radical skeptic? He appears to take skeptical scenarios seriously, and, as I indicated above, he has explicitly ranked himself among the skeptics. Yet that does not make him a radical skeptic in the philosophical sense of someone who thinks the knowledge game cannot be won. A description of some imagined possibilities, or an invitation to engage in some imagining, is not in itself an argument for skepticism.[5] In order to build a skeptical argument, one must rely on various premises that take us from an imagined possibility to some thesis about the impossibility or inexistence of some significant category of knowledge. And if the skeptical argument is to be sound, those premises cannot beg the question whether we in fact have any such knowledge or belief. It is arguable that many influential skeptical arguments do beg that question. If the point in dispute between anti-skeptics and skeptics is the meditator's actually having knowledge of the nature of the world – and if the denial of such knowledge follows directly from, or is logically entailed by the skeptical hypothesis or other assumptions – then only a dogmatic and circular skeptical argument can be based on the hypothesis that the meditator's experience in no wise indicates what world the meditator is in.

Now it is important to observe that Lem neither presents nor defends any skeptical arguments. He in fact argues against the possibility of a wholly "phantomized" society on the grounds that it would sooner or later fail to maintain its own survival in the natural environment, a contention that implies prior acceptance of various naturalist tenets concerning the way things really work. On the other hand, Lem also asserts that it is impossible to prove solipsism false. What follows from this latter concession about solipsism? The answer depends in part on one's notion of what would constitute a *proof* of solipsism's falsehood (or of any non-trivial claim, for that matter). Lem is not forthcoming on this topic, so we can only extrapolate.

A key question here is whether the absence of such a proof is any way incompatible with our actually having knowledge of the external world. Skeptical arguments are sometimes developed precisely along these lines. If it is conceded that the demon or brain-in-a-vat scenario is not only conceivable but also logically incompatible with our knowledge of ordinary facts about the external world – such as the proposition that I have two hands or that Stanislaw Lem is not an illusion – then perhaps it follows that we do not in fact know such ordinary things. If that sounds fishy, just consider an analogous argument: if you don't know that you haven't lost your keys, and if not knowing that entails that you don't know that your keys are still on your desk where you usually leave them, then it follows that you don't in fact know whether your keys are on your desk. Apart from somehow short-circuiting or limiting the validity of this rather common form of reasoning, it looks like the best way to resist the skeptic's conclusion is to disprove the first premise, which is that we don't know that the demon hypothesis is false, or to attack the second premise, which is that the possibility that the skeptical scenario obtains is incompatible with our knowledge of ordinary facts about the external world. (I here pass over other options in the literature – such as Moorean, contextualist, and relevant alternative lines of argumentation – because none of them resonates very strongly with Lem's work).

Lem's preferred option, I surmise, is what Crispin Wright calls "The Russellian retreat."[6] This amounts to giving up on the idea that we strictly know a lot of things about the external world, given, that is, high standards for knowledge. Yet that doesn't mean epistemological distinctions are all nullified, for we fall back on the difference between unjustified and justified belief, or what Bertrand Russell called "probable opinion." That this would be Lem's move is, I think, motivated by Lem's overt expression of fallibilist leanings.[7] If one's understanding of justified belief is that justification requires that the logical possibility of error be *completely* ruled out, then the skeptical scenarios, which perversely yet coherently conjoin evidence and falsehood, represent a serious stumbling block to our having knowledge in a strong, high-standards sense. Yet on a fallibilist understanding of justification, beliefs can be adequately justified even if error is still possible, provided they are correctly attuned to, and grounded in, sufficient evidence and reasons. Having beliefs that are justifiable in this sense is a necessary but insufficient condition of knowledge. The other conditions on our having knowledge will have to include luck, or the good fortune of not having fallen under the control of a demon or device that determines all of one's perceptions.

Lem seems willing to concede that we cannot, in principle, rationally determine whether we are in this kind of bad situation, or in the happier one where our perceptions give us some reliable indications concerning aspects of the external world. In other words, he appears to allow that the higher-order question as to what sort of scenario we are actually part of is ultimately undecidable. The radical skeptic cannot be proven wrong, he indicates, but this does not mean that we have good reason – or perhaps even any reason at all – to take the skeptical scenario for an accurate description of our world. The only evidence we have to work with indicates, on the contrary, that human beings evolved within, and interact with, the natural universe of which they are a part and that some of our rational beliefs are likely to be true. It is in such a fallibilist context that it makes sense to opt, as does Lem, for scientific enquiry's self-critical pursuit of probable opinion or rational belief, since it is the best move we can make in the game of knowledge. And insofar as we have any real way of keeping score at all, it is also the winning move.

There is, however, another cluster of considerations that could seem to challenge this strategy in which we make a concession to skepticism and retreat to a weakened, fallibilist conception of justified belief. The brain-in-a-vat situation described by Corcoran is but one type of skeptical scenario, and it can be contrasted to scenarios in which the manipulation of the victim's cognition is far more extensive. An example is Robert Nozick's evocation of an "experience machine" capable of determining the sum totality of the subject's experience (42–5), including all beliefs, thoughts, and memories.[8] The scientists who operate the machine allow you to choose the sort of life you want to experience; if you give yourself over to the machine, the next thing you know, the scenario you picked is up and running. Nozick's experience machine determines as well that the subject cannot even remember having chosen to be subjected to the machine and cannot possibly know that the experiences are governed by it. Choosing to give oneself over to this device, one must, then, voluntarily sacrifice crucial memories and epistemic capacities so as to obtain the desired phenomenological payoffs, a price that many – Lem included – would find too high to pay.

It may be worth noting that Nozick's thought of the experience machine was anticipated by another prominent American philosopher, Keith Lehrer, in 1971, the year in which *A Perfect Vacuum* appeared in Polish. Lehrer imagines superintelligent creatures named "googols" who "amuse themselves by sending out a peculiar kind of wave that affects our brain in such a way that our beliefs about the world are mostly incorrect. This form of error infects beliefs of every kind, but most of our beliefs, though erroneous, are nevertheless very nearly correct. This allows us to survive and manipulate our environment."[9] The manipulative googols, by the way, are themselves victims of the manipulations of googolplexes, and so on, in a possibly unending hierarchy similar to the abyss imagined at the end of Lem's Corcoran narrative.

Although to my knowledge Lem never slows down to justify or explain this stance, in his works true, rational belief and authentic action take absolute priority over artificially stimulated payoffs, even when the latter are phenomenologically equivalent, and qualitatively superior to, the experience of realities – whence Lem's harsh critical asides about a phantomized society and Tichy's dogged efforts to tear aside the "mascons" and return to an ever-elusive reality. The attachment to an ever-elusive truth is also central to the thematics of *Solaris*. Here we encounter a strong, realist affiliation in Lem, for if one were truly carried away by skeptical worries, giving oneself over to the pleasures of illusionism and the experience machine need not represent any great sacrifice. One may ask, however, how such a strong desire for truth can be squared with a weakened, fallibilist epistemology: why would justified belief be good enough when the skeptical possibility has not been fully ruled out? Why worry so much about illusion if one can never know for sure?

Two basic kinds of skeptical scenarios can be contrasted, then. On the one hand there is a deceiver or inanimate process that *directly* controls and vitiates perception and only indirectly influences belief, while on the other hand there are skeptical scenarios in which cognition, reasoning, and belief are also directly manipulated. This is a distinction that is often obscured or glossed over in philosophical discussions of skepticism, but I maintain that it has significant implications for both skeptical and anti-skeptical argumentations.

As I noted above, Lem tends to work with skeptical scenarios in which only perceptual input is manipulated. Yet his 1971 skeptical fiction *The Futurological Congress* constitutes a rather interesting hybrid case. When Tichy drinks the tap water at the Costa Rica Hilton and inadvertently takes a powerful psychotropic drug, it is not just his perceptions but his emotions and thoughts that are immediately influenced or altered, as when the drug causes him, as he puts it, to experience "a sudden surge of the categorial imperative" (18). He does, however, seem to retain sufficient memory and reasoning capacities to be aware of the anomaly and to investigate the causes of these unusual thoughts and feelings with which he can hardly identify; he is even capable of combatting the drug's influence by purposefully flagellating himself.

In the subsequent hallucinations Tichy recounts in this story, these vestiges of rational control slip away. The drugs induce not only perceptions but extremely intricate cognitions, such as the experience of acquiring large amounts of information by taking a pill, an experience that could hardly be achieved by means of purely sensorial input. Tichy has inklings that all of his experiences in this dystopic future are one vast hallucination, but the drugs are too powerful for him to latch onto this hypothesis or to reason his way to lucidity. When – or better, if – at the end of the story Tichy plunges back into the sewage and believes that he has not left the bowels of the Hilton Hotel in Costa Rica, this is again not a result of any rational victory but presumably an event that befalls him only because the drugs – or perhaps some of the drugs – have worn off. The entire narrative is, by the way, so overdrawn and parodic that it is hard to believe that any of it provides any foundations in relation to which the various levels of illusion could reliably be plotted. Thus I agree with Swirski (1992) that crucial aspects of the narrative undermine the very ontological distinctions that other aspects of the story invite us to attempt to draw. The narrator of this tale cannot reason or perceive his way out of the epistemic labyrinth, and, as he is our only guide, we are lost along with him.

It could seem to follow that, in the case of Lem's elaborate deployment of a skeptical scenario of the hybrid type, the conclusion to draw is that of a radical skepticism: the meditator necessarily loses the game of knowledge – and of ontology – since the very process of meditation is vitiated. It would follow that, in the fiction of *The Futurological Congress*, Lem expresses his deepest skepticism.

Yet I am not persuaded that either such conclusion should be drawn. If we are really going to try to reason through the implications of such scenarios, we must add as well that this entire train of thought is unreliable and self-defeating since its every premise is subject to doubt. For all thoughts, feelings, and inferences that occur to the meditator, the meditator can wonder whether these items figure among those artificially implanted by a demon. This doubt covers the very grounds of doubt as well, the key implication being that such a scenario can hardly provide a basis for a solid, skeptical argument, or any argument at all. Sound and fury, perhaps, but no meaningful proofs or arguments. Here lies madness, or the sort of subjective condition that Descartes explicitly ruled out at the outset of his exercise in hyperbolic doubt, because it would undermine the entire enterprise of a theoretical investigation of the grounds of belief.[10] So if there is to be a game of knowledge at all, it must be played by an at least minimally rational meditator, which means the only cogent skeptical scenario is a restricted, perceptual one. If a sharp perception/cognition distinction cannot be maintained, perhaps there is no cogent skeptical scenario at all. If, however, there is one, Lem's option is, as I have suggested, to retreat to a weaker, fallibilist understanding of knowledge, which means that he would be a skeptic only about knowledge, given rather high standards of knowing. Lower standards, however, allow the possibility of falsehood, which may explain Lem's occasional expression of a skeptical self-understanding.

In conclusion it must be said that, while Lem takes skeptical hypotheses seriously enough to mobilize them in various fictions, he is not really to be taken at his word when he declares himself a skeptic, as his more basic epistemological inclination is a kind of fallibilism. If it is granted that a scenario based on a distinction between perceptual input and autonomous doxastic agency – i.e., a capacity to guide one's own thinking – is coherent, as Lem seems to allow, his response is to retreat to a "low standards" account of knowledge that blocks the skeptical inference. Scientific knowledge, construed as the systematic pursuit of justified belief, is Lem's preferred strategy. On the other hand, such a move entails that there is no refutation of radical skepticism about our knowledge of the external world, and hence no strong, "high standards" claims to knowledge. Skeptical scenarios in which doxastic agency is tampered with may be coherent, but, as Lem's fictions suggest, they do not allow a non-dogmatic skeptical argument, as the very conditions of possibility of a "game of knowledge" are not satisfied. An outstanding question to be considered is whether skeptical imaginings based on a sharp perception/cognition distinction are genuinely compatible with the totality of our actual evidence; if not, the skeptical argument would fail, even with regard to high standards.

NOTES

1 The Latin and French versions differ slightly here, but both texts strongly support the basic idea that control over assent is retained in spite of the demon's vast powers. Descartes has been interpreted as having espoused a strong, voluntarist conception whereby belief or judgment is something the subject directly and freely wills (otherwise the omnipotent deity might be responsible for our errors). There is textual evidence to support this line; but for a more moderate and plausible explication, see Cottingham.

2 Commentators are not always clear on this point, no doubt because of Descartes's evocation, earlier in the same meditation, of God's power to deceive one about simple mathematical truths. See, for example, Hookway's contention that the Cartesian demon is "all powerful" (58). Another philosopher who extends the powers of the Cartesian demon is Stephen Cade Hetherington, who writes that: "Descartes suggested the possibility that there is an evil demon, or evil genius, who can put any thought at all into your mind and mislead you on any subject whatsoever … He would give you false thoughts, cause you to think confusedly, and make your thinking completely unreliable. If there was such a demon, you would lack all knowledge" (113). For background on Descartes' predecessors and possible sources in this regard, see Groarke, who usefully identifies various lesser-known sources, but tends to run together what I would characterize as significantly different types of skeptical scenarios. See also MacDonald; Nadler.

3 Lem (quoted in Swirski, *A Stanislaw Lem Reader* 88); for background on doxastic agency and indirect rational control of belief, see Robert Audi.
4 For background, see Baily; Hankinson.
5 For background on the steps needed to get from a skeptical scenario to an interesting argument for some form of skepticism in the theory of knowledge, see Brueckner; Greco; Pritchard; Klein.
6 Wright's claims are discussed in Brueckner, "Problems"; Tymoczko and Vogel.
7 For background on fallibilism in epistemology, see Feldman.
8 For commentary, see Sober and Wilson, 281–7.
9 A more recent speculation in this vein can be found in Bostrum.
10 For background, see D'Amico; Frankfurt.

8

Lem, Central Europe, and the Genre of Technological Empire

ISTVAN CSICSERY-RONAY

A list of the nations that have produced most of the science fiction in the past century and a half shows a distinct pattern: they are precisely those that have attempted in modern times to expand beyond their national borders in imperialist projects: Britain, France, Germany, Soviet Russia, Japan, and the United States. The most obvious exception to this pattern is the science fiction of Central Europe, represented mainly by Karel Čapek and, even more importantly, Stanislaw Lem. Their works were written for audiences and in languages not only without hegemonistic ambitions but, on the contrary, anxiously placed in the midst of imperialist conflicts. As their writing has, nonetheless, had a profound influence on the genre, I would like to examine this exceptional world-historical position of East-Central European, and specifically Lem's, science fiction.

It is necessary to place this investigation in the context of a larger set of proposals about science fiction as a manifestation and mediation of technoscientific "imperial culture." My main claim is that the genre of science fiction is an expression of the political-cultural transformation that originated in European imperialism and was inspired by the fantastic ideal of a single global technological regime. The conditions for the emergence of the genre were made possible by three historical factors: the technological expansion that drove imperialism, the need felt by national audiences for literary-cultural mediation as their societies were transformed from historical nations into would-be hegemons, and the fantastic cultural model of the technoscientific empire to be.

Some core elements of the genre appear in every science-fiction culture, but there are significant differences at the margins. Imperialist projects took different forms in different national cultures, depending on when they were embarked upon, the character of the home culture, and their material technological relations. I approach the matter as a complex evolution from imperialist expansions of nation-consolidating modernizing projects – i.e., attaching territories to the nation-state with the naive belief that the metropole would not be affected – toward the condition of global technical rationalization of power, currently most evident in the transnational market capitalism that Michael Hardt and Antonio Negri, in their book *Empire* (2000), treat as postmodern empire. Science fiction has been driven by a desire for the imaginary transformation of imperialism into empire, viewed primarily not in terms of political and economic contests among cartels and peoples but as a technological regime that affects and ensures the global control system of denationalized communications. It is in this sense that empire is the fantastic entelechy of imperialism, the ideal state that transcends the national competitions leading toward it. For most commentators, imperialism is the ideological justification for attempts by a nation-state to extend its power over other, weaker territories, in competition with similar nation-states striving for the same goals. Expanding on Hardt and Negri's concept of empire as the more or less achieved regime of global capitalism, I argue that the imaginary empire at the heart of imperialism is a regime that fatally restricts the power of nation-states and maintains itself through institutions of global governance and exchange, information technologies, and the military dominance of a technoscientific superpower.

As a world-model, technological empire is simultaneously an ideological fiction and a way of experiencing the world. It is also what Peter Stockwell calls an architext: a complex cognitive metaphor onto which one can map both readers' sense of reality and the many different parts of the science-fictional megatext – the shared body of works and assumptions of the genre of science fiction (204). In this sense, the idea of empire is like that of utopia. Indeed, I will argue that the utopian architext is closely linked to the model of empire; I will emphasize this by treating real imperialism as the real growing pains of imaginary empire.

SCIENCE FICTION AND IMPERIALISM

The role of technology in propelling imperialist projects is often neglected. Yet technological development was not only a precondition for the physical expansion of the imperialist countries but an immanent driving force. It led to changes of consciousness that facilitated the subjugation of less developed cultures, even as it wove converging networks of technical administration and established standards of "objective measurement" that led inevitably to myths of racial and national supremacy (Adas 145). It stands to reason that science fiction, a genre that extols and problematizes technology's effects, would emerge in those highly modernized societies where technology had become established as a system for dominating the environment and social life.

Imperialist states were at the wavefront of technological development. Their projects had what Thomas P. Hughes calls "technological momentum" (111). The tools of exploration and coercion as well as the tools of administration and production in the colonies formed gradually meshing systems. Colonial territories were treated as free zones where new techniques and instruments could be tried out by companies and bureaucracies far from the constraints of conservative national populations. These innovations then fed back into the metropole, inviting more and more investment, technical elaboration, and new applications. The exponential growth of mechanical production and the production of mechanisms continually widened the gaps between imperial agents and their subject peoples. Supremacy became a function of the technological regime (Adas 134).

There can be no doubt that, without constantly accelerating technological innovation, imperialism could not have had the force it did, nor would it have progressed so rapidly. Without steamships and gunboats, repeating rifles and machine guns, submarine cables, telegraph lines, and anti-malarial medicines, the power of imperial adventurers would have been greatly limited and perhaps not even possible.[1] But imperial technology was not only a set of tools used for exploitation of the colonies. Imperial future shock blew back into the home country, consolidating a new idea of political power linked to technological momentum, essentially colonizing the homeland, too, and at a speed that made resistance futile. Each global technological success brought power and money to technological projects, creating a logrolling effect that drove irrational political and economic exploitation beyond tolerance in grand-scale uncontrolled social experiments. It also fuelled ever more focused and complex technological momentum – until social conflicts, both within and beyond the national borders, could only be seen as politically manageable through technological means. With imperialism, politics became technological.

Let us look at this proposition from the perspective of literary history. It is generally accepted that the novel was an instrument for establishing bourgeois national consciousness. In Benedict Anderson's well-known formulation, the novel was one of the tools for constructing the imaginary sense of national community in modernizing societies. Novels were projects of national consolidation and normalization. They were attempts to reconcile at least two great competing cultural desires: to preserve the knowledge of a society's present in its language and collective memory (what Balzac called "the archeology of the present") and to ascend into the world community of modern players; i.e., join the Club of Nations at the wavefront of historical progress.

The arena for effecting this reconciliation in fiction readers was the social constitution of the bourgeois national subject. Through the techniques of realism (on a broad spectrum, from satirical to naturalistic styles), readers were trained to conceive of agency in the world in terms of a dialectic between, on the one hand, the possessive individualism and control characteristic of capitalist social relations and, on the other, the spiritual-ethical and even transcendental dependence of the pre-bourgeois Christian worldview. Thus the modern bourgeois subject was typically modelled on characters who were *physically* negotiating a world of concrete objects and property relations; *socially* navigating through class and power systems in which control over objects and institutions was increasingly the source of meaning; *politically* manœuvring in a world where the power to compel others was a matter of personal-individual interests; and *psychologically* defining themselves in dialectical terms in the conflict between the desire for power to compel others in one's own interest and the desire to submit to romanticized love's transcendent ethical power. These constituent aspects were also concretely national inasmuch as their subject was linguistically constituted. Each protagonist and narrator demonstrated the ability of the national tongue to articulate and compel the dominant institutions, which were themselves linguistic constructs. It is relevant to our discussion of Central European science fiction that the realistic novel did not steer toward social concreteness as unambiguously as in Western Europe. Well into the twentieth century the major exemplars of the Polish, Czech, and Hungarian novel tended toward lyrical romanticism, historicism, and satirical abstraction, thus relying on the premodern models of the tale and the chronicle far longer than in the West.

I am not proposing that science fiction replaces bourgeois realism as the main mediating agent of late modernist national culture in the West. (Even so, some versions of that argument will make sense, if instead of science fiction we put forward a larger class of fantastic writing that incorporates science fiction's traditional devices and world-pictures, a version of slipstream writing in which bourgeois realism, the non-Western fantastic, visionary satire, and science fiction are blended.)[2] Aspiring technocratic audiences did not replace the bourgeois national publics wholesale. But science fiction did take on some of the role of mediating between the national pasts and the late modern "future present," and it is important to establish the role national traditions had in this cultural work.

Students of imperialism know from the work of Hannah Arendt and Edward Said that imperial expansion had a profound effect on culture in the home countries, even when the effect was hardly noticed at the time. Since most bourgeois nation-states had completed their political consolidation only recently, and their social consolidation in many cases not at all, their underlying conflicts were often still active and menacing. Imperialism attempted to resolve domestic problems by exporting them beyond the borders of the homeland. As these "offworld" colonial constituencies established themselves, they put great pressure on the metropoles to give up certain constraints that went with the nation-state and to adjust to the "facts" of occupied territories: technological violence justified by ideologies of supremacy (Arendt 136–8). The corrosive effect that this justification, and the reliance on technological violence, had on the most positive institutions and values of the nation-state is seen climactically in the attempt by the home powers to reproduce their offworld successes on the Old Earth of Europe in the First

World War (Adas 365–6). At that point, the colliding would-be empires revealed that their technosystems had determined their identities more than their histories did. Their national traditions could not extend to the colonies, mainly because the colonists themselves refused to accept the constraints they placed on their liberty. For adventurers like Rhodes, the national flag had been merely an "asset" in the work of imperial accumulation; for the home populations, it had represented the very reason for that accumulation.

For imperialists, the twentieth century's world wars proved merely that national identity is a volatile investment instrument; for national populations it catastrophically undermined the politics of reality itself. For the imperialist subject, people are as malleable as matter; resistance is an alternative set of techniques. Political power is rarely a matter of personal interests made manifest in the public sphere; indeed, the notion of the public sphere is replaced by the field of action, where nature and social life are consolidated in the struggle for power over science, technology, or institutions that become the means of global cognitive control. For the imperialist subject there is strikingly little psychological agency, since the scale of the collision between different gnostic/technical worlds reduces nuance in the midst of struggles between radically differing worldviews. Romantic love, which plays a central mediating role for the modern subject, is much diminished since, in a universe where consciousness is malleable, love loses its transcendental charge. Desire for the non-instrumental means a longing for the archaic. The imperialist subject is, in sum, less a dialectical synthesis of historical conflicts as it is a – sometimes naive, sometimes ambivalent – wielder of technologies of control and/or resistance. One of science fiction's roles in the twentieth century has been to instil in national audiences a sense that its modernist struggles of national identity have been superseded by global struggles of technoscientific reason against nature and magic. The language of this position – like its concept of psychological agency – is primarily one of power; its narratives concern the adventure of domination.

Science fiction raises some very specific questions in this historical context. One is: are the differences in national traditions of science fiction due primarily to the desire to retain traditional cultural values against the engine of technological expansion? If so, then science fiction may have much the same function that novelistic realism had in bourgeois national modernization: managing the abstract techno-political leap forward out of "domestic" culture from a nation among nations to a global culture. Has science fiction been a privileged thematic genre – perhaps in the way that film has been a privileged material medium – for expressing and representing the dialectics of this imperial process because of its central fascination with technology? Has science fiction laboured to manage the technological momentum inherent in imperialism by infusing it with national cultural "dialects" – symbol systems, literary forms and formulas, artistic techniques, and discourse practices? If so, what difference did it make whether the expansion was a gradual and articulated process, as with the British and French; or intense, short, highly artificial, and self-reflective, like the German and the Japanese; or a smooth accession and aggrandizement of economic and military power, as in the US; or imported from abroad in the process of economic and intellectual colonization, as in Russia and Central Europe? From the rear-view mirror of the imperialist projects, what role did a given technoculture occupy: that of dominant agency, marginal latecomer, counter-imperialist adversary, or historical sublation? Finally, what was the character of the literary-cultural traditions that infused the fiction of SF?

National literary or artistic forms can lead us to the traditions that distinguish the styles of different nations' science fiction. Clearly the genre is identifiable by the icons it uses: the spaceship, the alien, the robot, superweapons, biomonsters, and the more recent additions: wormholes, the net, the cyborg, and so on. It is not difficult to link these to colonialist and imperialist practices. They represent the power tools of imperial subjects, the transformations of the objects of domination, the ambiguities of subjects who find themselves with split affinities. In these terms, science fiction's icons are abstract modern universals, free of specific cultural associations. Yet when we view or read SF of different national styles, we detect marked differences. The same icons are cast in the mode of political and/or visionary fantasy in Soviet science fiction and as scientific romance in British SF and its slapstick, dancehall *Red Dwarf* inversions. They are cast as fanciful ironic surrealism in post-Verne French science fiction and its vertiginous inversion, the camp of *Métal Hurlant*; as supersaturated nationalist romanticism in German science fiction and its militant ecophile science fiction descendants; as catastrophism in Japanese science fiction and its hidden puppet-theatre traditions; and as galactic Edisonian problem-solving and its wired beatnik bourgeois-bashing US twin of tech noir. These are, of course, crude characterizations. National styles develop along with social life and change constantly in response to influences, both domestic and foreign. There are also clear signs that these currents are intermingling, precisely because of the delight in diversity that Negri and Hardt consider characteristic of capitalist globalism.

SCIENCE FICTION AND EMPIRE

If we look at science fiction's connection with technoscientific empire only from the perspective of historical imperialism, we will see an exoskeleton: the genre as the interface between the pressures of global capitalist evolution and national technoculture. To take a truly dialectical view, we also need to look at the internal space of the genre, its world-model, its assumptions of conceptual design through which it makes politics, society, ontology, and technology science-fictional. I believe that this imaginary world-model is technoscientific empire: sustained and justified, but also riven, by simultaneously interlocking and competing technologies of social control and material expansion. Science-fiction artists construct stories about why this empire is desired, how it is achieved, how it is managed, how it corrupts (for corrupt it must), how it declines and falls, how it deals with competing claims to imperial sovereignty, and how it is resisted. The history of science fiction reflects the changing positions of different national audiences as they imagine themselves in a developing world-system constructed out of technology's second nature.

To see this connection concretely, let us take a quick look at the qualities that Hardt and Negri attribute to empire. Where imperialism is about unlimited growth, embodied in unlimited expansion of capital, markets, and production, empire is also about the consolidation of the expansions of the past and the irresistible attraction to imperial order. Its expansion is driven not necessarily by greed or national pride but by the superior ability of the imperial order to deliver peace and security.

Empire seeks to establish a single overdetermining power that is located not in a recognizable territory but in an ideology of abstract right enforced by technologies of control. Its characteristic space is horizontal, expansive, and limitless; it exhausts and suspends historical time, pragmatically (i.e., cynically) taking up typological justifications from the past and the future as the occasion demands. Its goal is the management of global conflict or "world peace." Empire continually reproduces and revitalizes itself through the management of local crises and, indeed, by the transformation of potentially global challenges into administrative conflicts. It eschews dialectics and transcendence, which are inherently destabilizing, in favour of constant intervention. It intervenes both in the social world and in the minds of private individuals, two spheres it fuses through pervasive communications technologies. Its physical space is limitless, open to perpetual expansion, and its social space is open to variety, hybridity, and relentless denaturing. Empire is the consummate replacement of nature by artifice. Empire is the fusion of force and legitimacy. Since order is its driving value, its driving motive is enforcement. Its laws are not the laws of God, but of science theorized globally and enforced locally, as exceptions. Technology pervades empire; it constructs a power grid, through which it distributes its force and, by doing so, converts the line of communication into a power cord.

As an imaginary political domain, empire is related to utopia. Utopia is an idealized image of the city-state, indeed nation-state, where internecine conflicts do not arise since the ideal congruence of right and law is an ontological given. Utopias resolve inherent differences through the irresistible logic of their order. They are spatially circumscribed, and so they easily contain their people, reinforcing their self-identity. Their hegemony may extend past their city walls, but they are essentially insular. They do not expand, and so their stability depends on their strict adherence to natural laws of balance. They are scientific and rational because their laws reflect a logic of stability inherent in natural reason.

The model of empire is grounded in the history of real empires. Utopia is crafted from an abstract conjunction of community and natural harmony; empire is energized by a more concrete relationship: the conjunction of might and right. Even in its most idealized form, empire is a complex machine that distributes – and thereby produces – force. In utopias, force is occasionally rationalized as a way of protecting the balance between people and state and of insuring the inviolability of the enclave. In empire all social and creative endeavours are shot through with the institutional violence that makes them materially possible. Imperial violence is so powerful, it must expand; contained, its society would implode like a black hole.

Science fiction's debt to utopia is great, but it owes more to empire: science fiction's technoscience – which is the basis of its icons, energies, and imaginary historical conflicts – has little to do with utopia's institutionalized balancing acts and containment strategies. Technoscientific projects expand, mesh with others, and gain power from grand-scale conflicts that inspire new resolutions, which then evolve into new mechanisms. This expansion is both internal (the logic of its technical applicability and improvement) and external (the logic of its universal application). Violently overcoming obstacles placed in its way by "nature" – which is nothing less than the world-as-given before imperial technologies go to work on it – technoscience charges all its claims to right and law with the irresistible expansion of its violence. The force is justified, however, in the name of peace and order. Before armies and proconsuls, technoscientific empire favours the adventurer, the Odyssean handyman far from home, whose desire for movement and conflict inspires his skill with tools. With each fight and each sociotechnical problem solved, the imperial handyman gains increased personal sovereignty and power.

As empire produces perpetual conflict on local levels – Hardt and Negri call it "omnicrisis" (189) – that invites its intervention, imperial fiction produces adventures, and science fiction is most comfortable with such imperial adventure-worlds. Even the classical genres to which science fiction is often traced (the pastoral, the romance, the utopian cityscape) originate in the imperial imagination (specifically from Alexandria, Byzantium, and Rome), as do their shadow genres, the slave's narrative, the journey through hell, and the dark city. Utopias demand placement, position, definition; they are, as Louis Marin calls them, games with spaces, real maps of imaginary territories. Empires are, by contrast, unbounded in space and restless in time. Empire is a model of constant, managed transition: its worlds are perpetually at some point on the timeline of imperial evolution, from initial expansion, through incorporation, then corruption, to decline and fall.

Even this is enough to see how much imaginary technoscientific empire offers science fiction. The genre's favourite counterfactual operations and mechanisms are all made rational by imperial ontology. Time machines, faster-than-light travel, galactic history, parallel universes, the restless reconstruction of relationships between the centre and the periphery endlessly replayed in the relationship between Old Earth and the offworlds, aliens and cyborgs, space opera, utopia and dystopia – these motifs, like many others in science fiction, rely on a cosmos governed by the laws and right of technoscience, and yet open to almost infinite variation. Science fiction is an endlessly productive engine of local crises in a highly tolerant universe from which it is impossible to depart.

This homology between empire and science fiction extends to formal levels. The cinematic serial form, for example, is particularly well-suited for imperial science fiction. It permits an enormous variety of elements to be juxtaposed with only minimal motivation. In each episode, yet another cultural metaphor of spatial or temporal disruption is managed. This has been true from the earliest versions, like *Flash Gordon*, to more recent ones, like *Star Trek* and *Farscape*. The serial permits alien and local elements to be acknowledged without threatening the order of things. The physically infinite expanse of space in such forms is generally controlled by forms of recursion and recapitulation – plot devices revealing that far-flung differences are related to the terrestrial metropole's perennial problems. At its most intellectual extremes, science fiction can even imagine that basic laws of nature are artificial, tools for the manifestation and communication of power.

Since the basic conditions of science fiction are made possible by the ontology of technoscience, the genre sets out to imagine the effects of any technology that might affect the way we live now. This includes not only the near-future applications of already operative communication/control technologies but also technoscience that might radically transform the most basic aspects of physical reality, such as nanotech, faster-than-light (FTL) propagation, genetic engineering, etc. The only restriction science fiction writers have historically set for themselves is that the powers in conflict must test technology as a basis for sovereignty. Sometimes the drama is explicit, as in overt imperial science fictions. In works as various as *The War of the Worlds* (1898), *The Day the Earth Stood Still* (1950), *Earth versus Flying Saucers* (1956), *Dune* (1965), *The Forever War* (1974), *Star Wars* (1977), *Ender's Game* (1985), *Schismatrix* (1985), *Hyperion* (1990), Le Guin's Hainish novels, and Banks's Culture novels, antagonistic technological regimes compete for dominance. Whatever their differences may be, however great the gulfs between them, they operate in the same social-ontological continuum, the most salient quality of which is the ability of sentient beings to construct technological cultures to manipulate and extend their power over the worlds in play.

In the human-against-nature variety of science fiction descended from Verne, heroic protagonists use their know-how to cope with problems posed by hostile natural phenomena. They may be ultimately successful, as in most catastrophe films, or they may fall to the superior power of the physical universe, as in works like the Strugatskys' *Far Rainbow* (1963) and Komatsu's *Japan Sinks* (1973). Whatever the outcome, each contest is a local test case (and often a parable) for the resilience and maturity of human technoscience as a species enterprise. Even in stories that take resolutely anti-technological stances, and where the instrumental empire takes an Ozymandian fall, like Stewart's *Earth Abides* (1949), the terms of struggle are determined by technoscience.

In the past fifty years, science fiction has come to occupy an important place in highly technologized cultures. In more and more areas, modernization wipes away premodern – and indeed pre-postmodern – hierarchical and transcendental worldviews that obstruct bureaucratic or market rationality and technological rationalization. Hypercapitalism and currently defunct "communist" internationalism labours to replace them with the "multicultural" coexistence of irresolvable, irreduceable, and intractable differences that must never develop into serious challenges to imperial sovereignty. The utopian ideal of universal right and law is replaced by the imperial practice of corruption, i.e., constant violation of universality in the interest of power.

Empire manages its populations by bombarding them with a multitude of slogans, hailings, and subject positions. Each one pretends to offer the prospect of unity, consummation, and the fulfillment of wishes, yet each is comfortably corrupt. They reproduce the imperial process of establishing sovereignty by creating and managing crises in individual subjects. In its purist forms, science fiction ultimately places its trust in the problem-generating and problem-solving capacities of technology and the ontology of science. The more such hegemony is consolidated, the more contradictions it seeks out and strives to mediate in fiction. The most characteristic imperial fantastic forms may then be world blends, in which the technoscientific ontology of science fiction is mixed with other kinds. This is a well-established element of the Japanese SF anime idiom. In many of the major works of the genre – *Neon Genesis: Evangelion* (1996–97), *Serial Experiments: Lain* (1998), *Ghost in the Shell* (1995), *Galaxy Express* (1996) – non-realistic domains of power or styles of representation infiltrate realism, creating hybrid worlds. It is also characteristic of much French science fiction, for which scientific plausibility is secondary compared with carnivalesque blending and philosophical metaphor. Many – perhaps most – important works of science fiction violate the strict rules of scientific plausibility and introduce heteronomic realities into their stories. Arguably, this signifies that the power to manage cultural differences is at least as important to science fiction as the cultivation of technoscience's mythology.

THE CENTRAL EUROPEAN EXCEPTION

Within this context, the science fiction of Central Europe stands out as a formidable exception, rather like the planet Solaris among mappable worlds. It does not fit comfortably in the techno-imperial scheme I have described, yet it cannot be ignored. Most Central and East European countries have avid readerships, but few have actually produced science fiction that has made an impression on the genre. Romanian, Bulgarian, and Hungarian science fiction has been written, but it has been predominantly "romantic" or "folk" science fiction. I do not intend this as disparagement, only to indicate that these national SFs reflect the gravity of traditional humanism and romantic nostalgia characteristic of Central European bourgeois literary culture and lack a concrete sense of technological modernization's power to undermine those values. In this, they resemble the science fiction of the so-called underdeveloped world more than of the techno-imperial cultures.

Moreover, the dominant influence on Central European science fiction since the Second World War has been Soviet science fiction, most of which projected an image of ethical imperialism based on a romantic, rhetorical, nineteenth-century vision of humanistic values in full control of science and technology. The writers of the Soviet SF thaw – Yefremov, the Strugatskys, Gansovsky, Savchenko, and others – challenged these empty rhetorical postures and with it the sham image of a humanistic communist scientific empire. Although their works were read avidly whenever they were translated, they nonetheless did not inspire interesting science fiction in most Central European countries. For most of that region in the twentieth century, the gap between the technologically advanced countries and their own development did not lessen appreciably with Soviet domination. Their forced industrialization was not a matter of internal development; their science and industry served one would-be empire and was not accompanied by the sense of intellectual agency and freedom that inspired in other populations the sense of political power through technology. In short, with no prospect of these peoples becoming free participants in the games of hegemony, science fiction had no mediating national function. On the contrary, under the Muscovite regimes the traditional function of literature to consolidate and conserve national identity was strengthened.

What was different in Čapek's Czechoslovakia and Lem's Poland? I will not dwell on Čapek here – suffice it to say that, when he wrote *R.U.R.* in 1920, Czechoslovakia was the tenth most industrialized country in the world. It was also politically a darling of the Entente, and Čapek's works were translated into the major European languages almost as soon as they saw print in Czech.[3] There is also a characteristic urbane ambivalence in Čapek about technological development, often remarked on even by his admirers. To put it simplistically, Čapek saw Czechoslovakia as a very junior partner in a pan-European modernization process, benefiting from the benign attitudes, investment, and cultivation of all the major Western and Central European states. Čapek was also not particularly interested in the world-historical effects of science and technology. Science fiction does not develop in societies where technological transformation does not occur at the level of daily life. Returning to the imperialist model, technoscience transforms all regions of a society equally, and the most active science-fiction literatures come from those cultures in which technological development has transformed the conditions of daily existence the most. In many Central European cities – especially the capitals – such transformations were limited to infrastructures, as in lighting and public transportation. Such modernization, detached from prospects of national cultural expansion, was ambivalently associated with urban anomie. (Čapek once said that he was inspired to imagine his robots by observing the anomie of passengers crowded into a Prague streetcar.) In Čapek's Prague, there appeared to be a tolerable balance between historical culture and the transformative force of modernization.[4]

But what about Poland and Lem? I am told that even after the end of the Second World War, streetcars in Kraków were horse-drawn. What could have inspired a man living in a famous medieval city, in a country devastated by war and the destructive application of technology, forbidden to write about the leading edge of science at the time by the forced mythology of Soviet science, to write the most influential science fiction to come out of non-techno-imperial culture? What was the cultivating medium of this science fiction, if not to mediate Polish national culture from an insular national role to that of a global culture? This question now takes on a surprising poignancy, if not urgency, as Polish troops are fighting under American command in the occupation of Iraq. For perhaps the first time in Poland's history, it has freely chosen to be a junior partner in the occupation of another country, facing a hostile population, and arguably in conflict with its famous tradition of resistance to foreign domination – to be, in effect, a partner state in the imperium of the most technologically advanced, and expansive, country in history.

Unlike all the other major science fiction cultures, postwar Poland's national identity had little to do with technoscientific expansion. Although it had a vibrant scientific and mathematics community during the Communist period, its scientists and theorists were governed by the proscriptions against leading-edge science promulgated by Moscow. The breaking of the intellectual quarantine occurred in Poland before anywhere else in the bloc, but Polish science could participate in the scientific-technological revolution only under the aegis of the Soviet scientific establishment, which involved restrictions of travel and public communication. In daily life, Poland experienced the Stalinist intensification of heavy industry, while resisting the collectivization of agriculture that in Czechoslovakia and Hungary created a mediating zone between rural and urban populations (which included the sometimes farcical cult of the tractor and the agricultural factory). The restrictions on applied science, consumer goods, and major national science projects apparently drove much of the Polish scientific imagination inward, into theoretical and metatheoretical research.

Before going further into the question of Lem and technoscientific imperialism, it is necessary to clarify the relationship between technoscientific empire and Soviet ideology. Postmodernist views of empire, like Hardt and Negri's, are predicated on the triumph of global capitalism over rival models. I must reiterate that the notion of empire with which we are working here is a fiction – what is more, a somewhat unconscious fiction that gives horizon and shape to technological development. In this sense, ideologies are pretexts for hypermodernization. The imaginary goal of global technological consolidation in the Soviet regime appears first in inverted form, in the utopian euphoria of the early post-Revolutionary years, with the dream that political-ethical emancipation will liberate science in terms not merely of the social organization of scientific investigation but the character of nature itself. This ethical determinism is then frozen in the bizarre Lysenkoite science fiction of "socialist science," an actually existing parody of historical imperialism that extended ideology into matter, making nature responsive to Party doctrine.

Soviet ideology "corrected" itself, returning in the 1950s to practical imperialist terms and conditions with the idea of the scientific-technological revolution (STR), which modified Marxism-Leninism sufficiently to permit technology (which under Stalin had, like science, been classified as an aspect of "superstructure") a determining role in historical evolution.[5] This immediately bore fruit in the space program, a source both of technological momentum and national pride. It was in this moment of transition in the Soviet bloc, when technology gained parity with ideology, that Lem wrote his most influential works. In the course of time, the technological logic of the arms race usurped, in Lem's view, all ideological justifications, transforming the entire world into a game of self-reinforcing competition determined entirely by the irrational power of technological rationalization.

Lem's science fiction stands out among the work of all other science-fiction writers. Were it not such a powerful synthesis of literary style and scientific-philosophical speculation, it could be labelled idiosyncratic, a distinction he shares with Calvino and Borges. It is especially risky to ascribe to one individual's writing traits characteristic of a whole nation, let alone a region; yet that is exactly what I propose here. This is because the characteristics of Lem's science fiction, when compared with the other national SF cultures, seem congruent with many of the contemporary interpretations of East Central Europe's historical position in the Cold War, viewed as an ordeal between two competing empires that sought to base their power entirely on technological domination justified by ideology. Poland, in this sense, played an active and exemplary role in this tug of war. It maintained a certain limited autonomy from direct Soviet intervention, yet obviously under tight colonial government. It was drawn culturally toward the modern West, and also to a memory of regional cultural autonomy and even hegemony, and it was placed several times by modern history in a vise between competing empires: Germany and Russia, "The West" and "The East." Dependent on imperial Soviet control for the infusion of technological rationalization, the Polish population practiced resistance simultaneously through the refusal of modernization (for example, in agriculture) and through mathematics and theoretical science.

In this sense, Lem is a recognizable exponent of Polish culture in the Soviet period. His synthesis of premodern literary forms like the tale and the fable (and the corresponding rejection of critical realism) and his theoretical speculation on the power of technology to transform the very conditions of thought, with very little reference to concrete social and political changes, is characteristic of a culture that observes the competition of technological empires close at hand and seeks to transcend them with the only means available: passionate commitment to theory and science, uncontaminated by ideology or self-interest. The above includes perhaps most of all his meditations on technology as a motive force of culture and evolution, told from the perspective of disembodied witnesses like Golem XIV or the Summalogist, or refuseniks of domination – explorers like Kelvin, Rohan, and Hogarth, who reject exercising physical power in order to maintain intellectual and ethical dignity in the face of resisting Others.

Lem's protagonists are almost never in a position of real power. They are not socially powerfully inventors or explorers. They are not warriors, governors, ambitious adventurers; they are not rebels, utopian founders, world-transformers; they are outsiders. This is not rare in science fiction – indeed one of the attractions of the genre is the way it imagines outsiders becoming endowed with power, either through technological changes that transform weaknesses into strengths, or through quasi-evolutionary changes, in which an ostensibly weaker organisms turn out to have greater adaptive capacities than the stronger. These are connected with the modern myths of world power: how a nation overcame obstacles to take a dominant place in the world. But Lem's outsiders are not beneficiaries of evolutionary transformations, or even of scientific gnosis. Their exceptional state – and they are all exceptional – has more to do with their eccentricity and exclusion from the mainstream and hence from power and influence in the world. Kris Kelvin is a psycho-Solarist who has few hard scientific skills. His strength is basically his debility, his "sentimental" innocence, and his capacity to let his feelings overcome his reason. Capable only of disproof, through persistent, desperate resistance to the militarization of research into the Letter from the Stars in *His Master's Voice*, Hogarth alone is able to purify the project of all ideological prejudices and thereby lay the groundwork for a belief in the ethical purity of the original Senders. The authors of *A Perfect Vacuum* and the grotesque sketches are mostly cranks, whose knowledge brings no lasting benefit to others. They exist, as the title tells us, in a perfect vacuum – the vacuum that Golem tells humanity is the zone of freedom and risk, where the politics of the past must be jettisoned.

Lem's aliens, too, are outsiders even among aliens, isolated in their corners of the universe. Solaris hangs in the cosmos signifying nothing. Its enormous powers are all self-intensive: even its effects on humanity (which is unable to extract useful knowledge from it, other than that such a thing is possible) are local and personal. The necroevolution of *The Invincible* is most likely the product of a universal law of evolution extended to cybernetic devices, but it is considered so local that the humans decide to leave it alone. Where most science-fiction cultures would be anxious about the cyberflies' imperialist potential – like Stapledon's Martians in *Last and First Men*, on whom they were partially based – for Lem they are not the problem. The desire to extend human hegemony over them is. The super-enlightened computers of *Golem XIV* sever their connections with humanity as soon as they are switched on and embark on a cosmic existentialist journey to discover the meaning of their own existence. Lem's most *frappant* aliens of all, the Great Players of "The New Cosmology" (in *A Perfect Vacuum*), are so great that they communicate by changing the laws of nature, a game in which the moves consist of changes of the rules, leaving minor beings like humanity not only forever ignorant but forever out of play.

This attitude changes in Lem's later work, as he becomes less interested in the toxic romance of scientific expansionism and takes as his theme the inexorable expansion of technological destructiveness, which he proposes, by the time of *Fiasco*, is out of the control of even the best-intentioned civilizations. There is much here that is well-known to Lem's readers: especially the recurring theme of autonomous technoevolution of weapons systems. The purest form of technoscientific imperialism is, after all, an arms race. It is perhaps too simple, but not entirely inaccurate, to speak of this as the point of view of the witness, the cool outside observer who affects a stance of detachment because there is no way to resist snowballing events.

Science in Lem is, moreover, almost always viewed as if it were autonomous from the human species' intentions. As Golem XIV tells it, humans are vehicles for the playing out of forces that require reason and consciousness but are not controllable by the latter. We might call this unsentimental faith in rational materialism, but the utter inability of Lem's human characters to affect political improvement of their paradoxical conditions – or rather his rejection of politics, national, or ideological, as a way to manage power – is also a rejection of any model of science as a creation of human society.

Lem has had significant influence on European and Japanese science fiction but considerably less on US writers. He seems to have acted as a model particularly to what we might call "rejection-front science fiction": fiction emphasizing the intractable paradoxes and defeats that technoscience leads to. From an abstract perspective, this is the modern version of the collision between the ideal and the real, between pure scientific ratiocination and "applied" science, between science as human creativity and technology as power and domination. But the great anxiety of the age is actually that science and technology are not really distinguishable in this way: that there is only scientific research encouraged, funded, obstructed, or neutralized by political-economic power; that the technoevolution described in *Summa* is not an abstract process viewed as if from a satellite but the actual form of contemporary political and cultural expansion, whether in the form of "scientific" collectivism or "scientific" capitalism. In either case, global politics is driven by a totalitarian ideal inherent not only in political ideologies but in the capacity of technology to intervene in and transform every aspect of human existence, from the global to the cellular, and all in the image of its own "evolutionary" tendency to consolidate and converge on the same "rational," and now informational, basis. Lem's science fiction has provided a model of hope in the inherent limits of technorationalistic expansion: that reason inevitably encounters its own contradictions. This point of view inspires anti-techno-imperialist writers and readers, who hold out for traditional non-technoscientific values. It is notable how powerfully Lem has influenced Russian, German, and Japanese science fiction – cultures where national-organic models are still very strong, alongside powerful technotransformative ones.

This is perhaps ironic from Lem's point of view, for his science fiction has almost no interest in the national-organic model, except perhaps in his use of language, a subject closed to me. Lem's science fiction represents the unique voice of the witness in the belly of the beast: the witness who has given up interest in the outcome of the collisions between competing political-technical forces. From his vantage point, the outcome is indifferent. In most national science fictions, the transition from a local to a global nation is tied to the expansion of a global technoscientific regime – hence galactic wars, colonization, management of empires, dissemination of inventions. For Lem the only thing at stake is the clear, dispassionate, ironic voice of the disinterested observer whose country and language cannot lay claim to power. If there is creative hubris in this role, it is in this disinterestedness that can observe destruction and evolution equally but preserves the edifice without laying claim to power. One might also argue that this is merely an illusion and that Lem's disgust with the trash of science fiction is a result of his exclusion from the exuberant, energetic cultural life of a populace engaged in a collective world-historical adventure. Even when writers of the leading science-fiction cultures critique myths of progress and power, they are engaged in a project in which much is at stake. Even trash art can reflect the ambitions of global power. Arguably, this is the trade-off of science fiction: clarity, elegance, and mordant wit at the cost of agency.

We are not accustomed to thinking of Lem's work in imperial terms – or, indeed, of technoscience as a unitary system with its own politics. Lem uses different models: one of the most comprehensive is the techno-evolution in *Summa,* treated with only minimal irony. There are, of course, others, such as the excesses of the human species' appetites when it builds tools of infinite satisfaction, or the infinity of paranoid weapons-construction. In almost every case, Lem's technoscience acts as if it were autonomous from the collective desires that produced it, as if humans were hosts of independent systems along the lines of natural evolution, or the insect kingdom, or the dynamics of games. This is partly the Swiftian diminishing of human pretensions and partly pure science fiction – in Gunn's and Aldiss's terms, the species' ironic encounter with its own power or its lack, which always has unintended consequences, whether it's the neurotic spaceship of "Ananke," the microcosmic implosion of the datasphere in "Prof. A. Donda," or others. At the same time, this purity and clarity comes at the expense of involvement, of influence, of the capacity to direct or divert technology to the species' benefit. Catastrophe may be averted, but not because of human intentions. When a quasi-utopian technical solution seems to have been achieved, like the betrization of *Return from the Stars*, the protagonist and the national audience-surrogate had nothing to do with it.

It is clear that this vision is closely linked to the Cold War position of Central Europe – frozen between competing would-be empires that increasingly follow the mutually shaping game logic of technoscientific acceleration, until destructive technoscience forms its own political sphere. Although Lem often writes as if he preferred to be among the "dwarves" of hard science versus the "elves" of the humanities, as a leading science-fiction writer he enjoys the cultural capital of being a scientific-humanist intellectual. Where technoscientific decisions are actually made, scientific intellectuals, including science-fiction writers, invest them with a sense of social power and participate in the illusion of contributing to collective will and decision-making. This is a postmodern phenomenon: attending a radical change in the concept of nation away from the image of historical collective (let alone a biological one) to the image of the nation as passengers of a vehicle ever on the move, ever picking up and distributing new passengers, ever extending its route and increasing its speed. Thus the technoscientific imperium is much like the hypermodern city extended to the whole world.

Lem's role in this has been, of course, as paradoxical as Poland's and Central Europe's has been. He lives in the city but, as he puts it, as a Robinson Crusoe, collecting the useful debris of the higher civilization, ever oppressed by his demanding scientific God and, because he's a Pole, without a servant Friday and forever resisting becoming anyone else's servant or a colonized subject. Moreover, the city he is most identified with is Kraków: a medieval preserve, a frontier town between Western Europe and the great village-world of Eastern organic society. He was embraced and put forward as an influential scientific intellectual in both the Soviet Union and later in Germany. But in each case his work was put to uses alien to his vision. His image of space exploration and the war-sphere had nothing to do with the utopian ambitions of the Soviet space program and the German eco-warriors.

There is a bitterness in Lem's vision that we don't expect in the science fiction of rising, previously marginal technoscientific cultures like India and China. Bitterness of being the victim of industrial scale destruction, of seeing one's countrymen willing partners in it, collaborating with the death-machines, the flexible prisons, and then watching the competing would-be empires threatening the existence of life itself, caring no more for the people below than dinosaurs for mammals scurrying under their feet. But here is where Lem, ever the paradox-monger, affords a positive answer, after all: not in the lofty critiques of degraded projects but in the travels of Ijon Tichy and the robot fables, in which the Münchausen-like extravagance of narrative excess returns science fiction to the folktale and the tall tale, to the "organic stratum," written in a language that is, in a sense, protected from the world, preserving the spirit of the national language without giving up knowledge of the world. This aspect of Lem, much as of Karel Čapek, is protected from universalizing critics like me, but that is precisely what gives me great comfort. This, indeed, may be the paradoxical gift of the science fiction of Central Europe.

NOTES

1 See Headrickm *The Tools of Empire.*

2 Brian McHale argues in *Postmodernist Fiction* that postmodernism replaces modernism's *epistemological dominant* (typified by detective fiction) with an *ontological dominant* (typified by science fiction). He elaborates on science fiction's privileges in *Constructing Postmodernism,* where he identifies cyberpunk as the quintessential postmodern genre. I have argued (in "An Elaborate Suggestion," my review of *Constructing Postmodernism*) that science fiction is not truly concerned with ontology, since the many worlds it admits are part of the single, albeit diverse and highly malleable, immanent world of scientific materialism. To the extent that there are significant world differences, science fiction posits that they were either created or discovered (and hence understood and

appropriated) by technology. McHale's notion of postmodernism's ontological dominant is strengthened, however, if we take not science fiction but the fantastic as the privileged genre of the age. Fantastic fiction and its various slipstream hybrids do not require any ontological decisions about the status of the imaginary worlds.

3 In 1923 *R.U.R.* was discussed on stage in London by a panel that included Chesterton and G.B. Shaw.

4 On Čapek, see Swirski, chapter 4.

5 On the history of Soviet "socialist" science, see Buccholz, Graham, and Greenberg.

9

Lem on Film

KRZYSZTOF LOSKA

Even if the story remains the same, it is impossible for a film to evoke the particular sign system employed in a literary work. It is therefore crucial to keep in mind that the process of adapting a book involves identifying the elements that should be transposed into a film, rather than following a literary original to the letter. According to Alicja Helman, a film adaptation implies that a literary text has been thoroughly read, even though deliberate changes and transformations made by a film director introduce meanings that may not have been intended by a writer.[1] A filmmaker grafts the original material into a new context that, in the case of Lem's works, is not only the context of science fiction but also that of a horror film, a psychological drama, or a detective story.

As the full scope of Lem's works comprises a great variety of genres, I shall focus on the most significant problems that must be solved by filmmakers adapting his novels. With this in mind, I will trace the evolution of Lem's narrative conventions from utopian concepts, influenced by socialist realism, through the elements of grotesque – in itself a challenge to the paradigms of science-fiction literature – down to the phase of psychological diagnosis of human condition in a crisis situation.

FIRST SPACESHIP ON VENUS AND *IKARIE XB-1*

First Spaceship on Venus (1959), a poor adaptation of Lem's novel *The Astronauts*, suffers from all the weaknesses of the original but lacks any of its virtues. In this respect, the Czechoslovakian film *Ikarie XB-1* (1963), loosely based on *The Magellan Nebula*, is a much more successful endeavour.

Both novels provide a peculiar type of development of a utopian theme, typically depicting a model of an ideal society or a fair political system. However, instead of being oriented socially and politically, Lem's utopian thinking demonstrates a strong biological and technological bias. The author's attitude is, in other words, unmistakably scientific, and his idealized vision of the future world serves no other function than as a background for detailed technological considerations. Traces of utopia in its pure form are thus absent both in *The Astronauts* and *The Magellan Nebula*; neither book presents contrasting social orders, nor, as in dystopia, shows an individual fighting against the system. The underlying reasoning is simple: there cannot be another promised land but Earth with its new ideal order based on the principles of communism.

Both adaptations allude to traditional conventions of science-fiction films produced in the 1920s and 1930s, with their typical understanding of science and its role in building a new world. In those days science fiction embodied a dream of developing a higher form of society, of transforming the material world and transcending its physical limitations. Not surprisingly, in films from that era, characters typically overcame all obstacles, often while travelling through space to remote worlds and civilizations (since their advanced technology – which included television screens, videophones, and, of course, spaceships – eliminated cosmic distances). All of the above seemed to anticipate a radical change and a new world order, while at the same time reflecting the pace of technological development, the process of industrialization, and the ideology of efficiency.[2]

Both *First Spaceship on Venus* and *Ikarie XB-1* use the narrative scheme of a scientific expedition, typical of US films of the early 1950s, such as *Destination Moon* (1950, dir. Irving Pichel), *Rocketship X-M* (1950, dir. Kurt Neumann), or *Conquest of Space* (1955, dir. Byron Haskin). Nevertheless, the belief in technological development, the triumph of reason, and a generally optimistic vision of the future were rarely present in the films of that period, as the stories more often than not focused on alien invasion, prehistoric monsters, or a threat to destroy the Earth. The adaptations of Lem's early novels do not, however, rely on such catastrophic scenarios. On the contrary, they never seem to undermine the utopian conviction of unlimited human development.

In his early works Lem approached techno-evolution from the perspective of a technocrat inviting support from an ideologue – in the same breath revealing the potential of science and the dangers resulting from a wrong social philosophy.[3] The influence of technology on human life and mind became the main preoccupation in Lem's books written in the 1960s and 1970s, in which his earlier optimism gave way to decidedly more anti-utopian themes (beginning already in 1959 with *Eden*). Gradually losing faith in humanity's progress, Lem warns us of the negative consequences of technological advancement while at the same time pointing out the limitations of our cognition.

Both *First Spaceship on Venus* and *Ikarie XB-1* concentrate on issues such as the conquest of space and the possibility of contact with alien civilizations. Like in US films of that time, personalities are less important than the course of events, which leads to the construction of a spaceship and a flight to Venus (or to the constellation of Centaurus). While both films convey a clear didactic message, this is especially true for *First Spaceship on Venus*, which includes a warning against the disastrous consequences of the arms race and of nuclear destruction. A typical element of utopia – namely, contrasting two models of society – is reduced here to attempts at reconstructing the past of the Venusians, whose devastating politics resulted in self-destruction.

Similar to German prewar films, such as *F.P. 1 Does Not Answer* (1933, dir. Karl Hartl) and *The Tunnel* (1933, dir. Kurt Bernhardt), technology plays a major role on the narrative level. Even as personal conflicts are reduced in significance, the plot movement becomes governed by the overarching ideology. Lem's *The Astronauts* and Kurt Maetzig's film are equally characterized by pathos and lack of dramatic conflict, both rooted in an overly idealized vision of the future in which people live in peace and harmony, while power rests safely in the hands of scientists. This last bit must have been inconsistent with the principles and the aesthetics of socialist realism, hence the wide criticism of the ideological message in both of Lem's books. On the other hand, they included such social-realist elements as monodimensional and schematic characters (particularly salient in *The Astronauts*) and a deterministic presentation of reality, with the ineluctable nature of laws of history made clear and explicit in these early novels.

All these elements are absent in *Ikarie XB-1*, in which social and political issues become replaced by psychological problems connected with long-distance space travel, such as stresses of being locked up in the stifling confines of a spaceship, physical and psychological fatigue, or illnesses caused by a mysterious radiation from a nearby star. The protagonists of the Czechoslovak film do not seem to embody the postulates of the socialist-realist doctrine, so, in the end, ideological considerations play only a minor role. Interpretation and diagnosis of the future is scarce, perhaps due to the limitations of narrative perspective. The problem of social conflict is not raised at all, presumably since conflicts of all kinds have already been solved in the past (as implied by numerous remarks from the crew members). The film is not devoid of educational overtones, but its didacticism is far from direct agitation or propaganda characteristic of ideological works.

First Spaceship on Venus offers a somewhat different vision – an idyllic reality where everybody works for the common good, cooperating rather than competing with one another. However, as Jerzy Jarzębski emphasized, "the victory of communism shown in the first novels is nothing but a declaration; in fact, political issues are actually evaded or dismissed with generalizations in order to make room for a 'technological utopia,' the issue which Lem was really fascinated with."[4] Absence of conflicts and one-dimensional characterization are particularly noticeable in the film version of *The Astronauts*, which seems much closer to the ideals of socialist-realist poetics, while its scientific context – crucial in the book – is of minor importance. In its place, the emphasis is put on adventures during the flight, on events that pose a threat to the astronauts' lives, and on the actual planet landing. The only remarkable aspect of the film is the presentation of the alien world and its dead scenery, the uncanny landscape the consequence of a nuclear disaster. All this does not mean, however, that the film is devoid of scientific context; though the role of technology is reduced to providing means to ensure humanity's happiness, in this world technical inventions serve to provide remedy for all problems.

The literary origins of *First Spaceship on Venus* and *Ikarie XB-1* derive from the nineteenth-century conventions of fantastic and adventure literature (i.e., detailed accounts of a scientific expedition or the didactic character of events), whereas their film adaptations refer to the typical structures of science-fiction movies. However, the adaptation of *The Magellan Nebula* departs significantly from its literary precursor both in its ideological and philosophical dimensions. The episodic narration used in the book is replaced by a clearly denoted storyline showing a group of people who must face up to a crisis. Personal relations gain priority, with particular attention paid to the inevitable conflicts resulting from being sequestered onboard a spaceship travelling through space. Contrary to Lem's novel, the emphasis is not so much on the scientific aspects of the enterprise but on psychological credibility and the description of everyday life in space. As John Baxter has written: "For the first time, life on exploratory space ship is examined, concepts like entertainment analyzed and given a futuristic twist. People on this ship go to dances, have parties, wash themselves and make love."[5]

This does not, however, imply that the plot lacks elements typical of science fiction. The two leitmotifs – a twentieth-century spaceship wreckage found by the protagonists and contact with alien civilization – were inspired by the book, though their function becomes fairly insignificant, partly because – just like in the novel – the aliens are never shown in "person." A collective protagonist presented in *The Magellan Nebula* turns into a group of strong individualities in the film – instead of a team of somewhat generic scientists and crew members, here the leading figures include the scientist Kubes, a biologist, and astronauts such as Harold, a pilot, and MacDonald, the ship's commander. Although the crew is multinational, the film does not provide any detailed information about the social and political situation of Earth or its current model of society (apart from the suggestion that wars and conflicts are things of the past).

There are significant differences between *First Spaceship on Venus* and *Ikarie XB-1* as far as the characters are concerned. In the former, they simply represent stereotypes of scientists and astronauts – nothing more than specialists entirely devoted to the cause and determined to accomplish their mission without questioning its motives. They are wise and good, and, since they have no weaknesses, they swiftly overcome all obstacles. The crew members have no real adversary, even though the expedition was organized in response to a threat from Venusians decoded from a mysterious message uncovered by archeologists in the Gobi desert. In the adaptation of *The Magellan Nebula* the characters also form a group, but this time they are presented as individuals with distinct personalities – they face doubts, must overcome the moments of weakness, and, finally, have time for love, leisure, and entertainment. The film provides an excellent depiction of a group of individuals plucked from their normal lifestyle and confined to a limited space where they must confront external pressures and accomplish their mission. The main theme becomes the development of a collective psychosis and the insight into individual fears leading to psychological breakdowns (Michał's case). All the same, the overall feeling of the film is optimistic, with such typical features as a strong belief in the power of human mind and humanity's ability to overcome difficulties and solve problems. Adding to the upbeat and positive mood is the focus on humanity's wish to find a solution to the mystery of the universe and to know the unknown.

SHORT STORIES: ADAPTATIONS

Lem displays a completely different attitude, both in terms of subject matter and the style, in his grotesque science-fiction stories. Adapted mainly for television by German and Polish filmmakers, they bring out the comical and satirical elements of his works. A perfect example may be the adaptation of the story "Wyprawa Profesora Tarantogi" made by German Television in late 1970s – with the script written by Lem – which plays on the theme of a wonderful invention typical of nineteenth-century fantastic literature (even though this time the attitude is parodic rather than scientific). Professor Tarantoga builds a machine that enables time-space to be curved in such a way that he may travel without leaving his flat. Accompanied by Chybek, his assistant, Professor travels to the constellations of Orion, Sagittarius, and Ursa Major, and finally to the Crab Nebula. On each journey he encounters the residents of the planets in these remote solar systems. The aim of all this is to ridicule the motives typical of science-fiction literature.

The uncanny, or perhaps one should say weird, character of the events stems from the internal inconsistencies of the grotesque form, where exaggeration or deformation reflects the lack of a homogeneous system of rules governing the world. This effect is achieved by introducing diverse, sometimes contradictory, modes of narration. Based on paradox and our inability to interpret facts "properly," the poetics of the absurd presents phenomena in a way that contradicts our common sense and deforms the world in order to reveal the relativity of our knowledge and the limitations of our popular beliefs. Moreover, in presenting encounters with alien civilizations or telling stories about robots, Lem aims to challenge the conventions of science-fiction literature. The events are but a pretext to undermine genre stereotypes and develop a satirical perspective, for example when describing cosmic bureaucracy or when referring to the super-figure of the Creator of the Universe and to life on other planets.

A grotesque exaggeration, aimed both at parodying particular conventions and at showing the consequences of scientific experiments, is also present in the short film *Profesor Zazul*. This 1965 movie unmistakably alludes to gothic romances, tales of the uncanny, and, above all, to mad-scientist stories – in this case, combining the characteristics of Victor Frankenstein and Doctor Moreau. Numerous motifs allude to the gothic tradition and to classical horror films of the 1930s: location (a dreary and dismal mansion), time (night), circumstances (rain, storm), traditional types of characters (a demonic scientist and an accidental guest – here, Ijon Tichy, the story's narrator). To complete the picture, the plot is based on a classical horror theme – an attempt to create an artificial lifeform, in this case, Professor Zazul's clone. As such, it offers a peculiar embodiment of alchemists' dream. At the same time, the story explores the motifs of split personalities and doppelgangers – typical of German expressionist cinema. However, the conventions of horror films are treated with a slightly perverse twist. As it turns out at the end, the real Professor Zazul has already been replaced by his doppelganger, whose intellectual capabilities surpass those of his creator and who decides to take his life in his own hands.

The same convention governs the world presented in *Layer Cake* (1968, dir. Andrzej Wajda), in which events assume a totally absurd dimension. The reason behind the absurdity is not, however, to introduce comic elements but to confront facts and show the discrepancy between commonsense beliefs and an extraordinary situation. Wajda's film follows not only the conventions of science fiction but also those of late modernist avant-garde, with particular deference to Pop Art and Godard's films (comic-book aesthetics). However, *Layer Cake* is not just a film that plays with conventions, inasmuch as it poses important questions about the essence of humanity in the face of inevitable scientific progress. Technology, which gradually transforms our environment, forces us to adapt to ever changing conditions. Plastic surgery, transplant operations, and genetic engineering make us revise our notions of identity. Invading the human body, technology modifies the latter's form and at times turns it into a mutated and grotesque entity. A human being is no longer complete, full, and perfect; instead, it is a form in the process of being (re)born – something unfinished, undefined, undergoing infinite modifications, and perpetually open to change.

This is the situation of the main character in *Layer Cake*. Richard Fox, a rally driver injured in numerous car crashes, must undergo many operations that keep him alive but that, at the same time, alter his life and his body. After so many transplants it is difficult to judge whether Richard is still himself or perhaps a mosaic of various personalities – male, female, or even animal. "We have created a new organic entity, perfectly adjusted," announces one of the doctors. The transformation affects not only the body but the mind as well, which leads to a paradoxical ending when the protagonist is no longer himself but a completely new man – a layer cake made from various elements that were at hand.

Humanity's limited cognitive abilities, its fear of unknown situations, and the complex notion of human identity have all been raised in *Test of Pirx the Pilot*, itself an unfortunate adaptation of Lem's long story "The Inquest." In the story the writer considered the question of whether we can create an artificial lifeform, thus underlining the problematic nature of providing a definition of humanity. In contrast, in Marek Piestrak's film, the motif of the rebellious machine gains primary importance, anticipating the extreme popularity of cyborg stories. The plot focuses on Commander Pirx, whose task is to determine the usefulness of these so-called "nonlinears" for space travel. Lem's story was an extrapolation of scientific theories developed by Manfred E. Clynes and Nathan S. Kline in the 1950s, in which they presented a project of transforming human body in such a way that it might endure the hardships of space travels. The model included psychological and physical changes necessary for human survival in extreme conditions.

In *Test of Pirx the Pilot* the main issue becomes the opposition between humans and cyborgs. A cyborg is an indefinite entity at the very centre of this confusion: it destroys the inherited conceptual system and stability of its boundaries, undermining the relation between the internal and the external by being neither a mechanical nor an organic entity. The presence of a cyborg produces fear of the Other and gives rise to moral and psychological problems. People dread that an electronic brain may become damaged or insane and threaten them. Indeed, cyborg menace has been the subject of numerous films since, including notably *2001: Space Odyssey* (1968, dir. Stanley Kubrick). In *Test of Pirx the Pilot*, "non-linear" pilot Calder suffers from megalomania as he is convinced of his superiority over human crew members. However, it is his apparent lack of weaknesses that becomes a shortcoming when, stuck in a dead-end situation, he cannot make a decision. "A human can hesitate, have doubts, but a robot cannot," claims Pirx, whose own passivity, hopelessness, and indecisiveness – typical human weaknesses – help in the end save at least a few crew members. Calder does not take into account the unpredictability of human reactions, nor is he himself able to make decisions based on intuition. The only way to defeat a cyborg is to await a situation in which human weakness will be an advantage over the perfection of a machine.

SOLARIS

Humanity's limited cognitive capacity, our inability to abandon fixed patterns of thought, and a tendency to impose an anthropomorphic point of view are recurrent subjects of many Lem's novels, some of which – among them *Solaris, The Investigation*, and *Hospital of the Transfiguration* – have been adapted for the screen. However, only *Solaris* belongs to the genre of science fiction.

Analyzing *Solaris*, critics usually bring out two dimensions of the novel: romantic and epistemological. In the book, the love story serves as the pretext for a general reflection on the nature of cognition; in the latest film adaptation (2002, dir. Steven Soderbergh) it is the emotional aspects that have been elaborated with much detail. Yet another approach was taken by Andrei Tarkovsky in his 1972 adaptation, with scientific issues giving way to philosophical questions of moral responsibility for one's mistakes and the chances for redressing them.[6] Neither version pays much attention to the motif of contact with an alien civilization, which in Lem's novels has reached a unique dimension, absent in popular science-fiction literature. Even as Lem rejects a typical view of aliens as members of a highly advanced civilization or monsters who threaten to attack humanity, he remains interested in the chances of communication with alien lifeforms, though he seems quite skeptical about those chances. "A contact with aliens seems to be impossible, and even if it happened, it might not be a 'real' one. A man is only capable of understanding something which is known to him, something that can be expressed within the framework of categories generated during the ages of cultural development of humanity."[7]

Neither adaptation – with crucial scenes taking place on Earth, not on board of the orbital station – devotes much attention to issues such as the inability to grasp the ultimate mystery of the unknown or the attempts to come to terms with such mystery by imposing human cognitive modes. What is more, the filmmakers seem to overlook crucial parts of the novel devoted to Solaristics, in which Lem treats scientific cognition with particular irony. A need for order based on the laws of reason is a dream deeply imprinted in our psyche. On the other hand – as the protagonist of *Solaris* discovers – our efforts aimed at classifying alien phenomena and explaining the secrets of the "thinking ocean" are doomed to failure. The lack of ultimate solutions does not, however, imply the lack of faith in the powers of reason, nor the author's underlying pessimism; it only emphasizes the awareness of the limitations that human thinking cannot escape.

In both adaptations, contact with the unknown hits a completely different tone. For Tarkovsky it is a test of human behaviour in inhumane circumstances that, from a broader perspective, forces us to consider a fundamental discrepancy between technological advancement and spiritual development; humanity seems to be morally unprepared for the consequences of technological progress. The "visitors" on the station are, after all, the embodied remorse of people who live there. Kelvin's primary goal is to overcome his own weakness, face the past, and expiate for his sin in order to be exculpated. In the concluding scenes, the Ocean creates an image of Earth that symbolizes both Kelvin's illusory home and a basic human need for a bond with nature. Tarkovsky's interpretation is to a certain extent anchored in Lem's original because, as the literary Kelvin states, "man has gone out to explore other worlds and other civilizations, without having explored his own labyrinth of dark passages and secret chambers, and without finding what lies behind doorways that he himself has sealed."[8]

As Tarkovsky wrote in *Sculpting in Time*, *Solaris* tells us about people lost in space who almost despite themselves must expand their point of view. This necessity, imposed on humanity by external forces, is painfully dramatic as it entails infinite anxiety, loss, bitterness, and disappointment, even as the absolute truth remains unattainable. "Man has been endowed with conscience which punishes him with suffering whenever his actions do not correspond to his moral principles. The presence of conscience is, then, in some sense, a tragedy. The characters of *Solaris* live in disillusionment, for the proposed resolution turns out to be rather illusory. It is implicit in their dreams, in the possibility of grasping the essence of one's own roots, in the ties that bind mankind's with Earth from which it was born. But even these ties, as they realize, are already an illusion."[9]

Solaris as directed by Soderbergh is different both from Tarkovsky's version and from Lem's novel. It does not introduce philosophical disputes on moral responsibility and on the essence of humanity – the issues so significant for Tarkovsky. Instead, we have an austere love story that lacks not only the epistemological doubts from Lem's novel but also the spectacular scenes typical of US science-fiction movies. Soderbergh uses the literary text as a starting point for psychological considerations on human condition, while the events of the plot become a sort of "therapeutic" exercise. That the protagonist cannot get over the suicide of his beloved is clearly denoted in the opening scenes of the film. His calm and indifference do not reflect scientific objectivism but serve as a disguise for a phenomenon that Sigmund Freud once called "the work of mourning."[10]

The process of "convalescence" is distorted by external factors that generate hallucinations leading to excessive guilt. George Clooney's character, trapped in the world of his illusions, cannot escape the temptation of pondering over his loss. In a sense, the plot combines the ghost story and the fantastical gothic romance. The protagonist hears strange voices, witnesses many inexplicable events, and feels the presence of an unknown force, but, instead of the uncanny (*unheimlich*) or horror, this creates the effect of the extraordinary. The dream sequences gain particular importance in the US film because they reveal the subjective truth about Chris and Rheya's relation, about their love and death. Chris becomes a slave to repetition compulsion. The image of past lost obscures the present, yet he neither turns despondent nor denies his identity, even though he cannot reconcile himself with reality. This makes his need for keeping an *ideal copy* of Rheya – created by the Ocean – justifiable.

The effect of mourning is reconciliation to the feeling of loss in order to get over the past; melancholy, on the other hand, induces pathological behaviour. In *Solaris* a unique mechanism created by the Ocean offers yet another possibility. The work of mourning is performed as if *à rebours*, resulting not in reconciliation but in *apophrades*, or "the return of the dead." All this seems consistent with a Dylan Thomas poem to which the characters frequently refer: "And death shall have no dominion. / Dead men naked they shall be one / with the man in the wind and the west moon; / When their bones are picked clean and the clean bones gone."[11]

THE INVESTIGATION AND HOSPITAL OF THE TRANSFIGURATION

In this final section, I would like to concentrate on two previously mentioned films, neither of which can be described as science fiction. *The Investigation* (1973) is a peculiar mixture of the tale of mystery and imagination with the thriller or detective story. London Metropolitan Police officers must investigate a case of corpses disappearing in mysterious circumstances. In Lem's novel the sensational events are the pretext for a theoretical discourse on investigative methods and the explanation of unknown phenomena.[12] The plot itself is affected in a particular way because, as Lem wrote in *Getting into Orbit*, "a crime story is a riddle whose last pages answer the question: who committed the crime, how and why? To comply with the conventions, an author is obliged to reveal a perpetrator of the crime, his motives and techniques."[13] However, it turns out that in *The Investigation* the perpetrator of the "crime" is never found because he simply does not exist, while the question of his motive is no longer pertinent – no matter how abhorrent the crime, no demonic forces can be blamed for it.

The film adaptation, even though it strictly follows the text, does not reflect the book's spirit. The film tries to play with genre conventions but the fundamental epistemological issue – showing various human attitudes in the face of a mystery and contrasting various methods of thinking – is not presented in a convincing way. The determinist approach, represented by Inspector Gregory, whose task is to discover the cause behind these phenomena, is shown in detail (investigating methods employed by the police, presented in a series of quasi-documentary flashback sequences). On the other hand, the statistical approach represented by Dr Sciss lacks sufficient basis in the plot. The conflict, as shown in the film, boils down to contrasting attitudes and characters rather than to confronting contradictory visions of the world. Sciss challenges the kind of rationalism that over-relies on stereotyping as it searches for the strange phenomena's causes, while rejecting any other motivation. A discovery of the relations between events, even if these relations exist only in the subject's mind, leads to the imposition of an order that does not exist in nature. Gregory rejects the possibility that the events are governed by the laws of probability – in other words, by a series of relations that have nothing to do with the crime itself. His desperate efforts to protect his world against disintegration imply the rejection of the "philosophy of chance" – the ending suggests that the detective will continue the investigation despite the lack of hope for finding a solution.

Consistent with Lem's intentions, the director does not leave out the fantastic elements of the world, thereby creating an uncanny atmosphere. He shows, for example, the weird aspects of ordinary events or objects (e.g., in the scene when Gregory pays a visit to Inspector Sheppard). In the film the effect of the uncanny stems from a subjective perception of the world: the protagonist sees a "living dead" wandering the streets of London; Constable Williams, who witnesses the "resurrection" of a corpse, experiences "terrible visions" reminiscent of the poetics of horror films.[14]

Hospital of the Transfiguration (1978) is an original and controversial adaptation of an early Lem novel that has no relation to science fiction. This tale of initiation depicts the process of one character's ascendance to maturity, both in epistemological and ethical terms. Stefan, a young physician working in an asylum, must face up to an extraordinary situation. In order to save his soul and perhaps even his mind, he is forced to make crucial and difficult choices. The demonic forces that compete for Stefan are represented by Sekułowski, a philosopher, poet (inspired by the Polish poet Witkiewicz, or Witkacy), and advocate of the "philosophy of chance." Sekułowski's rivals are two doctors: Rygier, who dreams of dictatorship and wants to corroborate with the German occupants, and Kauters, a neurosurgeon cut in the mold of gothic mad scientists, even to the point of carrying out forbidden experiments. In the literary text one can detect strong influences of Thomas Mann's *The Magic Mountain*, with the protagonist's search for his identity accompanied by philosophical discussions or monologues. On the other hand, Edward Żebrowski's film – not univocally realistic but rather presented in a visionary apocalyptic style – contains elements of political allegory and morality play that cannot be traced to the novel.

Insanity, both in its individual and collective form, becomes a major threat to Stefan's integrity, especially when he must confront the madness of the two doctors, whose main motivations are hatred and envy and who treat – perhaps one should say, torture – the patients with sadistic pleasure. The abhorrent events witnessed by Stefan justify his view on psychology as the art of trapping and eliminating individuals that society cannot cope with. The young man's doubts are fuelled by Sekułowski's questions about the borderlines between what is and is not normal and by his views on the significance of insanity for the development of art. The isolation of the hospital (suggested by Lem's novel) is another factor contributing to the effect of unreality. This feeling is intensified since the film does not contrast order and chaos; once more, unlike the book, it does not include traces of the external world that might be identified with normality or order.

In addition, by changing the ending and introducing a love scene during the sequence of the evacuation of the patients and staff, the director modified the message of the text. Everything is contaminated by disease; there is nothing rational or sane that might aid Stefan's struggle for the truth – a pessimistic vision that has nothing to do with the conclusion of the novel. With each event in the film, reality becomes more and more demonic, distorted, and misshapen. The pathological character of reality aggravates the hero's loneliness, his existential tragedy, and intensifies his feelings of loss and hopelessness and his inability to challenge the ambient absurdity. The collective insanity of the world terrifies Stefan, but all his efforts and choices are futile. The only solution is escape.

FILMOGRAPHY

FIRST SPACESHIP ON VENUS
DER SCHWEIGENDE STERN / MILCZĄCA GWIAZDA
GDR-Poland 1959, 104 min.
Director: Kurt Maetzig
Script: Jan Fethke, Kurt Maetzig based on *The Astronauts*
Photography: Joachim Hasler, Jan Olejniczak
Music: Andrzej Markowski
Editor: Lena Neumann
Special effects: Helmut Grewald, Martin Sonnabent, Ernst Kunstmann, Vera Kunstmann
Producer: Martin Sonnabent, Henryk Szlachet
Cast: Gunther Simon (Brinkmann), Ignacy Machowski (Sołtyk), Yoko Tani (Sumiko), Oldrich Lukes (Hawling), Michail Postnikov (Arsenev), Julius Ongewe (Tulus), Kurt Rackelmann (Sikarna), Tang-Hua-Ta (Tschen-Yu), Lucyna Winnicka (reporter)
Production: DEFA Berlin / Zespół „Iluzjon"

IKARIE XB-1
Czechoslovakia 1963, 81 min.
Director: Jindřich Polák
Script: Pavel Juraček, Jindřich Polák based on *Magellan Nebula*
Photography: Jan Kališ
Music: Zdeněk Liška
Editor: Josef Dobřichovský
Producer: Rudolph Wohl
Cast: Zdeněk Štěpánek (Abayev), Radovan Lukavský (MacDonald), Dana Madřicka (Kirova), Jiři Vrštala (Svenson), Otto Lackovič (Michal), František Smolik (Hopkins), Martin Tapak (Kubes), Rudolf Deyl (Herold)
Production: Studio Barrandov

PROFESOR ZAZUL
Poland 1965, 22 min.
Director: Marek Nowicki, Jerzy Stawicki
Script: Marek Nowicki, Jerzy Stawicki based on the story "Professor Zazul" from *Memoirs of a Space Traveler*
Photography: Marek Nowicki, Jerzy Stawicki
Music: Edward Pałłasz

Cast: Stanisław Milski (Zazul), Piotr Kurowski (Tichy)
Production: Studio Filmowe Se-Ma-For

LAYER CAKE
PRZEKŁADANIEC
Poland 1968, 35 min.
Director: Andrzej Wajda
Script: Stanislaw Lem
Photography: Wiesław Zdort
Music: Andrzej Markowski
Editor: Halina Prugar, Grażyna Pliszczyńska
Producer: Barbara Pec-Ślesicka
Cast: Bogumił Kobiela (Richard Fox), Ryszard Filipski (lawyer), Anna Prucnał (Thomas Fox's wife), Jerzy Zelnik (Dr Burton), Piotr Wysocki (Dr Benglow), Tadeusz Płucinski (priest)
Production: Zespół „Kamera", WFD Warszawa

SOLARIS
Soviet Union 1972, 165 min.
Director: Andrei Tarkovsky
Script: Andrei Tarkovsky, Friedrich Gorenstein
Photography: Vadim Jusov
Music: Eduard Artemev
Editor: Luba Feiginova
Special effects: A. Klimenko
Producer: Vatcheslav Tarasov
Cast: Donatas Banionis (Kris Kelvin), Natalya Bondarchuk (Harey), Anatoly Solonitsin (Sartorius), Nikolai Grinko (father), Vladislav Dvorzetsky (Burton), Sos Sarkisian (Gibarian), Yuri Jarvet (Snaut)
Production: Mosfilm

THE INVESTIGATION
ŚLEDZTWO
Poland 1973, 53 min.
Director: Marek Piestrak
Script: Andrzej Kotkowski, Marek Piestrak
Photography: Edward Kłosinski
Music: Włodzimierz Nahorny
Editing: Alina Fafik

Producer: Grzegorz Woźniak
Cast: Tadeusz Borowski (Gregory), Edmund Fetting (Sheppard), Jerzy Przybyłski (Sciss)
Production: PRF „Zespoły Filmowe", Zespół „Pryzmat"

JOURNEY OF PROFESSOR TARANTOGA
DIE SELTSAMEN BEGENUNGEN DES PROFESSOR TARANTOGA
Germany 1978, 99 min.
Director: Charles Chuck Kerremans
Script: Nico Werhahn, based on an original screenplay by Lem (*Wyprawa profesora Tarantogi*) published in *Noc księżycowa* (1963)
Photography: Lothar Stickelbrucks
Cast: Richard Muensch (Tarantoga), Manfred Seipol (Chybek), Kurt Beck (Professor Zazul), Claus Fuchs (Wissenshaftl. Direktor), Dietmar Mues, Stephan Stroux

HOSPITAL OF THE TRANSFIGURATION
SZPITAL PRZEMIENIENIA
Poland 1978, 93 min.
Director: Edward Żebrowski
Script: Michał Komar, Edward Żebrowski
Photography: Witold Sobocinski
Music: Stanisław Radwan
Editor: Urszula Śliwinska
Producer: Tadeusz Drewno
Cast: Piotr Dejmek (Stefan), Jerzy Bińczycki (Andrzej Nowacki), Henryk Bista (Kauters), Gustaw Holoubek (Sekułowski), Ewa Dalkowska (Nosilewska), Zygmunt Huebner (Pajączkowski), Wojciech Pszoniak (Marglewski), Klaus Piontek (Thiesdorf), Zbigniew Zapasiewicz (Rygier)
Production: Zespół "Tor"

STRANGE GUEST OF PROFESSOR TARANTOGA
PROFESSOR TARANTOGA UND SEIN SELTSAMER GAST
GDR 1979, 90 min.
Director: Jens-Peter Stoll
Script: Albrecht Boerner based on an original screenplay by Lem (*Dziwny gość profesora Tarantogi*) published in *Noc księżycowa* (1963)

Photography: Siegfried Peters
Music: Bernd Wefelmeyer
Cast: Eberhard Esche (Tarantoga), Volkmar Kleinert (Nowak/Hipperkorn), Ruth Glöse (Sianko), Herbert Sievers, Hannelore Erle (Mrs Nowak)

TEST PILOT PIRX
TEST PILOTA PIRXA
Poland – Soviet Union 1979, 104 min.
Director: Marek Piestrak
Script: Marek Piestrak, Wladimir Wałucki, based on story "The Inquest"
Photography: Janusz Pawłowski
Music: Arvo Pärt
Editor: Roman Kolski
Special effects: Jerzy Snieżawski
Producer: Edward Kłosowicz, Karl Levoll
Cast: Sergey Desnitski (Pirx), Bolesław Abart (Jan Otis), Vladimir Ivashov (Brown), Aleksandr Kaidanovsky (Tom Nowak), Zbigniew Lesien (Calder), Ferdynand Matysik (director of UNESCO), Igor Przegrodzki (McGuirr)
Production: PRF „Zespoły Filmowe", Tallinnfilm

SOLARIS
USA 2002, 99 min.
Director: Steven Soderbergh
Script: Steven Soderbergh
Photography: Peter Andrews (Steven Soderbergh)
Music: Cliff Martinez
Editor: Mary Ann Bernard
Special effects: Brooke Breton
Producer: James Cameron, Rae Sanchini, Jon Landau
Cast: George Clooney (Kelvin), Natasha McElhone (Rheya), Jeremy Davies (Snow), Viola Davis (Gordon), Ulrich Tukur (Gibarian)
Production: Lightstorm Entertainment, 20th Century Fox

NOTES

1 Cf. Helman, *Twórcza zdrada* (1998): 12–17.

2 Cf. Telotte, *A Distant Technology* (1999).
3 Czaplinski, *Stanisław Lem – spirala pesymizmu* (2003): 139.
4 Jarzębski, *Science fiction a polityka* (1992): 171.
5 Baxter, *Science Fiction in the Cinema* (1970): 207.
6 For a critical comparison between Lem's, Tarkovsky's, and Soderbergh's versions, see Swirski (2003; reprinted in this volume).
7 Jarzębski, *Wszechświat Lema* (2003): 222.
8 Lem, *Solaris* (1984): 79–80.
9 Tarkovsky, *Czas utrwalony* (1991): 137–8; translation by Peter Swirski.
10 Cf. Freud, *Trauer und Melancholie.*
11 Thomas, "And Death Shall Have No Dominion," (1974): 75.
12 For a sustained discussion of the novel and its problematics, see Swirski, *From Lowbrow to Nobrow,* chapter 3.
13 Lem, *Wejście na orbitę* (1962): 53.
14 In a similar vein, the notion of chance, or the crisis of rationality combined with the conventions of the crime story or thriller, are also included in a script written by Lem and Jan Józef Szczepański, based on the novel *The Chain of Chance.* The story also presents a series of mysterious deaths and an unexpected solution to the case: a string of unconnected factors that happen to occur at the same time and in the same place, causing the death of a few people.

10

Solaris! *Solaris*. *Solaris*?

PETER SWIRSKI

"Initially Faber and Faber did not want to publish my *Solaris* at all…"
Stanislaw Lem to Peter Swirski, 1992 personal interview

If you visited Moscow in the early 1990s, for a couple of dollars you could buy one of the most trivial yet symbolic fruits of the revolution that swept away the USSR together with the Berlin Wall – a new and improved matrioshka doll. In the olden days the best you could get was the politically correct variety: a tiny ruddy peasant woman in a babushka, inside a small ruddy peasant woman in a babushka, inside a medium-size ruddy peasant woman in a babushka, inside … anyway, you get the point. After 1991 and the dissolution of the Soviet quilt, some things were still too sacrilegious to touch, but political leaders at least lost their halos, so street peddlers began to proudly hawk the new matrioshka: a minuscule Lenin doll inside the paunch of a slightly larger Stalin, inside the equatorial bulge of Brezhnev, inside the belly of Gorbachev, inside the overhang of the then presiding, vodka-ruddy Yeltsin.

Full of folk wisdom, these glasnost-savvy matrioshkas preserved the transitive relation between the Soviet and Russian-era politicos (some things, like Khrushchev and Chernobyl, were still too hot to handle). Each, after all, contained within himself the legacy of his predecessor. The dissolute Yeltsin had to manage the patrimony left him by the Western darling "I Like Mike" Gorbachev, himself inheritor of the centrifugally outflying Soviet collective from Brezhnev, who presided over the empire cobbled together by Stalin, who in turn … anyway you get the point.

What does this have to do with Stanislaw Lem's celebrated novel *Solaris*? Simple: the relation between Lem's original and its subsequent motion-picture reincarnations by Tarkovsky and Soderbergh is the obverse of the canny Russian dolls. Masterful in its own right, the 1972 Cannes-triumphant Russian adaptation already truncates Lem's slim (two hundred pages in paperback) classic, while Tinseltown's "thirty years later" remix delivers no more than selections from these selections. In matrioshka-speak, where Lem's book contains within itself Tarkovsky's movie as well as all those things that got left on the cutting room floor, poke inside Tarkovsky and you'll find the entire Soderbergh/Clooney/Cameron cut. This progressive tunnel vision is no surprise. While Mosfilm was still shooting Lem, Hollywood was merely interpreting Tarkovsky, shutting Lem entirely out of the filmmaking process and – if you don't count the opening credit – failing to acknowledge his protean role in this cultural pyramid.

In Plato's metaphysics, you have first-tier ideal objects (say, tables), then second-tier real objects (say, kitchen tables on which you might read your *Critias*), then the third-tier, poets' descriptions of tables, twice removed from the ideal and thus twice corrupt. The old Hellene bequeathed us a potent metaphor to describe what befell *Solaris* on its mini-odyssey through the turbulent ocean of film adaptations. So, to set the record straight, let us first take a look between the covers.

SOLARIS 1.0 (ORIGINAL MIX, 1961 VERSION)

"If you take *Solaris* as a concrete example, I still maintain that the novel is well constructed because it – more precisely the library scene – clearly suggests the existence of an enormous body of professional literature on the subject of the planet and the ocean. The entire plot of the novel is, in a certain sense, an aftershock. The book records the twilight phase of solaristics; there had been thousands of hypotheses, and they all came to nothing."

Stanislaw Lem to Peter Swirski, 1992 personal interview

Lem's *Solaris*, translated into English from a French translation of the original, is all sparse prose, stylistic understatement, and reined-in emotions. The novel begins with Kris (not Chris as in the Hollywood adaptation) Kelvin being sent to a scientific station hovering over the gigantic "ocean" that covers the planet Solaris, somewhere yonder in space. The station is an eerie, desolate mess, reminiscent of the wreck of the Condor in Lem's 1964 novel *The Invincible*. Snaut (not Snow as in the English translation) reacts with dread until persuaded that Kelvin is not an apparition. An apparition? Kelvin's inquiries bog down in evasive, almost garbled answers from Snaut and Sartorius, even as one thing becomes clear: the third scientist, Gibarian, has met with an "accident."

Trying to decipher Gibarian's cryptic instructions left before his suicide, Kelvin becomes aware of "visitors" on the station in a series of haunting, disquieting episodes. Then "it" happens. Waking up, Kris discovers next to his side Harey (not Rheya as in the translation and the Hollywood version), his dead wife who had killed herself years before. She is everything he remembers her to have been ... and more. In a heart-stopping moment during which she casually recalls an old friend, Kelvin realizes his beautiful visitor is a copy reconstructed from his memory of her. His wife could not have known Pelle. Kris encountered him only after his return to Earth from an expedition, three years after she had died ...

Questions mount, pain and confusion hijacks Kelvin's emotions, while, against all odds, he tries to build a relationship with the new Harey. The stakes get even higher when, to his horror, he witnesses her smash through steel doors or become "resurrected" after gulping liquid oxygen in a vain attempt to die again. Investigations reveal that the apparitions, who in all other aspects are shockingly, indistinguishably human, are neutrino-based (unlike us, cobbled together from protons, neutrons, and electrons). A project is hatched to irradiate the ocean that somehow manufactures these visitations with images culled from a human brain. Kelvin volunteers. The experiment succeeds. Harey and other visitors who had haunted Snaut, Sartorius, and Gibarian vanish forever. In the tantalizing last scene, the protagonist lingers by the ocean's shore, part scientist and part broken-hearted man who, in the novel's final words, persists "in the faith that the time of cruel miracles was not past."

If that was all there was to Lem's masterpiece, even Soderbergh's *2002: A Love Odyssey* adaptation might have made more sense than it does. But it is not. Any *récit* of the *plot* will leave out what in some sense Lem's masterpiece is really about – interpolations, some chapter-long, that amount to a third of the book's length and make it so rich in cognitive and narrative terms. Caught in the love-drama of the plot, Kelvin struggles to find a *modus vivendi* with a living copy of his dead wife in a ghastly twist to the theme of remembrance of things past. But Lem is not Kelvin. Where his protagonist is but a pawn in a macabre game in which human rules of mortality do not apply, the author is more like the solaristic ocean, studying the human guinea pigs as they thrash in love and pain when face to face with the Alien.

Lem's novel is but one movement in his literary œuvre about contact with the utterly convincing – because ultimately incomprehensible – manifestation of alien intelligence. It is a harrowing tale about the age-old problem of resurrection and multiplication of self, hotly debated in the philosophical and analytical circles, especially since the two-slit experiment confirmed the wave-particle sensible nonsense. It is alienscapes, lit up by Solaris's two suns and by impeccable science hardware. It is metaphors and neologisms labouring to translate the visual experience of the ocean even as its language-defying formations remain unknown and unknowable. In the end, as Lem made it plain during our talks, it is as much a love story as a novel about cognition, about wrestling with concepts and discoveries that slip through the net woven out of anthropomorphic and Earth-bound science, philosophy, and culture. That's why the fulcrum of the book may lie not in the harrowing story of love's second chances, but in the actionless drama of the encounter with the unknown. Lem's exhaustive, detailed chronicles of investigations of the planet and its enigmatic ocean, full of conflicting reports, speculations, hypotheses, and outright guesses, model with cold accuracy what science is about: the process of moving one small step at a time into impenetrable darkness, lit only by the faint flicker of our minds' candlelight.

In an interview with Andrzej Ziembiecki – published in 1979 in *Polish Perspectives* under the telling title of "... Knowledge Is the Hero of My Books ..." – Lem afforded a rare glimpse behind his creative process. His central device, he revealed, has always been a puzzle approached as if through "a network of contrary hypotheses and suggestions" (64). It is for this reason that any filmmaker who discards his philosophical interpolations commits an act of artistic violence. Take Byron's *Childe Harold's Pilgrimage*, a digressive poem where the ostensible plotline occupies only about a quarter of its length. To dispense with Byron's digressions as a mere hindrance to the plotline is to misunderstand his entire work, much as to dispense with Lem's hypotheses-filled speculations about the true nature of Solaris is to invite *Mystery Science Theatre 3000* to quip: "The plot thinnens."

More than forty years after original publication, Sunday readers and academic scholars alike, we have good reasons to return to Lem's science thriller. Whatever else good literature is, it is also a radar system sensitive enough to point how our culture is a tool that reflects the limitations of its creators. Given how remarkably accurate Lem's *Solaris* is in offering us a ringside view of our scientific limitations, this is the one book you don't want to miss.

SOLARIS 2.0 (DOSTOYEVSKIAN MIX, LONG VERSION)

"*Solaris* is about love and the mysterious ocean, and that is what is important about it..."

Stanislaw Lem to Peter Swirski, 1992 personal interview

As a middle matrioshka, Andrei Tarkovsky's *Solaris* is poised somewhere between the intellectual density of the original and the artistic paucity of the current remake. Even as it tries to do justice to Lem's vision, the 1971 film swiftly establishes that it's not just a visual recreation of the novel. Where the Polish author gets his hero to the station on page 2, the Russian director lingers on Earth for a full forty minutes before sending Kelvin into space. The film's opening shot is of a stream, then the surface of a pond, then the pond itself. Images of water, suggestive of the Solaris ocean, permeate the entire Earth sequence, set mainly in a picturesque Russian country dacha, contrasted with Burton's apparently aimless drive through a city. The first pilot to have fallen prey to the ocean's power to create "living" beings from human memory, Burton is on his way back after briefing Kelvin (played to frowning perfection by Donatas Banionis) on his experience.

The centrepiece of this part of the film is a fifteen-minute reportage sequence, built around Burton's halting account of this first encounter of the third kind. While the pale, uncomprehending pilot struggles for words in front of a panel of scientists, their skeptical, if not hostile, reactions convey the essence of Lem's work:

the accretion of clashing hypotheses, philosophies, and vested interests that is solaristics. The participants in Tarkovsky's mini-symposium make no bones that their investigation is but a parting gesture to the moribund scientific program Kelvin is sent to *de facto* terminate. So much safer to ascribe Burton's report to an illusion.

Here and in the protracted philosophical discussions on the station, the European filmmaker does not neglect aspects of Lem's novel that will evaporate from the 2002 movie. Still, not everything is picture perfect. Tarkovsky's library scene, for instance, in which Snow, Kelvin, and Sartorius ponder the mysteries of the cosmos and humankind, is typical Dostoyevskian bombast, as overdone as a nine-hour roast. You can hardly be blamed for thinking the actors got a bonus every time they uttered words like *Cosmos, Man, Science,* or *Philosophy.* Another problem is the film's overall drift, which Lem – never one to mince words – openly condemned as a spurious exercise in psychoanalysis. Clinically and artistically false, the ocean's actions are taken out of its scientific context and made to carry an unconvincing burden of quasi-Freudian guilt. Thus in the final scene at the dacha Kelvin falls to his knees in front of his father in an archetypal prodigal-son tableau, implicitly begging forgiveness. Lem's *Solaris,* of course, is not about oral fixations or Oedipal guilt. It is about how, in the midst of the cosmic void, people finally glimpse the parabolic face of the universe – their own.

But for all this, Tarkovsky's adaptation is a gem on par with Kubrick's *2001: A Space Odyssey.* Even thirty years later it stuns (again like the Kubrick film) with the minimalist beauty of its sets. The docking scene a masterpiece of understatement, while its choreography of movement – much like that of the actors – is a triumph of the director's elliptical vision. Kelvin's inner-station room, a backdrop to his inner turmoil, is designed so well that Soderbergh preserves it in essential outline. In the end it's hard to pinpoint any one thing that elevates the 1971 *Solaris* to the level of art. Maybe Europeans are better actors than Hollywood graduates; maybe Tarkovsky was more faithful to Lem, maybe this, maybe that. Whatever the reason, his movie – languid to the point of ponderousness at times, visually self-indulgent (some scenes look for all the world like 35 mm études in still-life photography), and occasionally rhetorically overblown – works in its mathematically precise drama.

SOLARIS 3.0 (H-WOOD REMIX, BORING VERSION)

"À propos *Solaris*: once I even got a letter from a Russian ex-psychiatrist in which she wrote a continuation of my novel, since I would not even hear about doing something like that myself."

Stanislaw Lem to Peter Swirski, 1992 personal interview

In 1991 a beautiful film swept around the world, pocketing awards from Cannes to Vancouver and everywhere in between. It was *The Vanishing*, one of the most haunting and wrenching love stories in the annals of modern cinema (not to be confused with Hollywood's rapid remake bearing the same title). This French-Dutch co-production, machined with the precision of a BMW gearbox, offered the ultimate vision of lost opportunities, unspeakable guilt, and second chances. Next to its raw emotional power, all the more effective inside a story about pure, isotropic human evil, Soderbergh's movie about lost opportunities and second chances cannot but appear remarkably monodimensional.

It's not different *vis-à-vis* Tarkovsky. If the 1971 *Solaris* was love story plus superlative cinematography plus space-age existentialism, Soderbergh's vehicle is little more than a sketch of the first link of Tarkovsky's triad. The plot rambles to the point of incoherence, the love that conquers all is spiritless and flat, and the casting problematic at best. Yes, we do get the affirmative-action point of replacing a white male scientist Sartorius with a black woman scientist Gordon; still, viewers outside the US are apt to wonder about the country or the director in need of such ham-fisted liberties with Lem's work. The overall impression is of a bad Hollywood version of a European art (or is it angst?) flick; adapting Pirandello, the new *Solaris* is four actors in search of a story and soul.

Not that Soderbergh's remix of Tarkovsky is without its flashes of serene, dignified beauty. Once again the lingering docking scene, when Kelvin's capsule approaches the wheel-in-the-sky station, while the vapour-blurred eye of Solaris watches from below, combines with an electronic score to evoke magic and mystery. But inside the station you are at the mercy of producer James Cameron's heavy-handed touch, not only in the *Alien*-style sets but in the gratuitous clone-murder mystery tacked on a project that was to push all the artistic envelopes. "This film probably won't open great, and probably will have a modest run," predicted Clooney in an uncharacteristic display of pessimism only days before the premiere. As a Cassandra, he was right. Not even the *Entertainment Weekly*-type controversy over his butt – shots that preceded the release – could generate interest in this "badaptation" (the bottom line is that Hollywood's Hays Commission is gone in name only).

When I asked Lem what he thought of the upcoming Hollywood remix of Tarkovsky's mix of his novel, his reply was drier than Bond's vodka-martini: "I hope not to live long enough to see it." Make no mistake: Soderbergh's *Solaris* is both good and original. Unfortunately, what's good about it, isn't original, and what's original … well, you can figure the rest. There are films that equal or even transcend the novelistic original: Coppola's *Godfathers* or, indeed, *The Vanishing*, spring to mind. But the only remedy for Soderbergh's well-meaning fiasco may be a dose of Lem himself. Take *Solaris* about three times a day and see what it can do for you.

Stanislaw Lem
A Brief Chronological Biography

1921 Born in Lvov, Poland, now part of Ukraine.

1931 Finishes elementary school.

1939 High School matriculation.

1940 Begins medical studies at Lvov's Medical Institute.

1940–44 War occupation by Nazi troops.

1944 Resumes interrupted medical studies.

1946 Moves to Cracow, Poland, where he continues his studies. First novel, *Man from Mars* published in a Cracow weekly.

1948 Completes studies. Publishes numerous stories and essays. Editor of a popular science magazine.

1948 Commences work as a research associate at Cracow's Science Council. Completes second novel of contemporary realism, *Time Not Lost.*

1951 First science-fiction novel in book form, *Astronauci.*

1953 Marries Barbara Leśniak.

1955 Publishes two novels and a collection of short pieces. Receives the Golden Cross of Achievement.

1957 Volume of nonfiction studies of cybernetics and politics, *Dialogues*; another science-fiction story compilation. Receives literary award from the city of Cracow.

1959 Publishes *Eden* and *The Investigation,* as well as another story collection. Awarded one of Poland's highest cultural awards.

1961 *Annus mirabilis*: publishes no less than four novels, including *Return From the Stars, Memoirs Found in a Bathtub, Księga Robotów,* and the acclaimed *Solaris.*

1961–68 One of the most prolific periods in the author's career, frequently dubbed as the "golden period": multiple novels, collections of stories and essays, volumes of philosophy and criticism, and the incomparable *Summa technologiae.*

1968 Son, Tomasz, born.

1971 Several new novels and story collections, including the groundbreaking *A Perfect Vacuum.* Receives multiple national and international awards. Joins the Science-Fiction Research Association.

1971 Presents a paper at the first SETI scientific conference and publishes *The Futurological Congress.* Joins POLAND 2000, think-tank of the Polish Academy of Science.

1972 Andrei Tarkovsky's film *Solaris,* based on the 1961 Lem novel, triumphs at the Cannes festival.

1972–82 Multiple belletristic publications, including the popular *Chain of Chance* and the experimental *Imaginary Magnitude,* as well as philosophy, ethics, futurology, criticism, radio scripts, polemical writing. In the wake of multiple appearances on radio and television, Lem becomes a national spokesman on cultural, literary, and popular scientific matters.

1981 Honorary PhD from Wrocław Technical University.

1982–88 Takes up residence in West Berlin, then Vienna.

1985 Receives Austrian State Award for Culture.

1986 Completes *Fiasco,* his last work of fiction to date. Since then Lem has been equally prolific, but writes only nonfiction. Recipient of multiple national and international awards and distinctions, including nominations for the Nobel Prize in Literature.

1998 Honorary PhDs from Lvov's National Medical University, Warsaw University, Opole University, and the Jagiellonski University.

2002 Hollywood's blockbuster production of *Solaris.*

2003 First North American conference devoted to Lem's legacy, "The World According to Lem: Science Fiction and Futurology," mounted by the Wirth Institute for Austrian and Central European Studies of the University of Alberta, Edmonton, Canada.

2006 Stanislaw Lem dies on 27 March.

Bibliography

HALES: (UN)MASKING THE AGENT

Barkow, Jerome H., Leda Cosmides, and John Tooby. *The Adapted Mind: Evolutionary Psychology and the Generation of Culture*. Oxford: Oxford University Press, 1992.

Brooks, Rodney. *Flesh and Machines: How Robots Will Change Us*. New York: Vintage, 2003.

Damasio, Antonio R. *Descartes' Error: Emotion, Reason, and the Human Brain*. New York: Putnam, 1994.

Deleuze, Gilles, and Félix Guattari. *A Thousand Plateaus: Capitalism and Schizophrenia*. Trans. Brian Massumi. Minneapolis: University of Minnesota Press, 1987.

Dennett, Daniel C. *Freedom Evolves*. New York: Vintage, 2003.

Guattari, Félix, "Machinic Heterogenesis." *Rethinking Technologies*. Ed. Verena A. Conley. Minneapolis: Univeristy of Minnesota Press, 1993, 13–27.

Hansen, Mark. *Embodying Technesis: Technology beyond Writing*. Ann Arbor: University of Michigan Press, 2000.

Hayles, N. Katherine. "Simulated Narratives: What Virtual Creatures Can Teach Us." *Critical Inquiry* 26.1 (1999): 1–26.

Johnston, John. "The In-Mixing of Machines: Psychoanalysis and Cybernetics." Unpublished ms.

Lacan, Jacques. *The Seminar of Jacques Lacan: Book II, the Ego in Freud's Theory and in the Technique of Psychoanalysis, 1954–55.* Trans. Sylvana Tomaselli. New York: Norton, 1988.

Langton, Christopher. "Artificial Life." *Artificial Life.* Ed. Langton. Redwood City: Addison, 1989, 1–17.

Lem, Stanislaw. "The Mask." *Mortal Engines.* Trans. Michael Kandel. San Diego: Harcourt, 1992. 181–239.

– *Solaris.* Trans. Joanna Kilmartin and Steve Cox. New York: Berkley, 1971.

Libet, Benjamin, Anthony Freeman, and Keith Sutherland. *The Volitional Brain: Towards a Neuroscience of Free Will.* Thorverton, UK: Imprint Academic, 1999.

Libet, Benjamin, C.A. Gleason, E.W. Wright, and D.K. Pearl, "Time of Conscious Intention to Act in Relation to Onset of Cerebral Activities (Readiness Potential); The Unconscious Initiation of a Freely Voluntary Act." *Brain* 106 (1983): 623–42.

Munneke, Derek, Kirsten Wahlstrom, and Linda Zaccara. "Intelligent Software Robots on the Internet." www.cis.unisa.edu/au/~cisdm/papers/iagents/IntelligentAgentsInternet.html (8 February 2004).

Moravec, Hans. *Mind Children: The Future of Robot and Human Intelligence.* Cambridge: Harvard University Press, 1990.

– *Robot: Mere Machine to Transcendent Mind.* New York: Oxford University Press, 2000.

Parker, Jo Alyson. "Gendering the Robot: Stanislaw Lem's 'The Mask.'" *Science-Fiction Studies* 19 (1992): 178–91.

Saarinen, Leena, "Chatterbots: Crash Test Dummies of Communication." Master's Thesis, Media Lab, U. of Art and Design, Helsinki Finland. www.mlab.uiah.fin~lsaarine/bots/frontpage.html (8 February 2004).

Smith, Brian Cantwell. *On the Origin of Objects.* Cambridge: MIT Press, 1998.

Swirski, Peter. "A Case of Wishful Thinking." *Between Literature and Science: Poe, Lem, and Explorations in Aesthetics, Cognitive Science, and Literary Knowledge.* Montreal: McGill-Queen's University Press, 2001, 127–32. www.scienceboard.net/community/perspectives.64.html (4 February 2004).

Turing, A.M. "On Computable Numbers, with an Application to the Entscheidungsproblem." *Proceedings of the London Mathematical Society* ser. 2 42 (1936): 230–65.

Varela, Francisco J., Evan Thompson, and Eleanor Rosch. *The Embodied Mind: Cognitive Science and Human Experience.* Cambridge: MIT Press, 1991.

Wald, Carol. "The Female Machine: From von Neumann to Richard Powers." Unpublished ms.

Wolfram, Stephen. *A New Kind of Science.* New York: Wolfram Media, 2002.

Zivkovic, Zoran. "The Future without a Future: An Interview with Stanislaw Lem." *Pacific Quarterly (Moana): An International Review of Arts and Ideas* 4.3 (1979): 255–9.

SWIRSKI: BETRIZATION IS THE WORST SOLUTION

Alexander, Richard D. *The Biology of Moral Systems.* Hawthorne, NY: Aldine de Gruyter, 1987.

Altman, Russ, et al. *Pacific Symposium on Biocomputing.* New Jersey, London, Singapore, Hong Kong: World Scientific, 2002.

Associated Press. "Patriot Act Denounced as Danger to U.S Liberties." *The Edmonton Journal* Sunday, December 22 (2002): A5.

Barrow, John, and Frank J. Tipler. *The Anthropic Cosmological Principle.* Oxford: Oxford University Press, 1986.

BBC News World Edition (online). "Brain Chips Could Help Paralyzed." 17 April 2004. news.bbc.co.uk/2/hi/health/3632855.stm.

BBC News World Edition (online). "US Gets Access to Airline Details." 17 December 2003. news.bbc.co.uk/go/em/fr/-/2/hi/americas/3326279.stm.

BBC News World Edition (online). "New Weapon Can Fire round Corners." 18 December 2003. news.bbc.co.uk/go/em/fr/-/2/hi/americas/3324893.stm.

DARPA. "Exoskeletons for Human Performance Augmentation." 2002. Defense Advanced Research Projects Agency. www.darpa.mil/dso/

Davis, Mike. *City of Quartz: Excavating the Future in Los Angeles.* New York: Vintage, 1992.

Graham-Rowe, Duncan. "World's First Brain Prosthesis Revealed." *NewScientist.com* (March 2003). www.newscientist.com/news/news.jsp?id=ns99993488.

Hayes, Brian. "Statistics of Deadly Quarrels." *American Scientist Online* (January/February 2002). www.americanscientist.org/template/AssetDetail/assetid/14426.

"High priced Security." *Canada and the World Backgrounder* 67:4 (January 2002): 24–7.

IEEE Computer Society. *Proceedings. 2nd Annual ieee International Symposium on Bioinformatics and Bioengineering (BIBE 2001).* Los Alamitos, CA: IEEE, 2001.

"Immigration Law." *New York Law Journal*, 27 January 2003, 1–5.

Katzenberg, Michael. "Patriot Act." *IOBA Standard: The Newsletter of the independent Online Booksellers Association.* 2003. www.ioba.org/newsletter/V11/IOBANL-BearPond-5-03.php.

Knowles, John. "Warfare." *PC Magazine*, 12 March 2002. www.pcmag.com/article2/0,4149,509,00.asp.

Lem, Stanislaw. *Return from the Stars.* Trans. Barbara Marszal and Frank Simpson. New York: Harcourt, 1980. [1961].

– *Dialogi [Dialogues].* Kraków: Wydawnictwo Literackie, 1957.

– *Eden.* Trans. Marc E. Heine. San Diego: Harcourt, 1989. [1959].

– *The Futurological Congress.* Trans. Michael Kandel. New York: Avon, 1976. [1971].

– *Wizja lokalna [On Site Inspection].* Kraków: Wydawnictwo Literackie, 1983.

Lemley, Brad. "Future Tech: Really Special Forces." *Discover.com.* February 2002. Discover Magazine Online. www.discover.com/feb_02/feattech.html.

Lorenz, Konrad. *On Aggression.* New York: Harcourt, Brace and World, 1966.

McConnell, Terry. "Liberty Is Dealt Another Blow." *The Edmonton Journal* Sunday, 9 March 2003, D2.

Meadows, Donella H., et al. "Technology and the Limits of Growth." *Technology and Man's Future.* Ed. Albert H. Teich. 4rd ed. New York: St. Martin's, 1986.

More, Thomas. *Utopia. Latin Text and English Translation.* Eds. George M. Logan, Robert M. Adams, Clarence H. Miller. Cambridge, UK: Cambridge University Press, 1995.

Nagel, Matthew. "Brain Chip Reads Man's Thoughts." BBC News World Edition (online). March 31, 2005. news.bbc.co.uk/2/hi/health/4396387.stm.

Pardalos, Panos M., and Jose Principe. *Biocomputing.* Dordrecht: Kluwer Academic Publishers, 2002.

Park, Dean, and John Wieser. "Summary of Field Studies Evaluating the Efficacy of Bio-Bond®, a Porous Polymer Sheath, on Radio Frequency Identification (RFID) Transponders to Prevent Migration from a Known Implant Site." 2000. www.animal-id.com.au/report.html.

"Radwanski Warns Right to Privacy Endangered." *Canadian Association of University Teachers (CAUT) Bulletin* 50:2 (February 2003): A1, A10.

Rapoport, Anatol. "Spin-offs of Game Theory to Sciences." *Evolution and Progress in Democracie: Towards New Foundations of a Knowledge Society*. Ed. Johann Gotschl. Dordrecht: Kluwer Academic Publishers, 2001. 241–72.

Richardson, Lewis Fry. *Statistics of Deadly Quarrels*. Eds. Quincy Wright and C.C. Lienau. Pittsburgh: Boxwood Press, 1960.

– *Arms and Insecurity: a Mathematical Study of the Causes and Qrigins of War.* Eds. Nicolas Rashevsky and Ernesto Trucco. Pittsburg: Boxwood Press, 1960.

Russell, Bertrand. "On Scientific Method in Philosophy." In *Russell on Ethics. Selections from the Writings of Bertrand Russell.* Ed. Charles R. Pigden. London, New York: Routledge, 1999.

Scott Tyson, Ann. "Rumsfeld: Moral Warrior." *The Edmonton Journal* Saturday, 4 January 2003, A12.

Sokal, Robert R., and James F. Rohlf. *Biometry: the Principles and Practice of Statistics in Biological Research. 3d ed.* San Francisco: W.H. Freeman, 1995.

Stoff. Andrzej. *Lem i inni: Szkice o Polskiej science fiction [Lem and Others: Sketches on Polish Science Fiction*]. Bydgoszcz: Pomorze, 1990.

Swirski, Peter. "Stanislaw Lem and the Art of Science." *From Lowbrow to Nobrow.* Montreal: McGill-Queen's University Press, 2005.

– *Between Literature and Science. Poe, Lem, and Explorations in Aesthetics, Cognitive Science, and Literary Knowledge.* Montreal: McGill-Queen's University Press, 2000. Liverpool: Liverpool University Press, 2000.

– "Stanislaw Lem." In *Science Fiction Writers; Revised Edition.* Ed. Richard Bleiler. New York: Charles Scribner's Sons, 1999. 453–66.

– "Stanislaw Lem: *The Chain of Chance.*" *Beacham's Encyclopedia of Popular Fiction.* Ed. Kirk Beetz. Osprey, Florida: Beacham Publishing, 1998. Vol. 9. 5267–76.

– "Stanislaw Lem: *Fiasco.*" *Beacham's Encyclopedia of Popular Fiction.* Ed. Kirk Beetz. Osprey, Florida: Beacham Publishing, 1998. Vol. 9. 5491–500.

– *A Stanislaw Lem Reader.* Evanston, IL: Northwestern University Press, 1997.

– "Playing a Game of Ontology: A Postmodern Reading of *The Futurological Congress.*" *Extrapolation* 33 (1992): 32–41.

Weber, Max. *Economy and Society*. Trans. Ephraim Fischoff et al. Eds. Guenther Roth and Claus Wittich. Berkeley: University of California Press, 1978. [1914].

Wilson, Edward. *On Human Nature.* Cambridge: Harvard University Press, 1978.

Wright, Robert. *The Moral Animal.* New York: Pantheon, 1994.

Ziembiecki, Andrzej. "'… Knowing Is the Hero of My Books …'" *Polish Perspectives* 9 (1979): 64–9.

KANDEL: A FREUDIAN PEEK AT LEM'S *FIASCO*

Erofeyev, Victor. "Dirty Words: The Unique Power of Russia's Underground Language." *New Yorker* 15 September 2003: 42ff.

Freud, Sigmund. *Interpretation of Dreams.* www.psywww.com/book/interp/toc.htm.

Geier, Manfred. "Fantastyczny ocean Stanislawa Lema: Przyczynek do semantycznej interpretacji Science Fiction 'Solaris.'" Trans. Ryszard Wojnakowski. *Lem w oczach krytyki swiatowej.* Ed. Jerzy Jarzebski. Krakow: Wydawnictwo Literackie, 1989. 143–217. Trans. of "Stanislaw Lems Phantastischer Ozean: Ein Beitrag zur semantischen Interpretation des Science-fiction-Romans 'Solaris.'" *Uber Stanislaw Lem.* Ed. Werner Berthel. Frankfurt: Suhrkamp, 1981. 96–163.

Hayles, N. Katherine. "(Un)Masking the Agent: Stanislaw Lem's 'The Mask.'" The World According to Lem: Science Fiction and Futurology. University of Alberta. 29 September 2003.

Jarzebski, Jerzy. *Wszechswiat Lema.* Krakow: Wydawnictwo, Literackie, 2002.

Lem, Stanislaw. *DyLEMaty.* Krakow: Wydawnictwo Literackie, 2003.

– *Dzienniki gwiazdowe.* 4th ed. Warsaw: Czytelnik, 1971. Trans. as *The Star Diaries.* Trans. Michael Kandel. New York: Seabury, 1976.

– *Eden.* Trans. Marc. E. Heine. San Diego: Harcourt, 1989.

– *Fiasko.* 1987. Afterword by Jerzy Jarzebski. Krakow: Wydawnictwo Literackie, 1999. Trans. as *Fiasco.* Trans. Michael Kandel. San Diego: Harcourt, 1987.

– *Golem XIV.* Krakow: Wydawnictwo Literackie, 1981.

– *His Master's Voice.* Trans. Michael Kandel. San Diego: Harcourt, 1983.

– "The Hunt." Lem, *Mortal Engines* 138–80.

– Letter to Michael Kandel (remarks on *Fiasco*). 9 May 1985.

– Letter to Michael Kandel (account of prostate surgery). 17 July 1976.

– "The Mask." Lem, *Mortal Engines* 181–239.

– *Mortal Engines.* Trans. and introd. Michael Kandel. New York: Seabury, 1977.

– *Niezwyciezony i inne opowiadania.* Warsaw: Wydawnictwo Ministerstwa Obrony Narodowej, 1965.

– *Peace on Earth.* Trans. Elinor Ford with Michael Kandel. New York: Harcourt, 1994.

BUTKO: SUMMA TECHNOLOGIAE

Adleman, Leonard. "Molecular Computation of Solutions to Combinatorial Problem." *Science* 266:5187 (1994): 1021–4.

Bak, Per. *How Nature Works.* New York: Springer, 1996.

Borges, Jorge Luis. "Kafka and His Precursors." *Other Inquisitions.* Trans. Ruth L.C. Simms. Austin: University of Texas Press, 2000. [1952].

Dawkins, Richard. *The Blind Watchmaker.* New York: Oxford University Press, 1986.

– *The Selfish Gene.* New York: Oxford University Press, 1976.

Ellington, A.D., and Szostak, J.W. "In vitro selection of RNA molecules that bind specific ligands." *Nature* 346 (1990): 818–22.

Franklin, Allan. *Are There Really Neutrinos? An Evidential History.* Boulder: Perseus, 2000.

Garber, Stephen J. "Searching for Good Science: Cancellation of NASA's SETI Program." *Journal of The British Interplanetary Society* 52 (1999): 3–12.

Gregory, Paul, and Earl Cox. *Beyond Humanity: Cyberevolution and Future Minds.* Rockland, MA: Charles River Media, 1996.

Hofstadter, Douglas. *Goedel, Escher, Bach.* Harmondsworth, Middlesex: Penguin, 1980.

– *Metamagical Themas.* New York: Bantam Books, 1985.

Kauffman, Stuart. *At Home in the Universe.* New York: Oxford University Press, 1995.

Laplace, Pierre Simon. *A Philosophical Essay on Probabilities.* Trans. F.W. Truscott and F.L. Emory. New York: John Wiley & Sons, 1902. [1814].

Lem, Stanislaw. *A Perfect Vacuum.* Trans. Michael Kandel. San Diego: Harcourt, 1983. [1971].

– *Summa technologiae.* Kraków: Wydawnictwo Literackie, 2000. [1964].

– *Tajemnica chińskiego pokoju* [*The Mystery of the Chinese Room*]. Krakow: TAiWPN Universitas, 1996.

– *Bomba megabitowa* [*The Megabit Bomb*]. Kraków: Wydawnictwo Literackie, 1999.

– *Okamgnienie* [*The Blink of an Eye*]. Kraków: Wydawnictwo Literackie, 2000.

– *Dialogi* [*Dialogues*]. Kraków: Wydawnictwo Literackie,1957.

– *Return from the Stars.* Trans. Barbara Marszal and Frank Simpson. San Diego: Harcourt, 1980. [1961].

– *The Invincible.* Trans. Wendayne Ackerman. Harmondsworth, Middlesex: Penguin, 1976. [1964].

– *The Cyberiad: Fables for the Cybernetic Age*. Trans. Michael Kandel. New York: Avon, 1976. [1965].

– *Memoirs of a Space Traveler*. Trans. Joel Stern and Maria Swięcicka-Ziemianek. San Diego: Harcourt, 1983.

– *His Master's Voice*. Trans. Michael Kandel. San Diego: Harcourt, 1983 [1968].

– *Golem XIV*. Krakow: Wydawnictwo Literackie, 1981 [published in English as part of *Imaginary Magnitude*].

– *Imaginary Magnitude*. Trans. Marc E. Heine. San Diego: Harcourt, 1985 [1973].

– *Peace on Earth*. Trans. Elinor Ford with Michael Kandel. San Diego: Harcourt, 1994 [1987].

Livingston, Paisley. "From Virtual Reality to Phantomatics and Back." *Electronic Book Review*, www.altx.com/ebr/ebr4/paisley.htm, 1997.

Lucretius. *On the Nature of Things*. Trans. John S. Watson. Amherst, NY: Prometheus, 1998.

Monod, Jacques. *Chance and Necessity: An Essay on the Natural Philosophy of Modern Biology*. New York: Random House, 1972. [1971].

Mota, Sue Ann. "The US Supreme Court Addresses the Child Pornography Prevention Act And Child Online Protection Act in Ashcroft v. Free Speech Coalition and Ashcroft v. American Civil Liberties Union." *Federal Communications Law Journal* 55:1 (2002): 85–98; www.law.indiana.edu/fclj/pubs/v55/no1/mota.pdf.

Plato. "Cratylus." *Dialogues of Plato*. Trans. B. Jowett. New York: Random House, 1937.

Robertson, D.L., and Joyce, G.F. "Selection in vitro of an RNA enzyme that specifically cleaves single-stranded DNA." *Nature* 344 (1990): 467–8.

Schroedinger, Erwin. *What Is Life?* New York: Cambridge University Press, 1992. [1944].

St Thomas Aquinas. *Summa Theologiae*. New York: Benziger Bros, 1947. [c. 1273]; www.ccel.org/a/aquinas/summa/home.html.

Stapledon, Olaf. *Last and First Men*. Harmondsworth, Middlesex: Penguin, 1973. [1930].

Swift, Jonathan. *Gulliver's Travels*. Franklin Center, PA: Franklin Library, 1979. [1726].

Swirski, Peter. *A Stanislaw Lem Reader*. Evanston, IL: Northwestern University Press, 1997.

Tuerk, C., and Gold, L. "Systematic Evolution of Ligands by Exponential Enrichment: RNA Ligands to Bacteriophage T4 DNA Polymerase." *Science* 249 (1990): 505–10.

US Supreme Court. www.supremecourtus.gov/opinions/01pdf/00-795.pdf.

JARZĘBSKI: MODELS OF EVOLUTION IN THE WRITINGS OF STANISLAW LEM

Czapliński, P. "Śmierć chaotyczna: 'Katar' Stanisława Lema." In: *Mikrologi ze Śmiercią. Motywy tematyczne we współczesnej literaturze polskiej.* Poznań: Biblioteka Literacka "Poznańskich Studiów Polonistycznych," 2001.

Dawkins, R. *The Selfish Gene.* Oxford and New York: Oxford University Press, 1976.

Huxley, T.H. *Collected Essays.* IX: *Evolution and Ethics.*

Jarzębski, J. "Naturalne, sztuczne i dziura w kosmosie." In: *Wszechświat Lema.* Kraków: Wydawnictwo Literackie, 2003.

– "Chaos, ład i literatura." Afterword to S. Lem, *Katar* [*The Chain of Chance*]. Kraków: Wydawnictwo Literackie, 1998.

Lem, S. *Filozofia przypadku. Literatura w świetle empirii.* Kraków: Wydawnictwo Literackie, 2002. [1968].

– *Summa technologiae.* Kraków: Wydawnictwo Literackie, 1964.

– *Dialogi.* Kraków: Wydawnictwo Literackie, 2001. [1957].

LIVINGSTON: SKEPTICISM, REALISM, FALLIBILISM

Audi, Robert. "Doxastic Voluntarism and the Ethics of Belief." *Knowledge, Truth, and Duty: Essays on Epistemic Justification, Responsibility, and Virtue.* Ed. Matthias Steup. Oxford: Oxford University Press, 2001, 93–114.

Bailey, Alan. *Sextus Empiricus and Pyrrhonean Scepticism.* Cambridge: Cambridge University Press, 2002.

Bostrum, Nick. "Are We Living in a Computer Simulation?" *Philosophical Quarterly* 53 (2003): 243–55.

Brueckner, Anthony. "Problems with the Wright Route to Skepticism." *Mind* 102 (1992): 309–17.

– "The Structure of the Skeptical Argument." *Philosophy and Phenomenological Research* 44 (1994): 827–35.

Cottingham, John. "Descartes and the Voluntariness of Belief." *Monist* 854 (2002): 343–60.

D'Amico, Robert. "*Sed Amentes Sunt Isti*: Against Michel Foucault's Account of Cartesian Skepticism." *Philosophical Forum* 26 (1994–95): 33–48.

Descartes, René. *Œuvres et lettres.* Ed. André Bridoux. Paris: Gallimard, 1953.

Feldman, Richard. "Fallibilism and Knowing That One Knows." *Philosophical Review* 90 (1981): 77–93.

Frankfurt, Harry. *Demons, Dreamers, and Madmen.* New York: Bobbs, 1970.

Greco, John. *Putting Skeptics in Their Place: The Nature of Skeptical Arguments and Their Roles in Philosophical Inquiry.* Cambridge: Cambridge University Press, 2002.

Groarke, Leo. "Descartes' First Meditation: Something Old, Something New, Something Borrowed." *Journal of the History of Philosophy* 22 (1984): 281–301.

Hankinson, R.J. *The Sceptics.* London: Routledge, 1995.

Hetherington, Stephen Cade. *Knowledge Puzzles: An Introduction to Epistemology.* Boulder: Westview, 1996.

Hookway, Christopher. *Scepticism.* London: Routledge, 1990.

Klein, Peter. "Skepticism." *Oxford Handbook of Epistemology.* Ed. Paul K. Moser. Oxford: Oxford University Press, 2002, 336–61.

Lehrer, Keith. "Why Not Scepticism?" *Philosophical Forum* 2 (1971): 283–98. *Contemporary Readings in Epistemology.* Eds Michael F. Goodman and Robert A. Snyder. Englewood Cliffs: Prentice, 1993. 224–37.

Lem, Stanislaw. *The Futurological Congress.* Trans. Michael Kandel. New York: Harcourt, 1976. [1971].

– *Memoirs of a Space Traveler: Further Reminiscences of Ijon Tichy.* Trans. Joel Stern and Maria Swiecicka-Ziermianek. New York: Harcourt, 1983.

– "Thirty Years Later." Swirski, *Stanislaw Lem Reader,* 67–92.

MacDonald, Paul S. "Descartes: the Lost Episodes." *Journal of the History of Philosophy* 40 (2002): 437–60.

Nadler, Steven. "Descartes' Demon and the Madness of Don Quixote." *Journal of the History of Ideas* 58 (1997): 41–55.

Nozick, Robert K. *Anarchy, State, and Utopia.* New York: Basic, 1974.

Pritchard, Duncan. "Recent Work on Radical Skepticism." *American Philosophical Quarterly* 39 (2002): 215–57.

Sober, Elliott, and David Sloan Wilson. *Unto Others: The Evolution and Psychology of Unselfish Behavior.* Cambridge: Harvard University Press, 1998.

Swirski, Peter. *A Stanislaw Lem Reader.* Evanston: Northwestern University Press, 1997.

– "Playing a Game of Ontology: A Postmodern Reading of *The Futurological Congress.*" *Extrapolation* 33 (1992): 32–41.

Tymoczko, Thomas, and Jonathan Vogel. "The Exorcist's Nightmare: A Reply to Crispin Wright." *Mind* 101 (1992): 543–52.

Wright, Crispin. "Scepticism and Dreaming: Imploding the Demon." *Mind* 100 (1991): 87–116.

CSICSERY-RONAY: LEM, CENTRAL EUROPE, AND THE GENRE OF TECHNOLOGICAL EMPIRE

Adas, Michael. *Machines as the Measure of Men: Science, Technology, and Ideologies of Western Dominance.* Ithaca, NY: University of Cornell Press, 1989.

Anderson, Benedict. *Imagined Communities: Reflections on the Origins and Spread of Nationalism.* London: Verso, 1983.

Arendt, Hannah. *The Origins of Totalitarianism.* New York: Meridian Books, 1951.

Buccholz, Arnold. "The Role of the Scientific-Technological Revolution in Marxism-Leninism." *Studies in Soviet Thought* 20 (1970).

Csicsery-Ronay, Istvan, Jr. "An Elaborate Suggestion." [Review of Brian McHale, *Constructing Postmodernism.*] *Science-Fiction Studies* 20.3 (November 1993): 457–64.

Graham, Loren. *Science and Philosophy in the Soviet Union.* New York: Knopf, 1972.

Greenberg, Linda Lubrano. "Soviet Science Policy and the Scientific Establishment." Survey. August, 1971.

Hardt, Michael and Antonio Negri. *Empire.* Cambridge, MA: Harvard University Press, 2000.

Headrick, Daniel R. *The Tools of Empire: Technology and European Imperialism in the Nineteenth Century.* New York: Oxford University Press, 1981.

Hughes, Thomas P. "Technological Momentum." *Does Technology Drive History? The Dilemma of Technological Determinism.* Ed. Merritt Roe Smith and Leo Marx. Cambridge, MA: MIT, 1994. 101–13.

Lem, Stanislaw. *Fiasco.* Trans. Michael Kandel. New York: Harcourt Brace Jovanovich, 1987.

– *Golem XIV.* Trans. Marc E. Heine. *Imaginary Magnitude.* New York: Harcourt Brace Jovanovich, 1986. 97–248.

– *His Master's Voice.* Trans. Michael Kandel. New York: Harcourt Brace Jovanovich, 1983. [1968].

– *Solaris.* Trans. Joanna Kilmartin and Steve Cox. New York: Berkely, 1971. [1961].

– *Summa Technologiae.* Budapest. 1976. [1964].

– *The Investigation.* Trans. Adele Milch. New York: Harcourt Brace Jovanovich, 1986. [1959].

– "The New Cosmogony." *A Perfect Vacuum.* Trans. Michael Kandel. New York: Harcourt Brace Jovanovich, 1983. [1971]. 197–229.

McHale, Brian. *Constructing Postmodernism.* London: Routledge, 1992.

Marin, Louis. *Utopics: The Semiological Play of Textual Spaces.* 1984. Trans. Robert A. Vollrath. New York: Prometheus, 1990.

Said, Edward. *Culture and Imperialism.* New York: Vintage, 1994.

Stockwell, Peter. *The Poetics of Science Fiction.* Harlow, UK: Longmans, 2000.

Swirski, Peter. From Lowbrow to Nobrow. Montreal: McGill-Queen's University Press, 2005.

Zádor András. *Karel Čapek.* Budapest: Gondolat, 1984.

LOSKA: LEM ON FILM

Baxter, John. *Science Fiction in the Cinema.* New York: A.S. Barnes & Co, 1970.

Czaplinski, Przemysław. *Stanisław Lem – spirala pesymizmu.* In *Stanislaw Lem: pisarz, myśliciel, człowiek.* Ed. Jerzy Jarzębski. Kraków: Wydawnictwo Literackie, 2003.

Freud, Sigmund. *Trauer und Melancholie.* In *Gesammelte Werke,* vol. 10. London: Imago, 1940–52.

Helman, Alicja. *Twórcza zdrada.* Poznań: Ars Nova, 1998.

Jarzębski, Jerzy. *Science fiction a polityka (wersja Stanisława Lema).* In *W Polsce, czyli wszędzie. Szkice o polskiej prozie współczesnej.* Warszawa 1992.

– *Wszechświat Lema.* Krakow: Wydawnictwo Literackie, 2003.

Lem, Stanislaw. *Solaris.* In *Philosophy and Science Fiction.* Ed. Michael Philips. Buffalo: Prometheus Books, 1984.

– *Wejście na orbitę.* Krakow: Wydawnictwo Literackie, 1962.

Swirski, Peter. "Solaris! Solaris. Solaris?" *Central Europe Review (CER)* Jan. 8 (2003). (See also this volume.)

– *From Lowbrow to Nobrow.* Montreal: McGill-Queen's University Press, 2005.

Tarkovsky, Andrei. *Czas utrwalony.* Translated by S. Kuśmierczyk. Warszawa: Pelikan, 1991.

Telotte, J.P. *A Distant Technology. Science fiction and the Machine Age.* Hanover: Wesleyan University Press, 1999.

Thomas, Dylan. "And Death Shall Have No Dominion." In *Wiersze wybrane.* Kraków: Wydawnictwo Literackie, 1974.

About the Authors

PETER BUTKO earned degrees in physics and biophysics in his native Slovakia and in Hungary before pursuing research in North America at, among others, the National Research Council of Canada and the Harvard Medical School. Currently with the Department of Chemistry and Biochemistry, University of Southern Mississippi, he is using physical methods and computer simulations to study self-assembly of biological macromolecules into supramolecular functional structures (funded, among others, by the National Institutes of Health, and the National Science Foundation). Literature is his second hobby. Dissatisfied with the dearth of Lem's books in Slovak, he taught himself Polish, translating one of Lem's short stories for the Slovak weekly *Life*; his projects of translating *A Perfect Vacuum* and *The Imaginary Magnitude* are in progress. Recently he published reviews of two books on Lem in *Canadian Slavonic Papers.*

ISTVAN CSICSERY-RONAY is professor of English and World Literature at DePauw University, USA. His articles on postmodern culture and science fiction have appeared in several languages. He is coeditor of *Science Fiction Studies,* as well as editor of a special Lem issue of that journal (1986), and currently has two books under contract, *The Seven Beauties of Science Fiction* (a theoretical study of the genre) and *The Aliens of Lem* (a study of Lem's alien contact fiction).

N. KATHERINE HAYLES, professor of English and Design/Media Arts at the University of California, Los Angeles, teaches and writes on the relations of literature, science, and technology. Her recent book *How We Became Posthuman: Virtual Bodies in Cybernetics, Literature and Informatics* won the René Wellek Prize for the Best Book in Literary Theory for 1998–99 and the Eaton Award for the Best Book in Science Fiction Theory and Criticism for 1998–99. Her latest book, *Writing Machines*, is a joint verbal-visual work in collaboration with Anne Burdick. She is currently at work on a book exploring the interrelation of code and natural language, *Coding the Signifier: Rethinking Semiosis from the Telegraph to the Computer.* She has been recognized by numerous fellowships and awards, including a Guggenheim Fellowship, a Rockefeller Residential Fellowship, a Presidential Research Fellowship from the University of California, and two National Endowment for the Humanities Fellowships. She has received Distinguished Scholar Awards from the University of Rochester and the Association for Science Fiction and the Fantastic, and the Medal of Honor from Helsinki University.

JERZY JARZĘBSKI, a literary critic and member of the board of directors of the Polish PEN Club, focuses mainly on twentieth-century Polish prose. He was a visiting fellow at, among others, the School of Slavonic and East European Studies, London University (1984–85) and the University of Cambridge (1989), as well as a research associate at the University of Salzburg (1992) and at the Institute of Human Sciences in Vienna (1993). In 1997 he taught at Harvard University, and in 2000–01 at the Hebrew University of Jerusalem. Editor of fifty-eight books (two about Lem), as well as some 360 articles, reviews. and forewords, he was awarded several national and international prizes, among them the Aleksander Brueckner Prize of the Polish Academy of Sciences (1983), the Kościelski Foundation Prize (1985), the Ministry of National Education Prize (1987), and the Kazimierz Wyka Prize (1991).

MICHAEL KANDEL has translated many of Lem's works into English. Two of them, *The Cyberiad* and *The Futurological Congress*, were nominated for the National Book Award. Kandel has also edited a Lem anthology (*The Cosmic Carnival*) and written a few articles on the author. He is currently putting together an anthology of short stories and novellas by a new generation of Polish science fiction and fantasy authors (e.g., Dukaj, Huberath, Sapkowski) on the theme of monsters. He is the author of several science-fiction stories (including "Wading River Dogs and More") and a few novels (including *Captain Jack Zodiac*) and has edited science-fiction writers for Harcourt; among his authors: Patricia Anthony, Kage

Baker, James Morrow, Jonathan Lethem, and Ursula K. Le Guin. Currently he works as an editor for the Modern Language Association.

PAISLEY LIVINGSTON is senior lecturer in Philosophy at the University of Copenhagen. His books include *Literary Knowledge, Models of Desire, Literature and Rationality*, and the forthcoming *Art and Intention*; one of the chapters of his *Literature and Rationality* includes a discussion of Lem's key 1968 novel, *His Master's Voice*. He has recently coedited, with Berys Gaut, a collection of papers entitled *The Creation of Art*. He has published essays on various topics in aesthetics, cinema, theory of knowledge, philosophy and literature, and, not least, on Stanislaw Lem in the context of virtual-reality technology.

KRZYSZTOF LOSKA, associate professor at the Institute of Audiovisual Arts at Jagiellonian University (Cracow), has written some fifty papers and dissertations on media, popular culture, and film theory. He has published numerous books, including *Genre Films, James Joyce and Audiovisual Communication, 100 Science Fiction Movies, McLuhan's Legacy*, and *Hitchcock – The Author and the Genre Movies*. In his writing he has focused on the problems of film genre, with a particular interest in science-fiction cinema. He has also published several volumes on science fiction in film and literature: *Waiting for Apocalypse – Visions of the Future in Science Fiction Films* (1998), *The Birth of the Electronic Body and the Pursuit of Subjectivity* (2000), *Women Seeking Identity – Notes on Feminist Science Fiction Literature* (2001), *Between Science and Fiction – The Birth of Science Fiction Cinema* (2001), *Solaris – Two Models of Film Adaptation* (forthcoming), and the just-completed *The Encyclopaedia of Science Fiction Films* (2003). He is currently working on a new book entitled *Science and Fantastic: Technological Imagination in Science Fiction*.

PETER SWIRSKI, associate professor, heads American Studies at the University of Hong Kong. Specialist in twentieth-century American literature and culture, popular fiction and film, and interdisciplinary approaches to literature, he has published fifty articles on both sides of the Atlantic. His books are *A Stanislaw Lem Reader* (1997), *Between Literature and Science: Poe, Lem, and Explorations in Aesthetics, Cognitive Science, and Literary Knowledge* (2000), and *From Lowbrow to Nobrow* (2005). Forthcoming are *All Roads Lead to the American City* (2006), a collection of interdisciplinary essays on the contemporary urban environment, and *Of Literature and Knowledge* (2007), a study of narrative fictions as thought experiments.